De...
Technology

Metal

Other books in this series:
Design and Technology (Wood)
Design and Technology (Plastic)

Prepared by the authors in collaboration with
R. Millett and E. W. Storey.

Acknowledgments
The authors express their grateful thanks to the students
in the Design and Technology Department of Gold-
smiths' College (University of London) for allowing
their work to be photographed for use in this book, to
J. Hunnex for the photographs, and to the following
for their general assistance: H. V. Bailey, Mr. and Mrs.
W. Osborn, The Aluminium Federation, British Railways,
The British Iron and Steel Corporation, Costains, The
Colchester Lathe Company, Olympic Airways, The
Welding Institute, Vauxhall Motors, Vinatex Ltd.,
Metalaids and Tottenham School. Fig. 3.39 is repro-
duced by courtesy of Popperfoto.

Design & Technology
Metal

by P. A. Bridge, G. M. Heddle and G. A. Hicks

PERGAMON PRESS

Pergamon Press Ltd., Headington Hill Hall, Oxford

Pergamon Press Inc., Maxwell House, Fairview Park, Elmsford, New York 10523

Pergamon of Canada Ltd., P.O. Box 9600, Don Mills, Ontario M3C 2T9

Pergamon Press (Aust.) Pty Ltd., 19a Boundary Street, Rushcutter's Bay, Sydney, New South Wales 2011

Cover photomicrograph: Typical ferrite/pearlite microstructure of steel plate. Courtesy The Welding Institute

First edition 1975

Printed in Great Britain by A. Wheaton & Co., Exeter

ISBN 0 08 016897 3

Contents

Introduction

Design can best be defined as the solution to a problem. In three-dimensional work, no matter how simple or complex the problem may be, and whether it is concerned with functional efficiency or visual beauty, its solution requires the same logical reasoning.

Throughout the ages, Man has advanced his civilization by the application of design in solving his physical problems. This has required a thorough and continuing exploration into the properties of the materials at his disposal, such as wood, bone, stone, wool, glass, metal, cement and plastics. No doubt early Man learned by trial and error, and much care would be expended. for example, in fashioning a harpoon from wood that would break on the first use. But as man gained mastery over materials he began to conquer and enrich his environment. He materially advanced his civilization by finding solutions to his material problems. This continuous process is called technology.

The practice of design and the technology of materials cannot be divorced from one another; nor can design be confined to the use of a single material. However, in order to provide a sound basis for later integrated design work, each book in this series deals in some detail with a single material.

This volume presents a series of graded problems requiring the exploration of the physical properties of metals and alloys, leading the student to gain design experience through the principles of analysis, synthesis and realization. Each section deals with a particular property, and specific design problems are posed. However, just as the solution of a design problem may require the use of more than one material, so it may also require an appreciation of more than one physical property of a metal or alloy.

At the end of the book a number of more sophisticated design problems are posed. The solutions to these problems should come from a wide-ranging review of the properties and shaping methods of the available materials. By working these and similar problems the student will develop his understanding of the design process, and, at the same time, rationalize his understanding of the properties of metals and alloys.

So far, reference has been made to materials in general and to metals and alloys in particular. These materials should now be considered in the wider context of the physical world.

Our physical world is composed of materials (matter) in a seemingly limitless variety of forms. In his early attempts to classify matter, Man used such terms as Earth, Air, Fire and Water; Solids, Gases and Liquids. Later, organic and inorganic compounds were recognized, but these broad categories proved to be inadequate. In this book, the detailed and accurate classification of the chemist's periodic table of elements will be used.

An element is a pure substance that cannot be broken down by *chemical* means into simpler substances. There are 103 elements in the periodic table, of which ninety-two occur naturally. All but eighteen of these are metals. From this it will be clear that mastery of our environment depends on our understanding of these metals, not only chemically in relation to their structure, but also physically in relation to their electrical, thermal, visual, acoustic and other properties.

Metals form about one-quarter of the earth's crust in mass. Some metals occur more abundantly than others, and very few (such as gold) occur as pure elements. The metals are usually found in combination with other elements, such as oxygen, sulphur and silicon, in the form known as ores, and elaborate industrial techniques are employed to separate out the pure metals.

The ores are not distributed evenly throughout the earth's crust but are usually found in substantial deposits in localised ore-bearing areas. Some deposits are commercially more important than others. The principal factors are the size of the deposit, the ease and likely cost of extracting it, the proximity of the manufacturing facilities and the relative usefulness and scarcity of the metal.

Few metals are immediately useful in their pure form

(the major exception being copper), and most metals have to be blended with other metals (or non-metals such as carbon, silicon and nitrogen) to give them the desired properties. Blended metals are referred to by the metallurgist as alloys, and the term metal is reserved for the pure element.

To avoid tedious repetition, all metals and alloys will be referred to in this book as metals, and no attempt will be made to differentiate between the two.

Early Man first discovered metals in two distinct forms. Firstly, as native metals; that is, as virtually pure metal in lumps or nuggets protruding from fissures in rocks, or lying on the beds of rivers. This metal glinted in the sunlight and attracted his attention. He found it interesting because it reflected light, was relatively heavy and strong, did not tarnish, and could be hammered into different shapes without breaking. There is reason to believe that gold was the first metal to be used by man.

Secondly, early Man discovered that metals could be extracted from certain types of rocks by heating them, and it may be that the first discovery was made by accident.

Throughout the ages, Man has experimented with these metals, first by trial and error and later by scientific research. He has not only been able to exploit the inherent properties of the metals in the solution of his problems, but has also found ways of changing those very properties by alloying the metals with other substances, by heat treatment and by working them in different ways.

Thus, by making the metals themselves more versatile, by learning to work, cut and join them, Man has brought them to his use in the solution of a wide range of problems.

Chapter 1
DESIGN VOCABULARY

For many people, mention of design conjures up a concern with aesthetics, an appreciation of the beautiful. On the other hand, technology is regarded as being concerned with the technical means of achieving a given end, the former being very much a theoretical and abstract activity, and the latter a practical, down-to-earth business.

There are many definitions of design, such as 'a purposeful plan before creative activity', and there are many variations on this theme. However, without some understanding of the technology of the material in which one is working, it is impossible to design effectively. There can be little doubt that design and technology are very close partners in any creative activity of a three-dimensional nature. Although the partners are not always equal, this close relationship will become evident through involvement in the kind of activities suggested in this book.

Since, throughout this book, frequent references are made to form, you must first examine it, and, through this examination, begin to develop a design vocabulary. So that the technology of materials does not obscure your view, when examining form you can limit yourselves initially to study in two dimensions. Indeed, since the elements from which form can be created are so numerous, it is better to understand two-dimensional form before moving on to three-dimensional work. The basic design elements include lines, planes, mass and colour, as well as the principles of composition, rhythm, contrast and symmetry.

Form is shape determined by structure or mass.

The skeleton of a leaf shown in Fig. 1.1 is an example of a natural form determined by its structure; it is held together by its members or limbs.

Fig. 1.1

9

Fig. 1.2

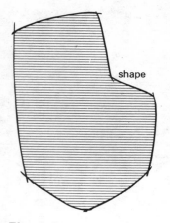

shape

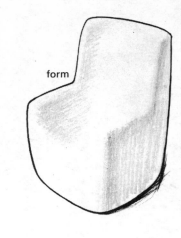

form

Fig. 1.3

The Forth Bridge (Fig. 1.2) is another example, this time man-made, where the members, struts, ties, etc., determine the final form of the bridge. A pebble is an example of form with no skeleton but determined by mass. In general, an object can be recognised by its dominating characteristic of either mass or line (skeleton), but it may, of course, be composed of both mass *and* line.

You must remind yourselves also that all objects fundamentally occupy space or possess volume. It is impossible to define form without understanding the part that space plays in perception. Any form must be surrounded by space, or, as in the case of the leaf skeleton, contain space within it. This space must be consciously used in your design work.

To illustrate this point, look at your hand with the fingers closed together. Now, spread your fingers apart. The spaces you have created between your fingers have helped you to become more aware of the shapes of your individual fingers as well as the whole of your hand. The form has become more positive now that you can see how space has defined it. You can now understand that form and space are two sides of a single coin.

The first element in creating a visual design is line. We use lines to enclose space and create shapes as shown in Fig. 1.3.

Lines can also be used expressively. For instance, in Fig. 1.4 vertical lines appear to climb or reach upwards, and

Fig. 1.4

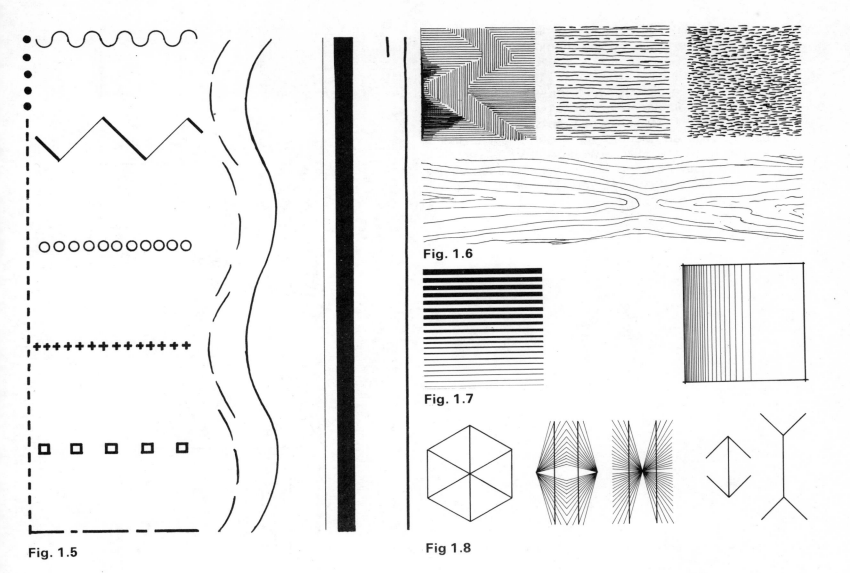

Fig. 1.5

Fig. 1.6

Fig. 1.7

Fig 1.8

slanting lines seem to be chaotic and sometimes aggressive. Lines, straight or wavy, can express motion, leading to rhythm as in Fig. 1.5. They may simulate texture as in Fig. 1.6, or light and shade as in Fig. 1.7. They can also deceive the eye or create ambiguity as in Fig. 1.8.

Usually, the first mark you will make when you start to design is a line. It may be an active line or a passive line. In any case, it radiates visual energy and serves as a beginning in your attempts to organise space.

Another word for shape, that is, space enclosed by a line, is a **plane.** You are probably familiar with this word from your technical drawing studies. The shape or plane

11

determined by the circumscribing line may be derived from geometry or nature, but will be two-dimensional as shown in Fig. 1.9.

When a third dimension is added, the form becomes volumetric—a three-dimensional form. Again, the simplest examples from geometry are a cube, a pyramid and sphere, as shown in Fig. 1.10. These may be solid, like a brick; transparent, like an electric light bulb; open, like a lobster pot; or twisted, like a wood screw. As shown in Fig. 1.11, you can work within the plane, overlap planes, penetrate planes and so on: your choice is enormous.

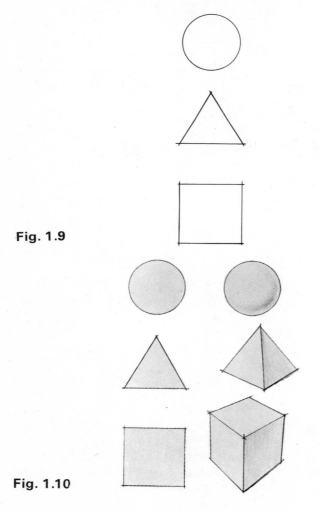

Fig. 1.9

Fig. 1.10

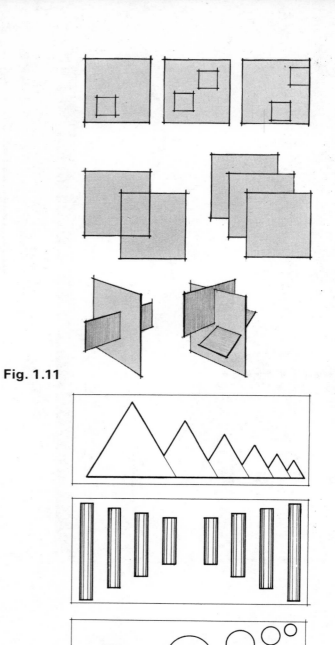

Fig. 1.11

Fig. 1.12

Remember that a plane may be solid, like a sheet of metal, transparent, like a sheet of glass; open, like a hoop; or twisted, like a leaf.

Before considering the principles of composition in design, you must think about the importance of size. Compare these three enclosed spheres—a football, a cricket ball and a table-tennis ball. Beside the football, the cricket ball is small: alongside the table-tennis ball, the cricket ball is large. A short line juxtaposed with a long line makes the long line seem longer and the short line shorter. Therefore, size must be relative. This size-relationship between parts of a form can help to give apparent depth where it does not physically exist, as seen in Fig. 1.12.

You will apply the principles of composition and use the elements of design whenever you wish to construct or create a design. The principles already mentioned—proportion, rhythm, contrast, symmetry, are now defined in verbal and visual terms. Knowledge of these principles is essential to the aspiring designer.

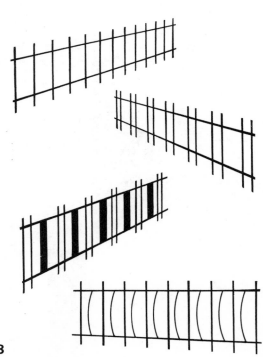

Fig. 1.13

Proportion means the relationship between parts of a whole or the relationship of one thing to another. This involves making comparisons and implies that the thing or parts must have some common characteristics. Sometimes these common characteristics are difficult to identify and comparison is virtually impossible. The degree to which things are similar depends on the number of factors being compared. For instance, it would be easy to compare one square with another; the only possible difference would be in their respective sizes. But if you compare an apple with a walnut you will find only limited similarities. They are both edible fruits and roughly spherical in shape, but the dissimilar characteristics are quite numerous. When considering proportion, the concern is with the visual correctness of an object: whether or not there is too much or too little of any characteristic, such as height to length, light to dark, rough to smooth, or simple to complex. If you agree with the relationship which you see between one element and another, you can say that the object has good proportions. A 'sense of proportion' may be developed by a careful examination of some of the established methods of determining proportions. However, these mathematical ratios and progressions should be regarded as tools and not as rules.

The rectangle is the most common of shapes indoors—windows, picture frames, books and envelopes—and some rectangles can be more interesting than others. For instance, a rectangle formed by two squares side by side, i.e. the sides of the rectangle have a ratio of 1:2, is quickly recognized as such and so interest in it is not maintained. From the architects of ancient Greece we have inherited a rectangle with a specific ratio of 1:1.618, which you will experience practically in Chapter 3.

Rhythm has two important contributing parts, repetition and emphasis. If a motif is made to recur, the sense of order is increased. A simple garden fence made from rods mounted vertically with even spacing, creates a very simple form of rhythm as seen in Fig. 1.13(a). There is greater emphasis when every third rod is removed as in Fig. 1.13(b) and more interest could be added by varying the width of the rods as well as the spacing—Fig. 1.13(c)—so that recurring differences as well as recurring similarities are used in the design—Fig. 1.13(d). Variety is achieved by using wider rods and contrasting the narrow with the wide —variety in size, shape, texture and interval is of infinite value to the designer. Fig. 1.14 is an illustration of rhythm and variety from several thousands of years ago. Rhythm has been created by variations of size, shape and position, suggesting a flowing movement as in Fig. 1.15.

Balance and *symmetry* are often regarded as synonymous. However, when a form is organized or constructed, symmetry is concerned with relating parts equally—as in a mirror image—and is relatively stable. (See Fig. 1.16). Balance, on the other hand, is an overall quality creating a sense of equilibrium and may contain within it various tensions, contrasts and dissimilar elements as in Fig. 1.17.

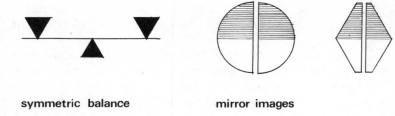

symmetric balance   **mirror images**

Fig. 1.16

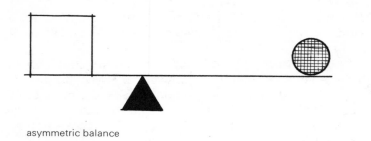

asymmetric balance

Fig. 1.14 detail of egg and dart—ancient Greek moulding

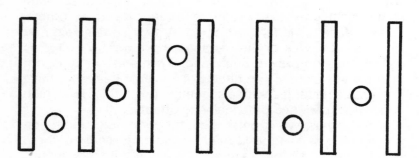

Fig. 1.15

The *tension* in this last figure is created by the variety of shapes and their different distances from the fulcrum. Visual tension is recognised when opposing forces create an area of stress as in Fig. 1.18.

asymmetric image

Fig. 1.17

(a) in position

(b) in shape

(c) in position and shape

Fig 1.18 visual tension

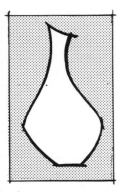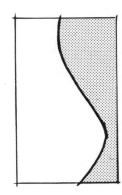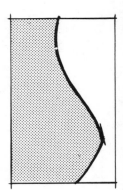

Fig. 1.19

You may achieve it by the use of variations of the same colour, by relating shapes, by limiting the actual materials or by surface treatment. In other words, you must have a sensitive control over the medium in which you are working.

The problems that follow have been arranged to enable you to attain this control gradually and then to practise using it wisely.

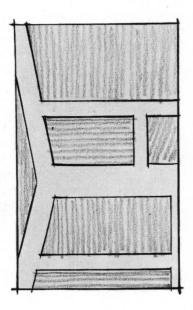

Fig. 1.20

A *positive* shape or form invariably means the form which actually exists in a solid material. A *negative* shape is the shape or form seen between or through the positive forms. As a positive form cannot exist without creating negative forms around itself, you must be aware of the negative shapes as well as the positive forms when you make three-dimensional objects.

Unity is said to be the prime design principle. The various principles and elements that have been discussed— form and space, rhythm and variety, balance and symmetry, line, shape, texture and contrast—are brought together in a design which, to be truly creative, must have a basic unity. The best way to achieve unity is to create with a definite objective in mind. The means by which you can establish this basic unity will vary with the problem.

PROBLEMS

1 Draw a series of lines which give the impression of diagonal movement.

2 Draw a number of shapes which depict rhythm.

3 Draw any skeleton structure which clearly shows the outer form.

4 Make sketches showing an asymmetric balance.

5 Within a square show how tension can be depicted using dots.

6 Make sketches to illustrate the meaning of negative and positive.

Chapter 2

THE STRUCTURE OF METALS

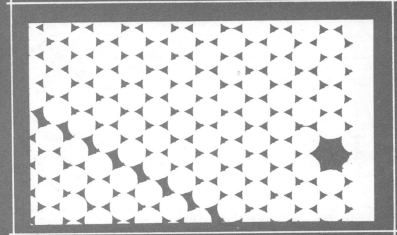

To understand what is happening to metals when they are being worked, it is necessary to explain their *structure*. You will then realize how it was possible for primitive Man to work metals in the way that he did and how a more scientific control over the structure of metals has made possible the present, advanced industrial techniques. Such an understanding will be of importance to you too, when designing and making articles in metal.

All metals, with the exception of mercury, are solid at normal atmospheric temperatures and are used in their solid state. Nevertheless, all metals at some stage in their extraction, refining and alloying, are molten, or liquid. While the metal is liquid, the atoms of the metal are in a disordered state and are highly energized.

It has been found in experiments that water may be in a liquid state when its temperature is below 0°C. So, too, can the temperature of a molten metal fall anything up to 10°C *below* its melting point before it begins to solidify. When a metal changes from its liquid to its solid state, we say that it freezes. When the liquid cools to below its melting point, the atoms release energy in the form of latent heat and the temperature of the metal rises momentarily to its melting point; the metal then solidifies and cooling continues.

Remember that an atom is the smallest quantity of an element that can take part in a chemical reaction. It should also be realized that there are about 5×10^{23} atoms of a metal in one cubic centimetre. Solidification begins with minute **seed crystals** or nuclei. These nuclei must not be confused with the nuclei of the metal atoms. The seed crystals are collections of millions of atoms which group together when they lose energy. Crystals may also grow from other nuclei in a liquid metal which is not of super-purity. These nuclei may be dust particles, slag or other impurities dispersed throughout the melt. The metal atoms begin to take up a three-dimensional orderly arrangement, forming cells. The cells grow to produce **dendrites** (Fig. 2.1), and the dendrites continue the three-dimen-

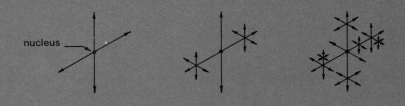

Fig. 2.1 growth of a dendrite

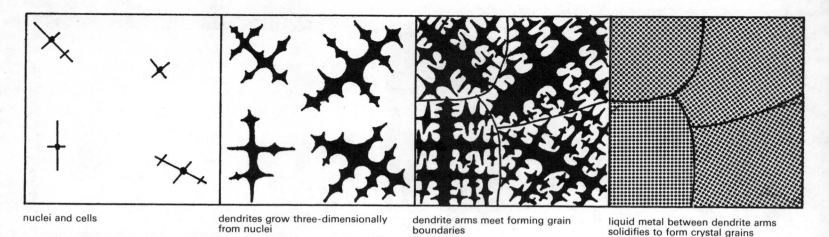

| nuclei and cells | dendrites grow three-dimensionally from nuclei | dendrite arms meet forming grain boundaries | liquid metal between dendrite arms solidifies to form crystal grains |

Fig. 2.2 growth of dendrites to produce crystal grains

sional growth to form metallic crystals, or grains, as in Fig. 2.2. The atoms of some metals group together, or **pack** in different arrangements from the atoms of other metals. There are three basic arrangements or structures: (Fig. 2.3) the face-centred cubic structure, the body-centred cubic structure, and the close-packed hexagonal structure.

Some metal crystals are easily seen with the naked eye; (Fig. 2.4) for example, zinc crystals on galvanised iron. You can also see crystals when the surface of a piece of metal is etched with acid—the crystals in gilding metal may be seen when the metal has been etched with nitric acid. It is necessary to carefully polish and etch the surface of the specimen before it is viewed under the microscope.

It is suggested that you make your own dendrites in the school workshop. The metals that will produce the best results are lead and antimony. These should be obtained from the Chemistry laboratory to ensure that they are of fairly high purity. Melt either metal in a small refractory crucible and remove the crucible from the heat source. The metal will then begin to freeze, starting at the sides and bottom of the crucible. When the metal has frozen to a thickness of about 3 mm, quickly pour out the still liquid metal. Dendrites may then be seen on the surface of the solid metal in the crucible.

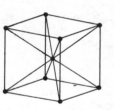

body-centred cubic lattice

face-centred cubic lattice

hexagonal close-packed lattice

Fig. 2.3

Fig. 2.4

18

Although the vast majority of atoms in metal pack three-dimensionally in organized arrangements, and are held in place by their interatomic force in a balanced way, the regular growth of the space or **crystal lattice** is occasionally interrupted. This interruption produces a flaw or fault line, called a **dislocation** in the crystal lattice structure (see Fig. 2.5(a)). Like other fault lines, a dislocation is a weakness in the general structure. Dislocations may be caused in several ways. For example, a group of atoms may be completely missing, as in Fig. 2.5(b) or a layer of atoms may form a line which is slightly out of phase with the others, as shown in Fig. 2.5(c). Experiment with a large number of small ball-bearings or lead shot in a flat-bottomed tray. The way in which the spheres pack, even in a single layer, will suggest the way in which metal atoms pack, and dislocations and grain boundaries may be produced.

The dendrites, which form the crystal grains, do not develop in a symmetrical form to produce regularly shaped crystals. As dendrites grow, their development is stopped

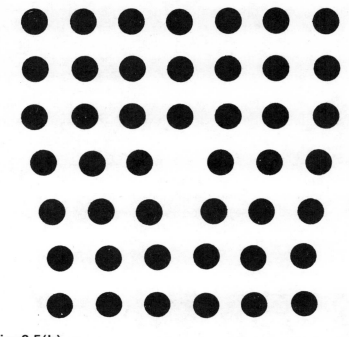

Fig. 2.5(b)

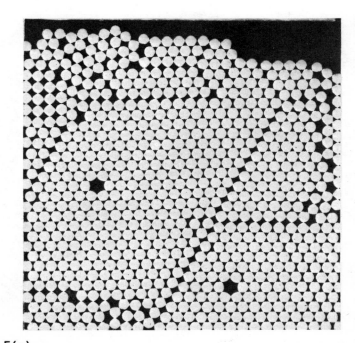

Fig. 2.5(a)

Fig. 2.5(c)

19

when they meet one another. The irregular surface where the crystal grains meet is called **the grain boundary.** The crystals are imperfect and yet they have strong bonds one to another (Fig. 2.6). The atomic character of a metal affects its strength and workability, its elasticity and lustre and its ability to conduct heat and electricity. This character depends on the interatomic force which binds one atom to another, the form in which the atoms arrange themselves into a crystal lattice and the imperfections in that lattice and even within each crystal.

If enough mechanical force is applied to the groups of atoms near a dislocation, they break their interatomic bonds, **slip** into a more regular position and re-establish more balanced and stable bonds. The metal is now stronger. The slip occurs gradually and progressively, and not suddenly by the whole group of atoms moving all at once (see Fig. 2.7). The metalworker relies on the fact that there are dislocations in the crystal lattice. Without dislocations, metals would be unworkable; they could not be usefully drawn, forged, beaten and cut. In order to satisfy the needs of design specifications that metals and alloys should be strong in certain ways, the metallurgist has found methods by which slip may be reduced or prevented.

When a metal cools from its liquid to its solid state, crystal grains are formed, as explained above. The size of the crystal grain is important to the metal's working properties. In general, the smaller the grain size the better the working property of the metal. Slip in the crystal lattice does not easily pass between one grain and another. Hence it will be more difficult to alter the shape of a piece of metal with small grains than one with large grains. This is a valuable property in castings, for example. Small grains are produced by quick and even cooling throughout the mass of the molten metal. Unfortunately, this condition is very difficult to obtain because metals lose heat from, and solidify at, their surfaces before the remainder of the metal freezes.

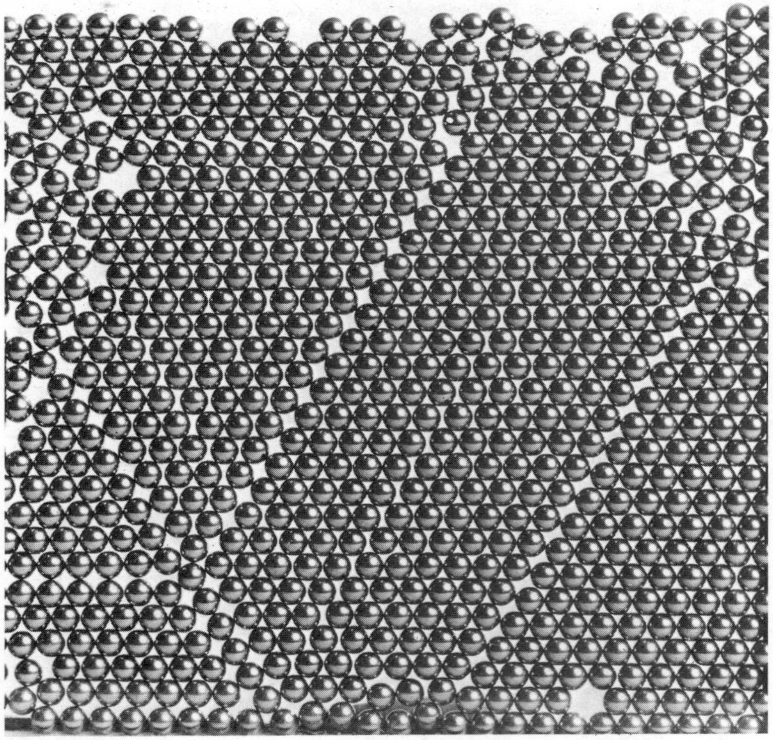

Fig. 2.6

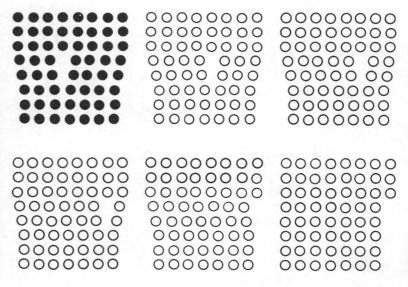

Fig. 2.7

The size of grain in a piece of metal can be changed by heating and cooling in a particular way, a process called **heat-treatment.** When metals, especially the steel which is used for forging, have been kept at a high temperature for a long time, the grains grow in size. Their size can be reduced by heating the metal and allowing it to cool. This process is called **critical,** or full **annealing.** Steel should be heated thoroughly to just above the upper critical temperature and then allowed to cool in the furnace or in hot sand.

In the Introduction the difference between metals and alloys was mentioned. In the school workshop, unless what is called 'commercially pure' aluminium or copper sheet or copper wire is used, the metals will almost always be alloys. This is because alloys are stronger than pure metals. When a small amount of a metal or some non-metal, is added to a larger amount of another metal it will usually mix completely with the second metal. It is said that it forms a **solid solution,** even though the mixing is done when the metals are molten. The presence of a strange atom in the orderly arrangement has the effect of stopping the movement of a dislocation. If the dislocation cannot completely correct itself, the metal is stronger. Another effect of the atoms of the alloying element is to distort the crystal lattice which also makes the metal stronger. You can take samples of copper and gilding metal (83 per cent copper and 17 per cent zinc) and cut them both to a size of, say, 50 mm x 10 mm x 0.95 mm. If you bend them with your fingers when both are in their softest condition, you can judge the effect of alloying for yourselves. This is a very greatly simplified statement: it does not cover all cases of alloying, but it gives the basic explanation.

As already mentioned, metals can be melted, but, with the exception of mercury, they are used in their solid state. An important fact which is linked with this is that different metals melt and solidify at different temperatures. The temperature at which a metal melts does not generally indicate other properties of the metal. Metals with high melting points can be as soft and workable as those with low melting points.

Another important point is that, with a few exceptions like constantin and antimony, metals expand when heated and contract when cooled. Different metals expand or contract at different rates. Over the range of temperatures in which we are interested, the expansion and contraction occurs at a constant rate. This is usually expressed as a constant known as the **coefficient of expansion.** Aluminium has a coefficient of expansion of 0.000023 per degree centigrade. So for each degree centigrade of rise or fall in temperature a unit length of aluminium expands or contracts by 0.000023 units.

When a metal is worked by bending, hammering or rolling, it becomes stronger; it is said that it **work hardens.** The metal loses its ductility and becomes brittle. If you bend a strip of gilding metal to and fro you will find that it soon requires more effort to bend the metal than it did for the first bend. This strengthening occurs in two ways; firstly, as a result of the grains having been broken into smaller grains, and, at the same time, because the slip plains within the grains meet one another, so that the atoms find it too difficult to sort themselves into a regular arrangement. As you will see in a later chapter, it is possible to make the metal soft and workable again by heating it to re-energize the atoms, making it easier for them to settle into a regular crystal lattice.

When a designer considers the use of metal as the material with which to solve his design problem, he has to make several decisions.

Firstly, he has to consider the type of metal to use and its properties. Not only is there a wide selection of basic metals, such as iron, aluminium and copper, but there are often a very large number of useful alloys of each metal. Mild steel, tool steel, stainless steel and cast iron are some of the alloys of iron, but there are also many different types of mild steel, tool steel, stainless steel and cast iron. Each particular alloy has its own particular properties, and you will find that they are often unlike the properties of the alloying elements.

Secondly, metals are produced in many different shapes, sections and sizes. It is possible to get plate, sheet, strip, bar, rod, wire, tube, rolled sections (angle, tee and H-section) and extrusions. These forms are produced because they meet the requirements of a very large number of manufacturers of different articles.

Again, the metals obtained in these forms may be shaped

Metal	Chemical Symbol	Melting Point	Density x 10^3 kg m^{-3}	Coefficient of linear expansion x 10^6 at 20°C
aluminium	Al	660	2.7	23.0
copper	Cu	1,083	8.9	16.6
gold	Au	1,063	19.32	13.9
iron	Fe	1,533	7.9	11.7
lead	Pb	327	11.3	29.1
silver	Ag	961	10.5	18.9
tin	Sn	232	7.3	21.4
zinc	Zn	419	7.1	33.0

Fig. 2.8 physical properties of some pure metals

in a variety of ways, such as cutting by hand or machine, or bending, rolling, hot or cold forging, drawing or pressing (see Chapter 4 on Malleability and Chapter 8 on Metal Cutting). In addition, metal may be shaped by casting. Each of these processes uses certain properties of the metal. Furthermore, the shaping process itself may alter the properties of the metal. When bright mild steel strip, or **flats,** are made, the black mild steel is cleaned and then rolled nearly to the required size. Finally it is drawn through a die to **size** the strip. The rolling and drawing processes rely on the malleability and ductility of the metal. The mild steel flats used in the workshop are in a work-hardened condition and are ideally strong for many of the things we make. But you may find that if you try to bend a piece of this steel to a sharp right angle it will crack. This is because the metal has become too brittle. In a bend formed when the mild steel is red hot, the metal will be softer when cooled than that in a bend made when the mild steel has been annealed and then worked cold.

Finally, there are many different ways in which pieces of metal may be fixed to one another. The assembly may be made by using soft or hard solders, rivets, threads, adhesives or force fits. Not all methods of joining or fixing may be used on all metals. It is not normally considered

possible to form a thread on components made from lead, for example, as it is too soft a metal. In the school workshop you may not be able to solder or braze together pieces of aluminium, as it oxidizes too readily, although these processes are used in industry. Each method of joining has its own advantages and disadvantages. Brazed joints (see Chapter 3) are relatively strong. They will conduct electricity and heat and can be made impervious to light, air, gas and water. They will withstand tensile, compressive, torsional and shear loads to various extents and will stand up to vibration fairly well. They may be plated, painted and plastic coated; they will not rust, but they may corrode. The disadvantages of brazed joints include the fact that they cannot easily be undone, that the colour of the joint may not match the colour of the pieces joined, and that the strength of the components may be altered by the heat required to melt the spelter. It is suggested that you start compiling a table giving the merits and drawbacks of all the methods of joining listed above.

Chapter 3
FUSIBILITY

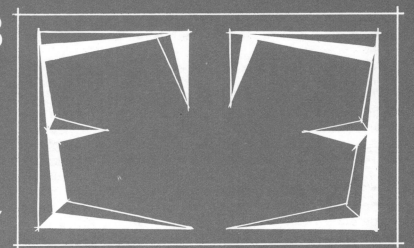

When a jelly is poured into a jelly mould and allowed to set, it assumes the shape of the jelly mould and retains this shape when it is turned out on a plate. Similarly, a molten metal, when poured into a mould and allowed to freeze, assumes the shape of its mould. This process of shaping metal is called **casting.** Shapes ranging from the very simple to the very intricate in form can be cast. By casting, it is possible to make articles whose shape cannot be achieved in any other way.

When a designer decides that an article should be of one piece of metal, rather than of several pieces joined together, he has to decide whether the article should be made by cutting it from a large piece of metal, or by casting it to the desired shape. Cutting or machining a shape from the solid piece is often wasteful in material, time and money, and the article made may not be the strongest that can be produced. When molten metal freezes, or solidifies—as we saw in Chapter 2—the crystal grains form in a definite arrangement. The metal starts to freeze at the outside and continues freezing towards the middle, and the crystals in the solid metal line up in a definite way. The shape of the crystals, and the direction in which they are lined up, help to strengthen the metal. If metals are cut across the crystal grain formation they will tend to be weaker than when the crystal grains are made to flow around, or follow the shape of the article produced, as in casting, forging, drawing, pressing and rolling. By controlling the rate at which metal freezes, the size of the crystals may be controlled. Small crystal grains are generally stronger than large ones. Small crystal grains are formed when metals freeze quickly. The article to be cast can often be planned so that the crystal grains may flow round the shape. This is one of the reasons why castings have rounded edges and corners.

Since nearly all metals and alloys may be cast—although some may be more easily cast than others—the designer can choose the most suitable metal in which to make the article from an extensive selection. Generally, the most important factors which control the selection of a metal are (i) its mechanical properties, such as strength and hardness; (ii) its relative weight; and (iii) the ease with which it may be cast. Some metals are not as fluid as others when they are molten, and so they do not run freely into the mould and fill it. This is important when a casting is to have thin or narrow parts in it or when it is to have fine detail of shape or surface texture, because such metals will not flow to cover the surface of the mould very closely. Other contributing factors to the choice of metal for a casting are its cost, colour, resistance to corrosion, and its melting point.

Note. The mould for a casting must be made from a material, such as sand, that will not be burnt by the molten metal.

To produce the correctly shaped hole, or cavity, of the mould, a **pattern** is usually used. The pattern is made to the exact shape, but not to the exact size of the required casting. When the finished size of a casting is important, the mould cavity must be made oversize so that when the molten metal cools and shrinks the casting will be of the desired size at room temperature. It is possible to calculate the dimensions of the cavity required for a particular metal to be cast to an accurate size. The pouring or casting temperature of the metal must be known, and room temperature must be given a value. Usually, however, a **contraction rule** is used when marking out wooden patterns or machining mould cavities. The graduations on the scale of the rule are made oversize by an amount calculated from the coefficient of expansion of the metal, the average casting temperature of the metal and average room temperature. Different contraction rules are required for each metal used. The rules are marked as normal rules. Any dimension set off using the contraction rule will be proportionally larger than actual size to allow for the contraction of the metal when it is cast.

Fig. 3.1(b)

Fig. 3.1(a)

Holes and intricately-shaped cavities, which would be time-consuming, difficult or even impossible to machine, can be included in a component by using **cores** during casting. Cores have to be strong enough to be handled and withstand the flow of molten metal, and yet easily broken up to empty the intricate hollow parts of the casting. They are made of sharp sand with a little flour and linseed oil and are shaped by ramming the core sand mixture into mould cavities in solid wooden moulding boxes called **coreboxes** (Fig. 3.1(a)). The shaped cores are carefully removed and baked hard. The core is positioned and supported in the mould cavity in recesses formed by **core prints** (Fig. 3.1(b)), which are additions to the pattern.

Cores may also be made from dry silica sand mixed with sodium silicate solution. This is rammed in the way described above, but the core is hardened by passing carbon dioxide gas into it. They can also be made by shaping an aerated concrete like Siporex. The aerated concrete must be dried thoroughly before use. Just as sand cores may be included, or trapped, in a casting, so, too, can pieces of metal, called **inserts.** For example, mild steel may be used as a bush or as a shaft in a cast aluminium alloy pulley wheel. The mild steel bush or shaft may be included in the casting when it is poured, instead of being fitted afterwards. A way has to be found of preventing the insert from slipping or rotating in the casting. Metal inserts may be included in sculptural castings, too, by adding them to the wax, expanded polystyrene or aerated concrete pattern before final moulding up.

These possibilities should be considered and explored when dealing with the design problems outlined later in this chapter, and when designing castings for engineering type components. An additional allowance must be given to surfaces which are to be machined after casting. Usually this is in the order of 3 mm. The completed casting must be **fettled**; that is the removal of the extra metal required in the casting operation in order to feed the molten metal into the mould cavity. Try to plan the position of these additions so that they are where the finished casting has to be machined or polished, leaving as many surfaces as possible in the as-cast condition.

Note. The metal must be completely molten when poured. It must also be clean, otherwise miss-runs and unsound castings will result.

MOULDS

Castings are made in either temporary or permanent moulds. The four materials generally used for making moulds of both types—and certainly the most appropriate for use in the school workshop—are sand, metal, cuttle-fish and investment plaster.

Sand Moulds

The essential properties of a moulding sand are:
 (i) resistance to high temperatures;
 (ii) a bonding strength so that it does not collapse under the flow or wash of the molten metal;
(iii) porosity, to allow steam and other gases to escape when the molten metal fills the cavity.

Greensand moulds are those made from a prepared sand and clay mixture to which water has been added. The clay provides the necessary bond, to hold the sand grains together.

The simplest way of making a mould cavity is to pack sand into a box and then to scrape, dig or cut sand away to form a hollow. Unfortunately, it is difficult to make the hollow of exactly the desired shape and size. Another drawback with this method is that when the molten metal freezes and contracts, the open surface of the casting develops a shrinkage cavity which is unsightly. In addition, the casting is often mis-shaped and too small. These disadvantages are overcome by using a pattern and packing the sand round it in a box, called a **drag,** so that the pattern may be removed. The drag in which there is the mould cavity, is covered with a second box, called the **cope,** which is then filled with sand. When a cope is used, provision must be made for pouring the molten metal through the cope and into the mould cavity. A means must be made for allowing the escape of steam and gas from the mould cavity. In Fig. 3.2 it will be seen that the molten

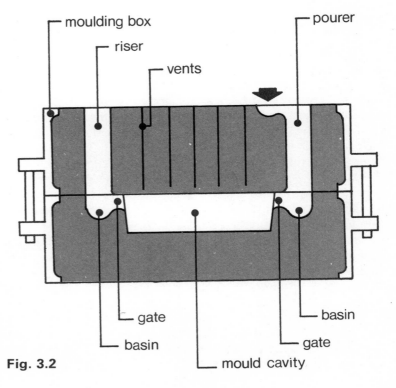

Fig. 3.2

metal is poured down the **pourer** into a **basin** before it is allowed to enter the mould cavity. This is to reduce the risk of sand being washed into the mould cavity and the sides of the mould cavity being damaged. The displaced air, the steam and gases escape through the vents and the risergate, basin and **riser**. As the metal is poured, the mould cavity fills and the metal rises up both the pourer and riser. Pouring is stopped when the metal reaches the top of the pourer and riser. This excess metal provides a weight, or 'head' of metal, to push the molten metal into the mould cavity, and also helps to feed the metal in the mould cavity as it solidifies and shrinks. When using sand it is possible to mould flat side, odd side and split patterns as shown in Fig. 3.3.

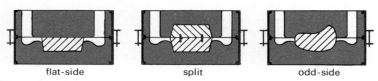

flat-side   split   odd-side

Fig. 3.3

After moulding, the faces of the mould cavity are dressed, either with French chalk for aluminium castings, or with coal dust for cast iron castings, so as to improve the finish on the casting. Proprietary dressings are available to coat the surfaces of the mould cavity. Some moulding sands are of such a fine grain size that a very good surface finish can be obtained without the use of a dressing. The quality of the surface finish largely depends on the surface finish of the pattern. Very fine detail can be reproduced when these fine grain sands are used. Fingerprints have been reproduced on pourers and basins when the sand has been rammed with the fingers.

Before use, greensand moulds are heated with a gas air torch to dry the sand, thereby reducing the amount of steam formed when the molten metal is poured. Excessive steam may penetrate the casting causing blowholes which will damage it and may also cause molten metal to be shot out of the pourer or riser. (A commercially produced oil-bound sand is now available which eliminates the problems caused by steam.)

A heated mould slows the cooling rate on the outer faces of the casting thereby making the crystal grain size of the metal more uniform throughout the casting. Before pouring, cast iron **chills** may be inserted in the mould to cool certain faces of the casting in order to produce a finer crystal structure in these areas. Chills locally harden some metals, and also help in the more uniform cooling of some cast shapes. Allowances must be made on the pattern to create cavities in the mould for these chills.

The versatility of sand as a mould material makes it economical for most types of casting, particularly where the number of castings involved is small. Often castings of very intricate shapes can be produced only in sand moulds because of the need to destroy the mould and the core in order to remove them.

Metal Moulds

When a large number of castings are required and the metals to be cast are of a suitable type, a superior product is obtained by casting into a metal mould rather than into a sand mould. The castings have a finer grain structure because they cool quickly. The metal moulds are called **dies.**

The required cavity, pourer and riser are machined into pieces of metal which are held together while the casting is made. In most dies the riser is omitted and is replaced by small vents. When the casting has solidified, the pieces of the die are separated so that the casting may be removed. Simple dies may be of only two parts, whilst complex dies may have ten or more parts.

When the molten metal is run into the cavity under its own weight the process is known as **permanent mould casting.** When the molten metal is forced into the cavity under considerable pressure the process is known as **pressure die casting.** This is shown in Fig. 3.4.

Die casting is confined mainly to the use of zinc based or aluminium based alloys and the process is extensively used in industry. Examples of die castings range from various well-known makes of toy cars to many of the components of real cars, such as door handles, carburetter parts and gear-box casings (Fig. 3.5). Very fine details, dimensional accuracy and surface finish can be obtained by casting in metal dies.

Although, in industry, special alloy steels are used to

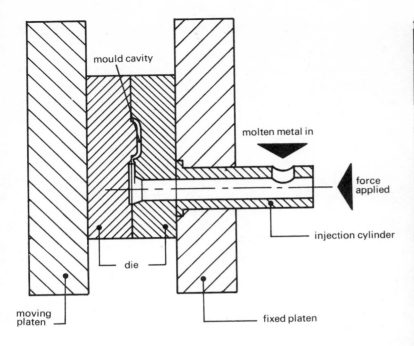

Fig. 3.4

make the dies, mild steel may be used for simple dies made in school workshops. When the die is used, it should be gently heated to ensure that it is completely dry and to prevent sudden freezing of the molten metal when it enters the mould cavity. (This may prevent the cavity being completely filled.) A **refractory wash** may be applied to the surface of the cavity (see p. 26). This will help the flow of metal and extend the life of the die.

Cuttlefish moulds

Pieces of cuttlefish bone may often be found on the sea-shore. Cuttlefish moulds are sometimes used by jewellers when they wish to cast small pieces of jewellery because fine detail can be reproduced. The bone withstands high temperatures and the mould cavities may be shaped easily by cutting or by pressing a hard pattern into it. Sometimes the texture of the cuttlefish itself may be used to advantage on the surface of the casting. (Fig. 3.6).

To make a cuttlefish mould, a flat joint is constructed

Fig. 3.5 the moving half of the die for the flywheel housing of the B.M.C. Mini Car

between two pieces of the material. These are located by means of small pegs pressed into the surface of one piece of the cuttlefish which in turn indent the other half, ensuring accurate alignment of the two halves. The chosen design is then cut or pressed into one or both surfaces of the mould. A funnel-shaped pourer is cut from the end of the cuttlefish to the mould cavity. Air vents are cut, radiating from the cavity, but not as far as the edge of the mould. The cavity faces are painted with a strong solution of borax and, when dry, with waterglass (sodium silicate solution) to toughen the surfaces against the effects of the hot metal. The two parts of the mould are then wired together.

A block of charcoal, in which a hollow has been cut, is used as a crucible. This block is wired to the cuttlefish mould. A channel is cut in the charcoal to connect the hollow to the funnel-shaped pourer in the mould. The metal is heated in the charcoal block until it is fully molten. The block-mould assembly is then tilted to allow the molten metal to flow into the mould cavity.

It is possible to use a mould of this material several times, and hence it may be classified as a permanent mould.

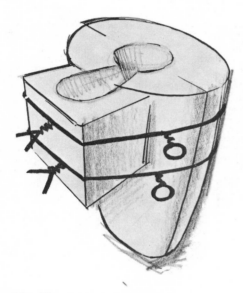

Fig. 3.6

Plaster moulds (Investment casting)
A jeweller can cast very intricate shapes, and reproduce very fine detail, using a mould made of **investment** plaster. Liquid plaster can be poured round an intricate pattern when **moulding-up.** Frequently, the plaster mould has to be broken from the solidified shape of the cast metal. Plaster moulds are therefore of a temporary nature. Because plaster may be used to form a one-piece mould, the pattern has to be burnt out before casting the metal.

Wax patterns are generally used in plaster moulds. The wax can be modelled to intricate shapes, thus using

the plaster mould to its fullest advantage. Wax patterns are easily melted and burnt from the plaster moulds.

The size of the flask used to contain the plaster, more correctly called the investment, must exceed the size of the pattern by approximately 6 mm in all directions to avoid a breakdown of the plaster under the heat of the metal. A larger amount of plaster may prevent the escape of the gases.

Bubbles must be removed from the wet plaster before it sets to ensure that a good finish is obtained on the surface of the pattern. The air is usually removed by placing the mould in a vacuum immediately after it has been poured. If a vacuum pump is not available, the investment can be painted onto the wax model before the flask is filled.

When set, the plaster is thoroughly dried. Drying is done slowly at first and then under sustained heat. This reduces to a minimum the possibility of steam bubbling through the wax pattern. It also melts the pattern from the mould.

The molten metal may be run into the cavity under its own weight, but greater success is achieved when the metal is forced into the cavity under pressure. Steam pressure can be generated by using a wet pad, as shown in Fig. 3.7.

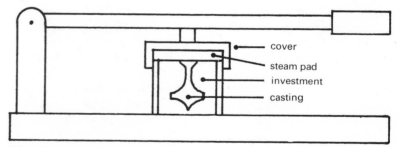

cover
steam pad
investment
casting

Fig. 3.7

Alternatively, centrifugal force may be used. A steam pad and a centrifugal casting machine can be made easily in a school workshop.

Precious metals, such as gold and silver, are usually associated with this type of casting, although cheap scrap metal can be used. This, and the fact that only small quantities of metal are involved, make investment casting a possible medium for work in schools.

This process has been used in the jewellery industry for a very long time. Other industries have recently shown considerable interest in the technique, and quite large castings are now being made in a variety of metals.

The disadvantage of this method is that the pattern is lost every time a casting is made. To overcome this difficulty, a mould is used to produce replicas of the original pattern. In industry, these moulds are made of vulcanized rubber, but in the school workshop Vinomould may be used.

Vinomould

This is a plastic which is poured and allowed to set around a pattern held inside a containing vessel. When set, Vinomould has a rubbery texture and is very pliable, making it possible to remove a pattern of complex shape. The Vinomould may be cut with a sharp knife to allow the easy withdrawal of complex patterns. It is then held together and molten wax is poured into the cavity and allowed to set. The process is repeated so producing replicas of the original pattern in wax.

If Vinomould is not available, simple moulds could be made from plasticine or moist clay.

PATTERNS

To make castings, either permanent or temporary patterns are used. Permanent patterns are used to form the mould cavity and are then removed and retained for further use. Temporary patterns are embedded in the mould material, so forming and filling the mould cavity, but are either melted out or burnt away before or during the casting process. New patterns have to be made when additional castings are required.

Patterns may be made from a wide variety of materials, but only the four most useful in the school workshop will be mentioned here.

Wooden Patterns

This type of pattern is generally associated with the casting of engineering type components. In school, a wooden pattern is made for each engineering design solution and therefore it is frequently used once only. It is possible, by selecting the most suitable type of pattern, carefully

making it and moulding it, to cast quite complex shapes. The problems involved in the moulding process will influence the type of pattern to be used, and may effect the design of the casting to be made. The four basic types of pattern used in sand moulds are shown in Fig. 3.8.—

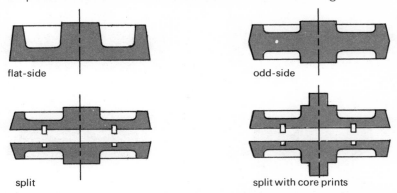

flat-side   odd-side

split   split with core prints

Fig. 3.8 types of pattern: cross-sections of pulley wheels

The pourer, basins, gates and riser are not included on the pattern but are cut into the sand after moulding up. **Sprue pins,** patterns in the form of tapered dowels, are sometimes used to mould the pourer and riser. On **plate patterns,** basins and gates are included to save time and effort when moulding up. When designing for wooden patterns, six allowances have to be considered:

(i) **Draft** or taper from the flat face, to allow easy removal of the pattern from the mould (Fig. 3.9, p. 30).

(ii) The avoidance of internal angles or sharp corners within a component, as this would result in weakness in the casting as it freezes. Furthermore, the wash of the molten metal may break off the corner of the sand mould. Such angles can be strengthened by the use of **fillets** (Fig. 3.10, p. 30).

(iii) Contraction of the metal when it cools. This affects the initial size of the pattern. As mentioned before, a contraction rule is generally used when making patterns.

(iv) An allowance must be made where a face of the casting has to be machined.

(v) The provision of core prints, if cores are to be used to make cavities in the casting.

(vi) The possible use of chills: this is unlikely to occur in the school workshop.

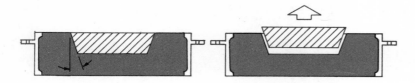

Fig. 3.9

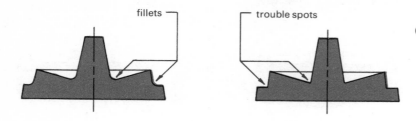

fillets

trouble spots

Fig. 3.10

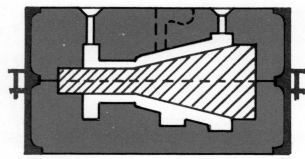

(i) conventional moulding

(ii) cavity-less casting

Fig. 3.11

Expanded Polystyrene

Expanded polystyrene vaporizes, leaving very little ash or residue when brought into contact with a heated object, or when molten metal is poured on to it. Intricate shapes cut from expanded polystyrene can be embedded in sand in a moulding box or flask, and left in place when the molten metal is poured. This technique is called **lost pattern** or **cavity-less** casting. The sand must be rammed firmly around the pattern, preferably with the fingers rather than with tools, to prevent the sand collapsing when the polystyrene foam vaporizes, but since expanded polystyrene is crushable, the sand must not be rammed too hard.

As the problem of removing the pattern from the mould is avoided with this technique, a wide variety of creative forms is possible.

The patterns may be shaped from blocks of the material by using a sharp knife, rasps, glass-paper, or a wire heated electrically or in a gas flame. The patterns may be built up by gluing pieces together. Care must be exercised in selecting an adhesive like PVA, which will not dissolve the polystyrene and will vaporize or burn out, leaving little ash. Pieces of expanded polystyrene may be dowelled together with a short piece of wire of the same metal as

that to be cast. Pourer, basins, gates and riser should be made from expanded polystyrene and fixed to the pattern.

It is best to position the pourer to feed the metal into the lowest part of the casting.

The structure of expanded polystyrene is of small, soft pellets compacted together to form the 'solid' material. In fact ninety-eight per cent of the volume of this material is air. When moulded-up and vaporized away by the molten metal, these pellets impart their own characteristic texture to the surface of the solidified metal. This texture can be exploited when sculptural castings are made—the contrast between textured and polished surfaces can be used. Remember that the casting must be fettled, leaving a sawn surface. Plan the position of the pattern in the mould, and hence the position of the pourer gate on the pattern, so that the pourer-gate is on a surface of the casting which is to be polished, or will be hidden. Experiment by using a pourer, basin and gate only, omitting the riser, but vent the mould to permit vapour, gases and steam to escape.

Fig. 3.12 expanded polystyrene pattern and casting

This will considerably reduce the number of unsightly fettling marks.

Aerated Concrete (Siporex)

Mention has been made of the use of cores when holes or cavities are required in castings. Sculptural forms incorporating large holes and cavities may be produced by using a dry aerated concrete, like Siporex, as the pattern material *and* as its own core. The solid pattern, usually of the odd-side type but possibly flat-side, is carved from a block of aerated concrete (Fig. 3.13(a)). Only old saws, chisels, rasps, surforms and drills should be used as the tools quickly become blunt. The pattern is then moulded up as if it were a wooden pattern, although extra care should be taken as the aerated concrete is rather fragile. The pourer, basins, gates and riser are prepared as for normal castings. The pattern and mould should be marked so that when the pattern is replaced in the mould it will be returned to its original position. Channels and cavities, according to the previously determined design are then carved into the pattern (Fig. 3.13(b)). Any features or grooves so carved must join one another and that part of the pattern which will be next to the pourer and riser gates, so that the metal will flow through them when poured. The pattern, now in the form of a core, is replaced in the mould cavity of the drag and the core is positioned on the drag ready for pouring. When the molten metal

Fig. 3.13(a)

Fig. 3.13(b)

has frozen, the casting containing the aerated concrete core is removed and fettled. The concrete core is then broken up leaving an open casting (Fig. 3.13(c)).

The structure of aerated concrete is that of a foam, the material being composed of millions of tiny air bubbles surrounded by the hard concrete. When the aerated concrete is shaped and moulded-up in a fine-grain moulding sand, the texture of the pattern material will be reproduced in the sand, and hence on the casting. In addition, when the metal is cast, the surface of the metal in contact with the channels in the pattern/core will be textured. Planning, similar to that suggested before for expanded polystyrene, is necessary when designing, moulding-up, fettling and finishing a casting using aerated concrete as the pattern material.

Wax patterns
The use of wax as a pattern material in casting is one of the oldest techniques known to man. A pattern was made in wax and then carefully enclosed in clay, an opening was left for the wax to be melted out and the metal to be

poured in. The process is known as the **lost wax** or **cire perdue** method, because the pattern is destroyed in the casting operation.

Today, instead of clay, plaster is used as the mould material. Superior results are obtained by using specially developed investment plasters.

Beeswax can be used for the patterns, but proprietary waxes are now available and these have better modelling properties and melt out and burn away without a residue.

The wax may be shaped by cutting the pattern from the solid, or by building up the form by adding molten wax to a basic shape and modelling it with a warm tool. Wax patterns may also be reproduced from a master pattern. A wax pourer must be attached to the pattern before the investment is made, i.e. before the plaster is poured round the pattern (see Fig. 3.14).

It is possible, by this process, to obtain very fine detail on castings, as the wax may be minutely detailed and as the plaster has such a smooth texture. The technique, therefore, is of value to both the jeweller and the engineer. An overall accuracy of 0.025 mm is possible on as-cast components, and the process is being used increasingly in industry for such items as car parts and electronic equipment.

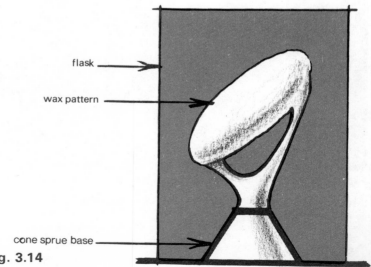

flask

wax pattern

cone sprue base

Fig. 3.14

Fig. 3.13(c)

METALS

A wide range of metals is available which may be cast using the relatively simple equipment of the school workshop. If melting facilities are limited, it may be necessary to extend the analysis of the problem and explore other tentative design solutions. For example, a number of bearings may be required in a cast component for which cast iron would be the ideal material. If it is not possible to melt cast iron, an alternative solution has to be found. It is then necessary to investigate the possibilities of using bronze, brass or aluminium alloys suitably bushed with steel or phosphor bronze, or ball races.

The metals most likely to be used in school foundry-work are aluminium alloys, e.g. LM4 and LM6; zinc alloys, e.g. Kayem 1 and Mazak 5; bronze, e.g. gunmetal; brass, e.g. English Standard; sterling silver and grey cast iron. Lead, tinman's solder, the zinc alloys and the aluminium alloys have relatively low melting points and may be melted in, and poured from a steel ladle or cast iron melting pot. The ladle or melting pot should be coated with a refractory wash to prevent the molten metal dissolving the containing vessel, so contaminating the melt and weakening the vessel. Such a wash is made from whiting mixed with water and sodium silicate, commonly known as waterglass. All metal tools used in contact with molten metal should have a refractory coating. The coating *must* be thoroughly dry before the article is used. It is preferable to melt these metals in a proper furnace. A gas-fired natural-draught furnace will provide enough heat for the purpose. Alternatively, the ladle or melting pot may be heated by brazing torches, in a forced air/gas hearth, or in a blacksmith's forge.

Brass, bronze, silver and cast iron are melted in refractory crucibles made of clay and graphite. These crucibles withstand the higher temperatures necessary to melt these metals, but they must be handled carefully to avoid cracking them. To melt these metals which have high melting points, a forced air/gas furnace is essential.

Fresh ingot or scrap must be thoroughly dry before it is placed in the ladle, melting pot or crucible. Pre-heated ingot or scrap should be used to 'top up' a melt. A damp ingot could well cause an explosion, and a cold ingot will cool the melt unnecessarily.

When metals are heated and melted, they oxidize rapidly and absorb gases. This process increases greatly with the rise in temperature and the metal should not be overheated. The formation of oxide in the form of dross wastes metal, and the oxide may be carried into the mould cavity causing imperfections in the casting. The absorbed gases are liberated when the metal solidifies and produce a porous, weak, unsightly casting showing blowholes. When a metal is overheated, it is likely that certain alloying elements will be burnt away so changing the composition of the alloy. English Standard brass, containing 65 per cent copper and 35 per cent zinc, melts at about 920°C. Copper melts at 1083°C, while zinc melts at 419°C and boils at 907°C. To minimize and try to prevent oxidation and gas absorption, **fluxes** are used to cover the molten metal. Fluxes are in powder form and are sprinkled onto the surface of the melt. Just before pouring, the flux and dross are removed with a heated, refractory-coated tool. To remove unwanted gases, a degassing agent in tablet form is introduced into the melt a few minutes before the metal is poured. The reaction of the degassing agent to the molten metal is vigorous. In school foundries it is usual only to de-gas aluminium melts, and then only when scrap and metal other than fresh ingot is used.

The grain structure of some metals may be modified, or refined, by adding certain chemicals to the melt just before pouring. Such cast metals have a greater ductility than unmodified castings.

It has been mentioned that metals melt at different temperatures, and the melting point of a metal may be changed by the addition of various alloying elements. The temperature at which a molten metal should be poured depends on the shape and size of the mould cavity. In general, the metal should be poured when its temperature, and hence its fluidity, is such that it will flow into, and completely fill the mould cavity, gates, basins, pourer and riser. For castings having thin sections, a higher pouring temperature is needed than for castings of larger section. In addition, it must be remembered that the gating system must not restrict the flow of the metal and so cause it to freeze before the mould cavity is filled. A metal with a large thermal capacity will cool more slowly than one with a small thermal capacity. So it is possible to pour a metal with a high thermal capacity at a temperature only a little above its melting point and it will remain liquid long enough to allow a sound casting to be made.

A summary, giving further details of moulds, patterns and metals is to be found in Figs. 3.15, 3.16 and 3.17.

Mould material	Production method	Pattern material	Metal feed	Industrial usage	Commercial examples	School application	Remarks
Green sand/ loam sand (clay and water bond). **temporary mould**	Moulded by skilled and semi-skilled craftsmen, or by machine (ram or vibration packed).	**Permanent:** Wood, metal, plastic, clay, plaster. **Temporary:** Expanded polystyrene.	Gravity	General foundrywork: production of moulds for casting nearly **all** metals. Bulk size of components almost unlimited.	Drain gratings, engine parts, e.g. cylinder blocks, etc.	Production of components in aluminium, zinc, brass, bronze, cast iron. Hand moulded.	Cheap. Easy to use. Sand is re-used. Some surfaces of castings can be made to cool more quickly than others (chilled) to produce fine grain structure. Faces of mould are lined with metal to chill castings. Pattern shape produces cavity for chills.
Oil bound sand **temporary mould**	As above.	As above.	As above.	As above, but gives reproduction of fine detail.			Expensive. Charred surface of mould is waste.
Investment Plaster **temporary mould**	Skilled craftsmen or semi-mechanized.	Wood, metal or plastic, if release agent is used. Wax: melted from one piece mould. Expanded polystyrene.	Gravity or by centrifugal force.	Specialized foundrywork. Quantity production. Many metals. Accuracy in size, shape and surface finish. Jewellery and silversmithing. Precious metals. Quantity or one-off production.	Charms for bracelets.	Jewellery.	Centrifugal casting machine may be made in school workshop. Use of scrap silver.
Metal **permanent mould**	Moulds or dies machined by skilled craftsmen using hand tools or machine. May be made on copying machines using a master pattern as a template.	Special alloy steels.	Gravity or by centrifugal force or **pressure** into pre-heated dies.	Quantity production. Accuracy in size, shape and surface finish. Die casting metals include lead, zinc, aluminium and brass alloys.	Dinky and Matchbox toys, many automobile parts, e.g. carburetter body.	Limited use for gravity casting of simple components for some projects, e.g. go-kart wheels.	Expensive and hence used only for mass production. Dies for school use may be made of B.M. Steel.
Fireclay/ refractory sands. (shell moulding) **temporary mould**	As for sand, often moulds are made in metal moulds and baked.	Metal plate, patterns.	Gravity.	Specialized foundrywork. Quantity production. Many metals. Accuracy in size, shape and surface finish.			Expensive moulds discarded as waste.
Cuttlefish **gradually expendable.**	Skilled craftsmen. Cavity cut by hand or made by squeezing hard pattern into surface.	(Engraving tools) Metal, wood, plaster, plastic or hard natural solid object.	Gravity.	Jewellery and silversmithing. One-off or very small number of components. Precious metals.		Jewellery.	Simple. Use of scrap silver.
Vinomould **permanent mould.**	Poured in liquid state around the pattern. When set, cut to release pattern.	Any solid material with higher melting point. Wax. Natural objects.		Quantity production of wax patterns for use in cire-perdue lost wax-casting.		Jewellery.	Makes casting of delicate and intricate components and enables repeats of patterns to be made if required.

Fig. 3.15

Pattern material	Production method	Industrial usage	Mould material	Allowances necessary	School application	Remarks
Wood Most commonly used are jelutong, white pine, cherry, mahogany.	craftsmen— Hand and Machine tools by skilled craftsmen— patternmakers.	Extensively used for general foundry work. Repetitive work. Plate patterns used to increase production rate.	Sand.	**Draft**—for ease of removal from mould. **Fillets**—for strength of casting; also strengthens mould. **Size**—**Contraction**, to allow for shrinkage of metal on —**Machining**: to allow for facing **Core prints**—provision of location registers for cores.	Excellent for most engineering design needs.	Pattern made for only one solution, hence in school, used only once, but available for re-use if first casting is a waster The four basic types of pattern are shown in Fig. 3.8. Cheap material: allows use of scrap wood.
Metal Often aluminium alloy for weight reasons.		Limited use but patterns stronger than wood and hence withstand hard wear.			Very rarely used if sand moulded, but could be used as master pattern for lost wax or cuttlefish castings.	Expensive material. Shaping processes could be expensive in labour and tools.
Wax	Modelled with warm modelling tools (see p. 32), or cast in Vinomould.	Centrifugal casting for mass production in engineering, e.g. carburetter parts, jewellery and silversmithing, e.g. rings, bracelets.	Usually investment plaster. Completely surrounding pattern which may be of an intricate shape.	Wax sprue or runner added to pattern to allow entry of molten metal when investment plaster surrounds pattern.	Jewellery and silver-smithing. Sculptural work	Wax pattern burnt out of mould material before pouring. Excellent for creative work. Simple and straightforward to use.
Expanded polystyrene	Shaped by hand tools, e.g. sharp knives, saws, or by hot wire. Patterns built up by gluing and dowelling. Industrial use of very high speed routers.	Components for engineering industries, see Fig. 3.12. Sculptural work, see Fig. 3.13.	Sand or investment plaster.	Foam sprue and rise added to pattern for entry of molten metal. Virtually eliminates need for cores. Contraction Machining.	Some engineering design needs—poor finish produced. Sculptural work. Surface texture of casting produced by expanded polystyrene may be exploited. Care therefore required in positioning pourer and riser gates.	Foam pattern burnt out in mould **during pouring.** Vapour given off; must be used in a well ventilated room. Excellent for creative work. Simple and straightforward to use.
Aerated concrete e.g. Siporex	Hand tools, e.g. old saws, files, rasps, drills.		Sand.	**Draft**—(Usually odd side patterns, but flat side patterns can be produced.)	Sculptural work. Surface texture of casting produced by aerated concrete may be exploited. Care then required in positioning riser gates. Surface may be filled to reduce texture.	Material crumbles and cracks if handled carelessly. Negatives cut in pattern become positives when metal is cast. Concrete core is chipped away after fettering. Can be used as cores.
Plastic	Hand and machine.	For Vinomoulds for mass production for cire perdue process.				

Fig. 3.16

Metal/alloy	Composition (approx.)	Melting Range °C / Pouring Range °C	Fluidity	Machinability	School Use	Remarks
Aluminium	Commercially pure	660 / 700 – 760	Fair	Poor	Simple sculptural castings only.	Little used because of poor working properties.
Aluminium alloys LM 4	3% copper 5% silicon Remainder aluminium and trace elements.	525 – 625 / 680 – 720 (750 for v. thin sects.)	Good	Good	General purpose castings	
LM 6	12% silicon Remainder aluminium and trace elements.	565 – 575 / 690 – 720 (760 for v. thin sects.)	Very good	Fair	Castings with thin walled sections.	Should be modified with small addition of sodium to refine grain structure and increase ductility.
Zinc alloys Kayem 1	Traces of lead, cadmium and tin. Remainder zinc.	378 – 390 / 400 – 440	Very good	Good	Blanking and forming tools.	Used for press tools, blanking and forming. Can be melted in a ladle over a brazing torch.
Mazak 5	4% aluminium 1% copper Traces of magnesium, lead and iron. Remainder zinc.	382 – 387 / 400 – 420	Very good	Good		Used for most die castings, e.g. car parts and toys. Can be melted over a brazing torch.
Lead	Commercially pure	327 / 340 approx.	Fair	Very poor	Very simple castings, such as weights.	Useful for demonstrations, may be melted in a ladle over a brazing torch.
Lead alloy Tinman's solder	50% lead 50% tin	183 – 204 / 220 approx.	Fair	Very poor		
Copper alloys Brass (English Standard)	65% copper 35% zinc	900 – 930 / 1020 – 1100	Good	Good		Addition of between 1% and 2% lead improves machinability.
Bronze (gunmetal)	90% copper 10% tin	850 – 1000 / 1200 – 1200	Good	Good		Addition of between 1% and 2% lead improves machinability. The addition of phosphorous lowers the melting point.
Iron alloy Cast iron (grey)	94% Iron 3% carbon 2% silicon Traces of manganese, sulphur, phosphorous.	1130 – 1250 / 1400 – 1500	Very good	Very good		Addition of silicon (e.g. ladeloy) prevents hard spots.
Silver alloy Sterling silver	92.5% silver 7.5% copper	779 – 890 / 990	Very good	Fair	Jewellery, usually centrifugally cast.	Economical use of scrap.

Fig. 3.17

PROBLEMS

The programme of your work in design is planned to introduce you to a systematic process of designing *abstract* forms before the additional problem of *function* is included. Problems requiring wooden patterns or metal dies for their solution are usually associated with functional objects and are left until later in the book. Here the problems suggested will involve you with the other mould and pattern-making materials. It is suggested that you use either aluminium alloys or zinc alloys for these castings.

Before starting any practical work, such as pattern-making, moulding-up and casting, it is essential to: (i) plan and organize the procedure thoroughly; and (ii) plan and organize the shapes, patterns and use of textures involved in the design of the article so that the final product will look right. See also Appendix A, pp. 169 to 179.

There are as many possible ways of starting to design an object as there are of casting it. Possibly the easiest way to begin designing is to take a simple geometric shape and explore and develop it.

EXPANDED POLYSTYRENE

1 If you start with a *square* as the basic shape, it is interesting to discover what can be done with it.

(A) Take a 150 mm square of paper and work entirely with scissors which you may find easier than drawing. Now remove areas systematically by cutting off strips of uniform width as shown in the diagrams 3.18 to 3.20 and gluing them down on to a different coloured paper.

What happens visually to the square if it is treated in this way? Study the remaining shape after the removal of each piece and write down your comments beside a similar drawn or cut shape in your design book or folder. Is the original square sufficiently satisfying? Does one cut alone make it sufficiently different?

Eventually, after several cuts, does the difference in side lengths become too excessive?

When do you think the shape appears to be most successful and satisfying?

(B) Having decided on what you consider to be a well-balanced shape, cut 10 mm strips from a different coloured piece of paper and apply them experimentally to the surface of your chosen shape.

(C) Arrange all strips at right angles to each other and to the basic shape and try to provide a visual link between any two shapes (see Figs. 3.20 and 3.21). Leave at least 10 mm space between the strips.

(D) Now make this pattern in expanded polystyrene 10 mm thick. The thickness of a normal ceiling tile will do for this purpose.

(E) In discussion, plan the best method of pouring such a casting as mentioned on p. 30 and apply the necessary pourer, basin, gate and riser.

(F) Mould, cast and fettle the casting.

(G) Mount for decorative use, either singly or by grouping several together as a panel.

(H) List and reconsider, or analyse every stage in your planning for making this project, taking care to get each stage in the right order. Do not write in essay form but use notes, like these:
   1 Pattern considered in connection with casting flask to decide method of pouring.
   2 Pourer, basin, gate and riser added to pattern in approved positions.
   3 Flask, moulding board, sand prepared . . .
   4 Etc.

(I) Conclude this work by asking yourself questions about your finished article:
Does it look as satisfying as a low relief as it did in two dimensions? If not what could be done to improve it?
Would you work differently if you were to tackle the problem again now?
Is the final product in the cast metal more interesting due to its colour, lustre and texture than the three-dimensional pattern of expanded polystyrene?
Could one surface be given a different texture, such as by

filing and polishing it, in order to provide a 'centre of interest'?

Could a 'centre of interest' be achieved by colouring one surface? (See Appendix A.)

Could the visual effects of the casting have been obtained by making the object by a means other than by casting? If so, list and sketch a few possible ideas of how you would do so.

Aerated Concrete

From the work you did on Problem 7, you will realize that the design process needs as much planning and logical development as the technical process involved. For the next problem, we will continue the exploration of a basic shape as the design source for our work, but we will add variety to our thinking by using the circle as our original shape.

2 (A) Prepare several 100 m diameter circles. Use either scissors or pencil, develop the shape by dissecting rather than adding to it. Explore the shape by experimenting with one straight line division in different places as before. Record each one in your design folder, and make notes on your findings as for Problem 1(H) on p. 38.

(B) Select the line which you feel makes the most visually interesting division.
Add to this line another at right angles to the first and again develop this technique progressively. Make notes as before.

(C) Select from your work the most interesting design, draw it again on tracing paper and relate the tracing to the original drawing as shown so that you can get an impression of the design as a three-dimensional object. You may need to modify your original idea slightly.

(D) To allow the metal to flow better when the shape is cast, the corners should be rounded off. Plan this carefully on paper also, varying the sizes of the curves, if necessary, to make this an improvement visually as well as technically.

(E) Carve a shape from a piece of aerated concrete,

the plan of which is a circle of 100 mm diameter, and which has a roughly elliptical elevation. On completion, heat the block to drive off any moisture and mould up.

(F) Remove your pattern from the mould and carve into it the final design you have developed. A groove should be cut all round at the widest part and all the grooves should be at least 8 mm wide and deep. Return it to the mould, making provisions for pourer, basins, gates, riser and cast.

(G) When the casting is cool, remove it from the mould, fettle and break out the core. Finish as required.

(H) As in Problem 1(H), evaluate in note and sketch form the success of the product. Keep these notes in your design folder together with, if possible, a photograph of the final piece of work. (See Figs. 3. 23–3.26.)

Cuttlefish

Once the process of working from a basic shape has been grasped, any shape can be used in connection with any of the casting processes, but to aid your progress further a *triangle* has been selected as the basic shape for the next problem.

3 (A) Within a rectangle 40 mm x 25 mm, see how many variations you can produce by placing a triangular form around the perimeter of this shape. (Fig. 3. 27).

(B) Continue the experiment by introducing two smaller triangles to touch any of the original ones (see Fig. 3.28).

(C) From all your sketches, select the one that you think would look most pleasing when cast in metal. Now repeat the unit. Redraw this, making each triangle appear triangular in section.

(D) Prepare a cuttlefish mould for casting and carve your final design on the inner face of one piece of the mould using a triangular shaped graver or similar tool, as shown in Fig. 3.30(b).

(E) Cast as directed on p. 27. Fettle and polish as required.

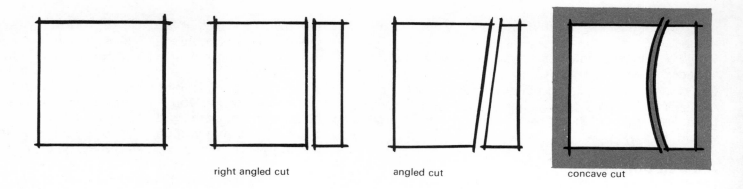

right angled cut   angled cut   concave cut

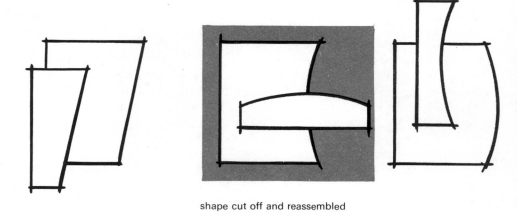

shape cut off and reassembled

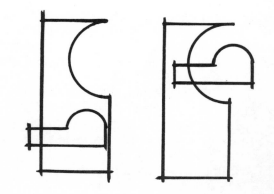

Fig. 3.18

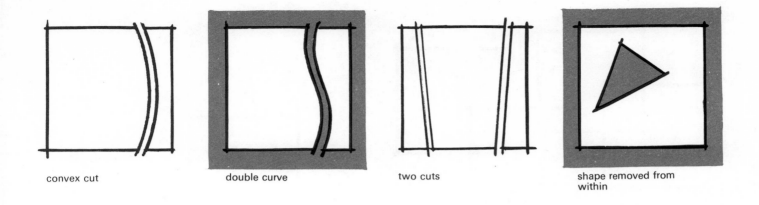

convex cut   double curve   two cuts   shape removed from within

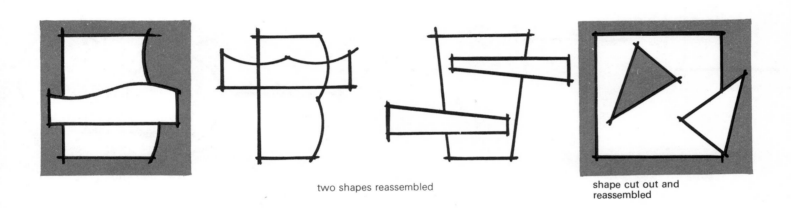

two shapes reassembled   shape cut out and reassembled

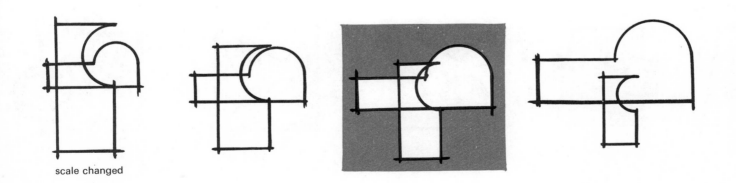

scale changed

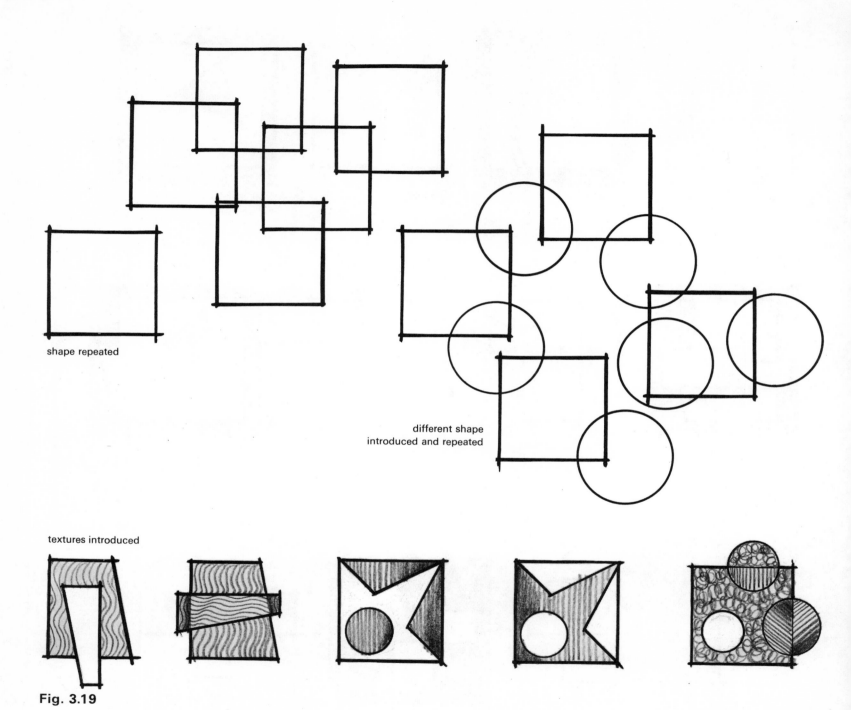

shape repeated

different shape
introduced and repeated

textures introduced

Fig. 3.19

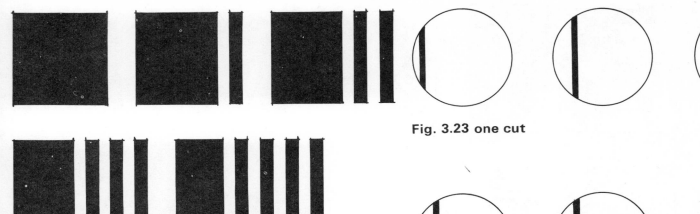

Fig. 3.20

Fig. 3.23 one cut

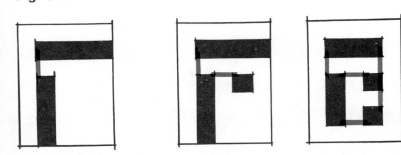

Fig. 3.21 visual link

Fig. 3.24 two cuts at right angles

Fig. 3.22

Fig. 3.25 near surface and rear surface related

Fig. 3.26 corners rounded

Fig. 3.27 triangles round the perimeter

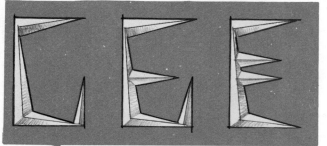

Fig. 3.28 one small triangle added   **two small triangles added**

Fig. 3.30(b)

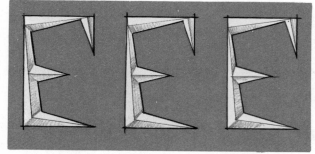

Fig. 3.29 shape repeated

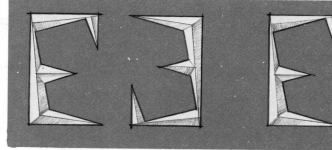

shape reversed and repeated

Wax

A similar development of shape can be used as with the cuttlefish casting but the use of wax will dictate a slightly different form. Whereas the graver was sharp and crisp, the wax is more mobile, softer and fluid, therefore the shapes will be softer also. (See Figs. 3.31 and 3.32).

4 As with the cuttlefish, design a unit which can be repeated to form a bracelet, or used singly as a brooch. Work out how many units you will need for the object you want to make (see page 45).

Fig. 3.30(a) shape cut into cuttlefish

44

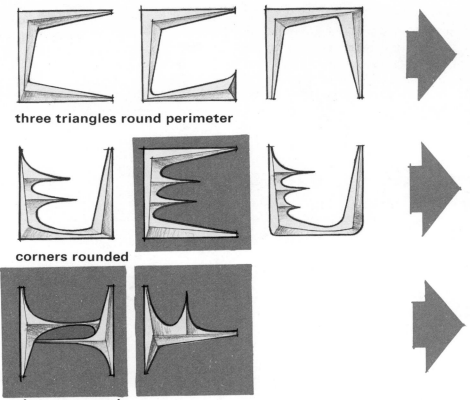

three triangles round perimeter

corners rounded

Fig. 3.31 shape repeated

Fig. 3.32

45

MIXING METALS—ALLOYS

Chapter 2—The Structure of Metals—mentioned that pure metals are rarely used and described how desirable working properties are obtained by alloying metals. Most alloying is done by mixing the ingredients of the alloy in their liquid state, and its success depends entirely on the property of fusibility. It is impossible to give an exact analogy to alloying, but at a very simple level it can be likened to the mixing of colours. The colour blue is said to be 'cold', and the colour yellow to be 'exciting'. When mixed, these two dissimilar colours produce green, which is said to be 'restful'.

In Fig. 3.17, the table of metals, there is a list of a number of alloys suitable for casting in school. The table, Fig. 3.33 below gives the basic details of other commonly used alloys.

Alloy	Composition		Properties	Uses
Copper Based **Brasses** Gilding Metal	copper zinc	85% 15%	Very malleable and ductile, easily soldered.	Cheap jewellery.
English Standard	copper zinc	66% 34%	Casts well and may be rolled and hammered.	General use.
German Silver (Nickel Silver)	copper zinc nickel	55% 27% 18%	Good resistance to corrosion. Solders well, good base for silver plating.	Fittings on ships and cars, etc. Cheap jewellery.
Copper Based **Bronze** **Bearing metals** Phosphor bronze	tin antimony copper	93% 3.5% 3.5%	Good wearing properties (see page 158). Can take heavy loads, high speeds.	Big end bearings. Motor and aero engines.
Tin Based **Bearing metals** White metals	copper tin phosphorus	88.7% 11.0% 0.3%	Obtainable as cast bar or tube for bearings: hard.	Bearings in very heavy machinery, worm wheels, gears, etc.
Aluminium Based Duralumin	aluminium copper manganese magnesium	95% 4% 0.5% 0.5%	Has the property of age hardening. Light but very strong.	Used for forgings, sheet, rods, tubes, rivets and castings.
Silver Based Sterling silver	silver copper	92.5% 7.5%	Malleable, ductile, easily soldered. High thermal and electrical conductivity.	Electrical contacts. General silversmithing; castings.
Britannia silver	silver copper	95.84% 4.16%	Very malleable, easily soldered.	Deep raising, drawing, spinning etc.

Fig. 3.33 (See page 111 for further details.)

JOINING METALS

The property of fusibility also makes it possible for us to join metals in a permanent way. Welding, brazing and soldering produce complete or at least partial fusion (alloying), at the surface of the pieces of metal being joined. A more or less continuous crystal structure forms across the area of the joint as seen in Fig. 3.34.

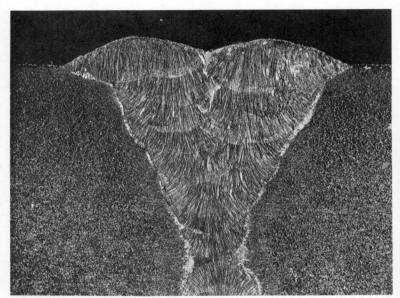

Fig. 3.34 etched micro-section of a welded joint

Welding

In each case the surfaces of the metals to be joined are melted either by the gas flame or the electric arc, and welding rod or filler rod, is used to fill the weld. The rod, which is usually of a similar composition to the metals being joined, is held close to the work and melted into the prepared joint. The edges of these pieces also fuse so that a strong, continuous joint is formed. The weld is really a miniature casting.

BRAZING

The temperature used for brazing is between 600°C and 900°C and is therefore attainable with a normal gas/air torch. Unlike welding, the metals being joined do not melt at all. As the heating is gradual, oxide tends to form on the surfaces of the joint. This prevents fusion between the brazing material and the metals being joined and so a chemical flux of the **borax** type is used. This is applied to the freshly filed joint and solder before heating commences and fuses at a low temperature to form a glass-like substance which spreads over and around the joint and prevents oxidization taking place. After soldering, this flux can be removed from the work by pickling it in warm dilute sulphuric acid, in the case of non-ferrous metals, and in a caustic solution, such as Jenolite, for the ferrous metals.

Fig. 3.35 etched micro-section of a brazed joint

Brazing solder or **spelter** is a brass containing fifty per cent copper and fifty per cent zinc and melts (or freezes) at a temperature of 875°C. This gives a tough, strong joint, but the work should not be quenched when still hot as it tends to make the brass in the joint contract at a different rate to the workpiece, creating a weakness. Brazing is used on most ferrous and non-ferrous alloys which melt at a higher temperature than the solder.

High grade brazing compounds—**silver solders**—contain a high but varying percentage of silver which lowers the melting point. Such a range of solders makes it possible to make several brazed joints on one piece of work without the fear of earlier ones remelting as the work is heated each time for soldering subsequent joints.

Silver solders are used mostly on non-ferrous metals, particularly on silver. Where the solder alloys with the silver to form a new alloy on the joint—which therefore becomes richer in silver—it results in a higher melting point than the original solder.

On the other hand, when used on a copper alloy, it alloys with the copper, forming a new alloy with a smaller silver content and therefore melts at a *lower* temperature than the original solder. It is important to remember this last point when planning a series of such soldering operations.

The table, Fig. 3.36, gives the brazing spelters available.

SOFT SOLDERING

As with brazing, a thin film of molten alloy is applied to the parts to be joined at a temperature below the melting point of these parts. In order that the solder should wet and flow freely over the surfaces to be joined and adhere firmly to the workpiece when frozen, the joints must be free from oxides. In this instance, a flux is used which will act as a solvent to the thin oxide layers which are liable to form before the surface can be wetted by the solder. The flux also prevents

the solder from oxidizing. Typical fluxes are zinc chloride ('killed spirits'), hydrochloric acid (dilute) or ammonium chloride (sal ammoniac) or a combination of these. These fluxes are corrosive and should be washed carefully from the work after soldering. As any trace of corrosion would be fatal to an electrical connection, a resin-based flux is used for soldering electrical joints and often a resin-cored solder wire is used directly onto the joint concerned. Solvent fluxes are often known as active fluxes and non-corrosive fluxes as passive fluxes.

It is the problem of removing the fast-forming oxides of aluminium and its alloys that makes soldering very difficult on this metal.

As the heat required to melt the solder is such that it can be applied to the work by a soldering bit, this must also be fluxed before the soldering operation commences. The copper bit must not be allowed to get red hot when carrying solder as the tin in the solder alloys with it to form bronze which does not adhere to soft solder.

When you are designing, work requiring metal joints of this kind must be carefully planned so that a correct sequence of solders is used. The exercises that follow later are prepared to help you with this planning. The stages in soldering must be included in your design analysis.

The methods of soldering are summarised in Fig. 3.38.

Group	Type	Grade	Composition		Melting Range °C Solidus–Liquidus
hard	Silver solder	Easy Flow No. 2	50% silver 15% copper 16% zinc 19% cadmium		620–640
		Easy	66.7% silver, plus . . .		705–723
		Medium	74% silver, plus . . .		720–765
		Hard	66.7% silver, plus . . .		745–778
		Enamelling	81.0% silver, plus . . .		730–800
	Brazing spelter		50% copper 50% zinc		875
			60% copper 40% zinc		900
			65% copper 35% zinc		915

Fig. 3.36

GENERAL PREPARATION

Prepare the two pieces of metal which are to be joined. Files, emery cloth, scrapers or chemicals may be used, as most appropriate. The gap in the joint should be as small as possible and the joint well-fitting.

Flux *both* pieces of metal. The corrosive fluxes should never be used if they cannot be easily cleaned off after soldering is complete. Flux the cleaned solder.

The joint must be held together firmly. The action of the expanding flux when heated, the pressure from the gas/air torch or the touch of the strip of solder or soldering bit can displace the joints. Joints may be held by their own weight, or by additional weights, magnets, clamps, soft iron binding wire, or stitches. However held, the joint must *not* be disturbed until the solder has solidified.

SOLDERING—HARD (brazing and silver soldering)

Position the work on the brazing hearth so that the joint is easy to get at.

Flat surfaces should be lifted from the firebrick to allow all round heating.

Heat the joint area generally and gently at first to drive off moisture from the flux.

Heat the joint strongly—*both pieces to the same temperature*. When the flux flows, feed the solder to the edge or the corner of the joint and allow it to flow along the joint. Use only sufficient solder to fill the joint. Whenever possible, apply solder to the outside of the joint rather than the inside. This makes cleaning up easier.

Reheating the joint to remelt and flush the solder can form a smooth joint line. Overheating of the solder causes a weak joint. Remove the flux by pickling (see p. 176) or by mechanical means.

SOLDERING—SOFT

Support the work to be soldered—preferably on wood to retain heat. Pick up solder on the newly tinned soldering bit. Press the bit on to one end of the joint until the

Fig. 3.37

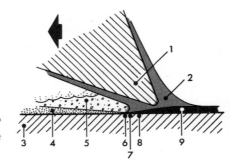

1 soldering bit
2 Molten solder
3 Base Metal
4 Flux
5 Boiling flux removes oxide
6 Base metal in contact with molten solder
7 Solder replaces flux
8 Solder reacts chemically with base metal
9 Solder freezes (solidifies)

Group	Type	Grade	Composition	Melting Range °C Solidus–Liquidus	Remarks
soft	Lead and tin	B.S. solder A	35% lead 60% tin	183–185	tinman's solder. Lowest melting point. Free running.
		B.S. solder K	40% lead 60% tin	183–188	
		B.S. solder B	50% lead 50% tin	183–205	tinman's ordinary
		B.S. solder G	60% lead 40% tin	183–234	blowpipe solder
		B.S. solder H	65% lead 35% tin	183–255	plumber's solder—wiped joints
		B.S. solder V	80% lead 20% tin	183–276	dipping solder

Fig. 3.38

D.A.T.–M.—C

conducted heat allows the solder to flow into the joint. Repeat this procedure at the other end of the joint. This process is called tacking and helps to hold the joint together.

Pick up solder on the re-heated bit and press it on to the joint at the first end. When the solder tacking melts and the solder flows, *slowly* draw the bit along the joint allowing the metal to be heated and the solder to flow. Re-charge the bit with solder and continue the joint until it is completed. Wipe or wash off the flux when the solder has solidified.

PROPORTIONAL RELATIONSHIPS

When creating objects such as buildings, furniture or pottery, the proportion of the whole and of the different parts has always been considered to be of the utmost importance.

Ideally, each part should have a proportional relationship to the rest if it is to appear well-balanced and visually interesting and many theories and formulae have been suggested to ensure this. For example, the proportions of the Parthenon in Greece and of most classical archi-

Fig. 3.39

tecture were based on the Greek Golden Section (see below), whereas those of St Paul's Cathedral in London were based throughout on a theory relating to musical harmony which suggests that aural harmony (or balance) and visual balance are similarly pleasing. Theories like these provide a foundation from which to make judgments concerning the appearance or visual success of an object, but it is doubtful whether they should be used indiscriminately.

An appreciation of beauty (aesthetics) belongs to the individual and is relevant only to him and his senses, whereas mathematical facts are complete in themselves and are not variable from one individual to another. It would seem, therefore, that aesthetics should not rely merely on numbers and that mathematical measurements can only be used as a starting point, or in an attempt to justify something which is already considered beautiful. Even this second point is doubtful, as it may be equally possible to justify some things that are not considered beautiful.

The Golden Section

Of the many formulae governing proportional relationships, perhaps the Greek Golden Section is the most popular. Here the ratio of the short to the long is the same as the long to the whole, or $a:b = b:c$ (see Fig. 3.40). Means of constructing this are shown in Figs. 3.40 and 3.41(a) and you will see that sub-divisions of areas within the original rectangle are possible using this formula. This allows a designer to consider every part of his design to ensure that a pleasing relationship exists between them.

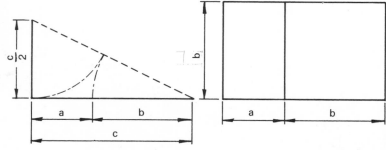

Fig. 3.40 the right-hand diagram shows how length 'b' is used to provide a main dimension of the required Golden Section

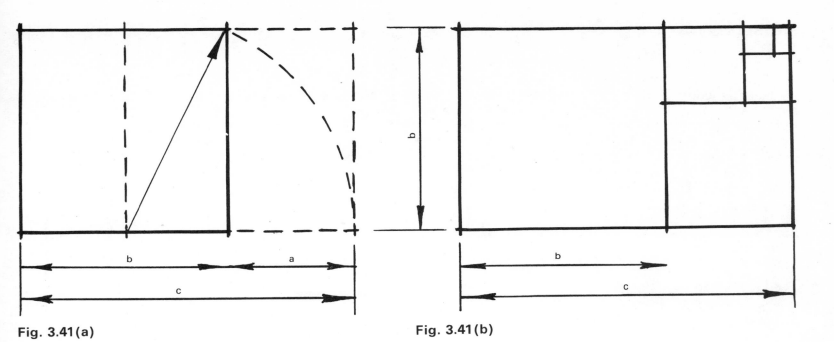

Fig. 3.41(a)   **Fig. 3.41(b)**

A second method is shown here, where in view (b) the process is taken to a second and third stage by the subdivision of some of the areas within the whole, using the same process over and over again.

Experiment with this technique by selecting any suitable length, developing it into a rectangle and sub-dividing this further into smaller areas as shown in Fig. 3.41 (b).

Experiment also with the visual appearances that a rectangle so proportioned can produce by reproducing it vertically instead of horizontally and by using lines instead of closed figures as shown in Fig. 3.42. Do these still look right? Do they still appear to have the same proportion? Results of experiments such as this are very important when designing. They show that aesthetics cannot be planned by mathematics alone, and that for final decisions you must rely almost entirely on your own sensitivity. This can only be developed by continually exercising your visual senses. As a musician practises over and over again to become proficient, so you must practise continuously to develop your powers of visual appreciation.

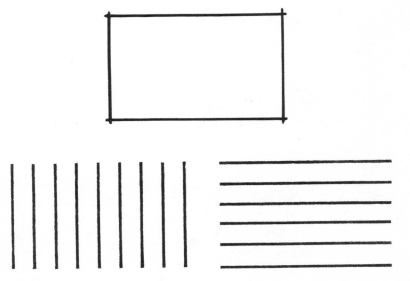

Fig. 3.42

PROBLEMS

1 Draw a line of length between 50 mm and 150 mm and, using the formula of the Golden Section, divide it it into two well-proportioned parts using a line at right angles. The length of this line should also be determined by the same rule of proportion. Repeat this exercise for four different lengths between 50 mm and 150 mm.

Make these up using 4 mm square mild steel. Carefully plan your method of joining them as the second part of this problem is to join these four shapes together by the same formula, thereby producing a well-proportioned space sculpture, as featured in Fig. 3.43.

2 Produce a space-frame construction, based on the shapes produced in Fig. 3.41(b) or your first experiment (page 51).

(A) Use number one rectangle for the main elevation and decide what proportion you will use for the side elevation, as suggested in Fig. 3.44.

(B) Having decided this, arrange either Nos. 2, 3, 4, 5 or 6 shapes within elevation number 1, as shown. Sketch and plan freely.

(C) When you have decided on this, take one of the remaining shapes and arrange it within the side elevation, which should give a space frame something like Fig. 3.45.

(D) If the frame is mild steel and one of the solid areas copper and the other tinplate how will you fasten these in position?

(E) Plan the whole construction carefully before starting the practical work, and make notes of this on your design sheet.

From the last problems set, we can learn a great deal about joining metals and about proportional shapes and areas in space. To work from the Golden Section rectangle is very rigid, and working to mathematical principles, which allow little room for personal judgments, can be very limiting. By now you should have sufficient experience and skill in joining metals and, possibly, in producing good shapes, so that you can work more freely with geometric pattern. Now work carefully through Problem 3.

3 Examine the possibilities for making structures using straight rods and sheet, and joining these together as shown in Fig. 3.46. From these suggestions, select your own method of planning and make such a space-frame.

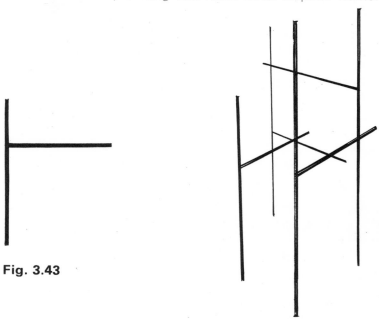

Fig. 3.43

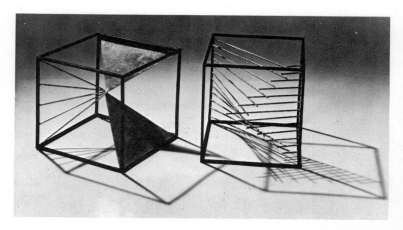

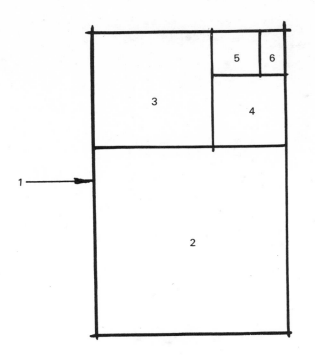

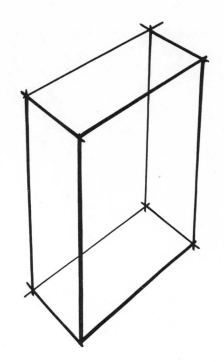

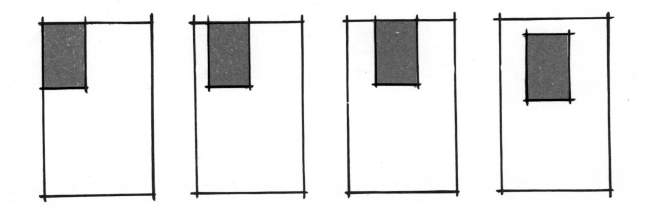

Fig. 3.44

Fig. 3.45

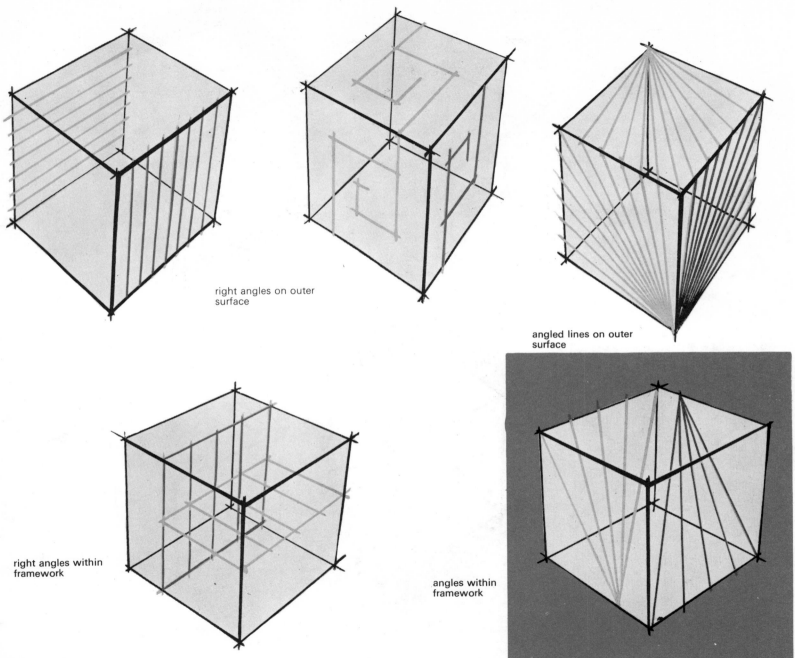

right angles on outer
surface

angled lines on outer
surface

right angles within
framework

angles within
framework

Fig. 3.46(a)

55

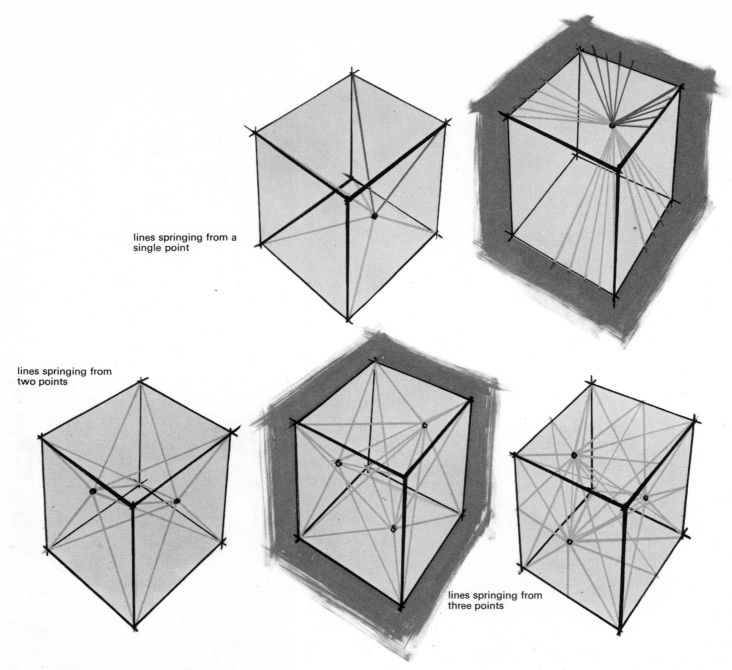

lines springing from a
single point

lines springing from
two points

lines springing from
three points

Fig. 3.46(b)

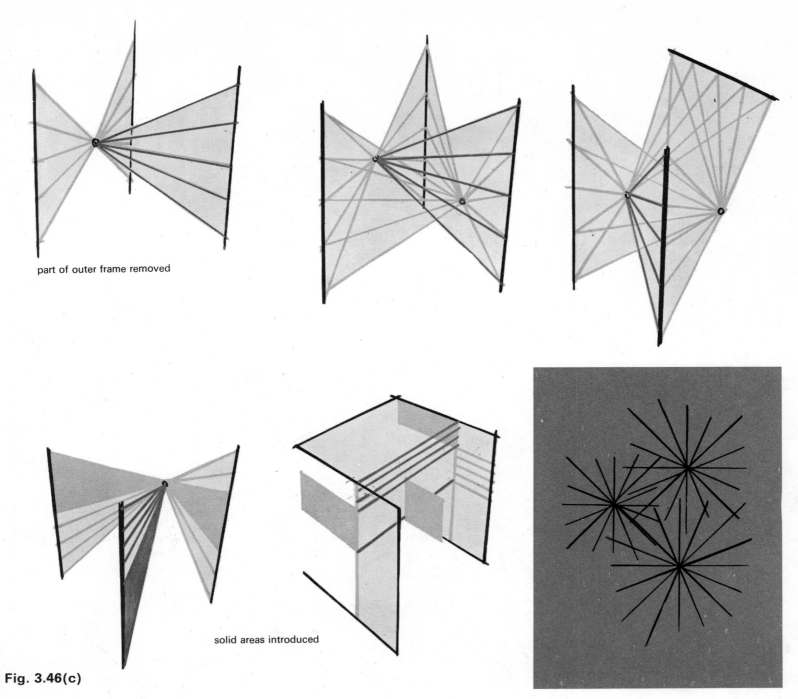

part of outer frame removed

solid areas introduced

Fig. 3.46(c)

57

Chapter 4

MALLEABILITY

What happens to a piece of metal when it is being worked, that is, when it is permanently deformed or displaced by hammering, pressing, rolling or by drawing through a die? Think back to what you have learnt about the atomic and crystal grain structure of metals. The highly-energized, freely-moving atoms in molten metal form into the organized patterns of the dendrites and then into crystal grains when the metal freezes. The regular growth of this crystal lattice is occasionally interrupted, producing dislocations (see Fig. 2.5); the directions of the atoms, as they pack, vary from crystal to crystal (see Fig. 4.1).

When the metal is in its frozen, solid state, it can be worked in the ways mentioned above. This working tends to move the dislocations to the grain boundaries and to make the atoms slide along their slip planes. So, working destroys the original crystal structure of the metal, squashing the grains or making them longer in the direction of working. These actions harden the metal and this is referred to as **work hardening.** The metal can be returned to its original state of softness by heating it, a process called **annealing.** During the annealing, recrystallization takes place so that the metal may then be worked again. The temperature at which recrystallization takes place varies from metal to metal. The recrystallization temperature for lead is so low that it takes place at normal room temperature while the metal is being worked.

When metals are worked hot, as when a blacksmith forges iron or steel at red heat, the deformed crystal structure continually recrystallizes under the effect of the heat. See Fig. 4.2(a) and (b).

The ability of metals to extend permanently in all directions by hammering, pressing or rolling, that is, under compression, without rupture and cracking, is called **malleability.** The metals must have plasticity and react like Plasticine or putty, but they need not be strong.

When a metal has the property which allows it to be permanently reduced in cross-section by being pulled through a die without rupturing, it is said to be **ductile.** Ductile metals must also have plasticity but, unlike Plasticine, they must be strong in tension, that is, they must withstand being stretched. This property of some metals to distort readily when compressed or stretched makes available a wide range of shaping processes. Each of the terms, hammering, rolling, pressing and drawing, may be subdivided into still more specific techniques. Some of these techniques will be discussed later.

There are two ways in which easily workable metals are available in design and production. Firstly, a very large proportion of the metals used are required in forms dependent on malleability and ductility in their production processes. Examples of these forms are sheet, plate, strip, bar, rod, wire, tube, angle and other sections, and extru-

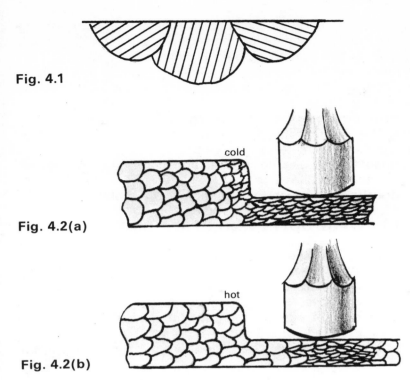

Fig. 4.1

Fig. 4.2(a)

cold

Fig. 4.2(b)

hot

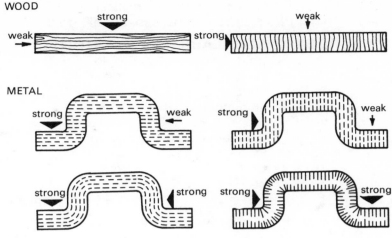

Fig. 4.3

sions. These are produced in an extensive range of standard stock sizes from a wide variety of metals and are available for the manufacture of metal objects which need specific properties to work efficiently. It is extremely important that the strength of the metal is retained, and even increased, when it is formed by these processes. This strength is due to the crystal grain flow caused during compression or stretching. When metal is worked, especially if it is worked in one direction (as in forging), the crystal grains are squashed into longer, thread-like forms. The grain-flow of some metals appears like the fibrous grain of wood, and improves the physical properties of the metal. Just as wood has more strength across its fibres than between its fibres, so metal components are stronger when the grain fibres are made to flow along the axis of the workpiece than they are in other directions.

In a forged crankshaft, the grain structure flows through the shape, as in Fig. 4.3, making it stronger than if it was machined from the solid, when the grain flow would be

cut, or if the metal were cast, when the grain direction would be perpendicular to the surfaces of the shape.

The general result of working metals is that they become stronger in the direction of working. However, if the metal is over-worked when cold, the work hardening increases until eventually the metal is so brittle that it cracks. Failure of components in aircraft, ships and cars through vibration, and known as fatigue, is the result of extended work hardening.

Other reasons why the properties of malleability and ductility are important, and therefore useful, are that the shaping processes used are frequently:

(a) more economical in material than if the components were machined from the solid, as in the case of the crankshaft mentioned above,

(b) carried out quickly. The initial roughing-out of the crankshaft would take a considerable amount of time,

(c) the only ones by which the form of the component can be obtained. The thin pressed panel of a car roof could not be cast or machined from the solid.

In addition, advantage is often taken of the work hardening, and hence the increase in strength of the metal caused by cold shaping processes. For example, to obtain the equal strength and rigidity required for a car roof panel, a thin, work-hardened pressing is both lighter in weight and cheaper than a panel made from soft, annealed metal. Fig. 4.4 shows the order of malleability of some metals starting from the most malleable of all, gold.

ORDER	MALLEABILITY	DUCTILITY	
1	gold	gold	
2	silver	silver	
3	copper	platinum	
4	aluminium	iron	
5	tin	nickel	
6	platinum	copper	
7	lead	aluminium	
8	zinc	zinc	
9	iron	tin	
10	nickel	lead	**Fig. 4.4**

The following ways of working metals depend on their malleability. The property of ductility will be examined later in the chapter.

HOT WORKING
Like casting, forging is one of the most ancient metal-working processes. The ability of the metal to recrystallize immediately after deformation makes hot working very relevant to heavy industrial processes of manufacture and shaping, for when hot the metal is more plastic and more easily moved under the hammer or press. In industry the difficulties of holding hot metal can be overcome by mechanical means.

During a forging operation, the coarse grain structure obtained from an original casting is broken down and replaced by a fine grain structure. Other metallurgical advantages will be illustrated when discussing the industrial method of drop forging.

The forging of metals ranges from the work of the jobbing blacksmith, using traditional hand tools on metal heated in an open coke hearth, to heavy engineering components shaped by hydraulic presses after heating in gas, oil or electrically heated furnaces.

The advantages of forging as a shaping process include both strength, in that the grain of the metal is made to flow and follow the shape of the component, and economy, for the metal is pushed and squeezed into shape rather than being cut and wasted.

In schools little use is made of hot working of metals,

with the important exception of hammering, or forging ferrous alloys, where forging is carried out in the traditional manner. In industry forging is done by a variety of processes including pressing, rolling and drop forging. There are three basic processes which are performed by forging. These are:

drawing down and **spreading** whereby the cross section of the metal is changed or reduced, but the length and/or width of the metal is increased;

upsetting, when the cross section of the metal is increased and the length reduced;

bending, in which the direction of the metal is changed.

DRAWING DOWN AND SPREADING
Drawing down is done by heating the metal rod to a bright red heat, holding it at an angle to the **bick** and striking on the end of the rod. Work is commenced at the end of the rod, otherwise piping or hollowing of the end will occur.

The process may be speeded up by working on the anvil bick, or edge of the anvil face and then smoothing off on the face of the anvil.

Work should only be carried out with the metal at full red heat.

UPSETTING or JUMPING UP
The metal rod is heated to a bright heat and quenched with water poured from a ladle, except where upsetting is to take place. It is then struck on its end, so forcing the metal into itself where it remains red hot and plastic.

The metal may be held in a vertical position on the anvil while it is hammered, or if it is long and heavy enough it may be jumped up and down with the red hot end on the anvil face. If the metal bends during the operation it must be straightened at once.

When strip or square section metal is bent a round external corner is produced (see Fig. 4.5(a)). If a square external corner is required as in Fig. 4.5(b), how would one gain the extra metal needed to fill the corner?

BENDING
Small section metal may be bent cold after suitable annealing. Larger section metal is bent by heating it to a bright red heat and then tapping it over the bick or edge

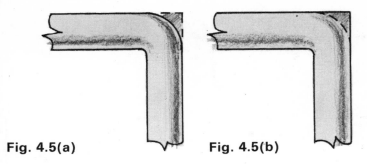

Fig. 4.5(a)   **Fig. 4.5(b)**

of the anvil depending on the tightness of the bend required. In some cases the work may be bent with tongs, or by placing part in a vice and pulling and/or tapping the metal round with a hammer. Heavy hammer blows should be avoided when bending red hot metal, as they will tend to dent it.

TWISTING

A decorative effect may be given to rectangular or octagonal sectioned metal by twisting it.

The metal is heated locally, along the length where the twist is required, and then, with one end of the length to be twisted firmly held, a twisting wrench is slipped over

the metal to the other end and the metal twisted with a continuous turning action. The operation must be carried out as quickly as possible, before the metal cools and retards the twisting. The edges or the faces of the metal may be treated first with punches and chisels to add interest to the effect of the twists as shown in the photograph.

Experiment with twisting metal using other forms of texturing or patterning. Extend these experiments to include the alteration of the cross-section of round stock then twisting it. (See Fig. 4.6.)

PUNCHING or DRIFTING

Long holes or splits may be made through metal by cutting it with a hot or cold set. Round, oval or square holes may be made by using a suitably-shaped tapered punch or drift. The metal is heated to a bright red heat at the point where the hole is to be made. It is then placed on the anvil face and the punch hammered into the metal until it can go no further. The metal is turned over and the end of the punch is placed on the tell-tale black mark left on the metal surface and driven through with a hammer. A pellet of metal is usually removed if the punch has a small flat end.

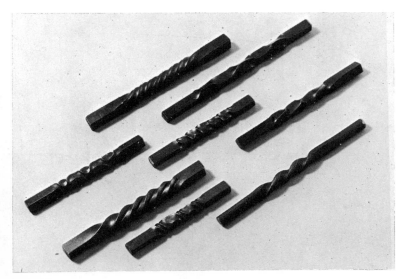

Fig. 4.6

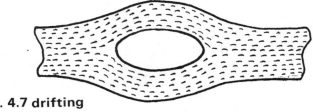

Fig. 4.7 drifting

The hole may be enlarged and further shaped by reheating the metal and driving a drift into the hole. To ensure symmetry, first work from one side and then the other. Work directly over the punch hole or hardy hole in the anvil.

INDUSTRIAL DROP FORGING

When a large number of identical forged components are required, as in the case of a woodworker's G-cramp, it is convenient to make them by drop forging. In this process, a shaped die is used, one half being attached to the hammer, which falls between two vertical guides, and the other half to the anvil. As the hammer falls it forges the hot metal between the two halves of the die, thus shaping the component.

Another familiar example of this technique using the two-part die is called heading and is used to form the heads on bolts, etc. Here the drawings speak for themselves, but note the advantage gained in grain flow.

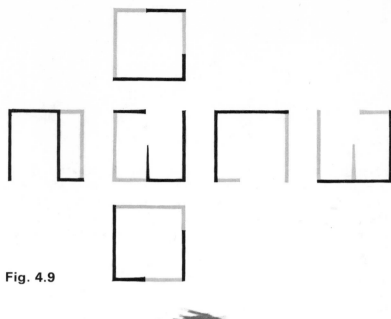

Fig. 4.9

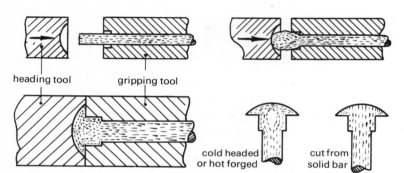

heading tool   gripping tool

cold headed
or hot forged

cut from
solid bar

Fig. 4.8

PROBLEMS

1   Plan a three-dimensional form that will incorporate drawing down, spreading, bending and upsetting. Base your ideas on a 150 mm cube and plan to bend a length of 8 mm square-section steel to form a pattern around or across the cube. All the bends must be at right angles and one end of the rod should be drawn down and the other upset. Start planning by using half-scale elevations and representing the metal by drawing with a thick black line.

Having decided on one elevation, see if you can link this up with the next elevation, then the next and so on. This will obviously become quite complicated and to clarify your ideas it may be necessary to make a model using thin gauge wire which is easily bent. It is possible that you will modify your first ideas when you see them in such a three-dimensional form (see Figs. 4.9 and 4.10).

Fig. 4.10

2 Design and make a screen or a standing panel which is to make use of a repeated unit for its form. Again, part is to be bent, part upset and part drawn down. Plan as before, using pencil first and then make a model using thin gauge wire.

Before finishing with your model decide what section metal you will use, what length of metal you will require, and what finish you will give the metal (see Fig. 4.11).

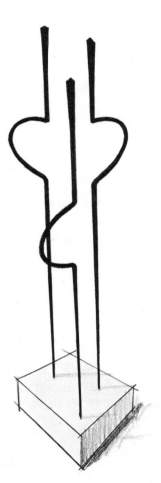

Fig. 4.11

COLD WORKING

Sheet metals such as copper, brass, gilding metal (which is a specific type of brass), nickel silver, aluminium and silver, which are malleable and ductile may be shaped cold by the use of hammer and mallet. The metals become work hardened as the crystal structure becomes distorted. This work hardening must be relieved by annealing from time to time. There are seven basic processes which are performed under the title of cold working. These are:

    hollowing and blocking,
    sinking,
    raising,
    caulking,
    planishing,
    spinning,
    stretch forming.

All of these processes are closely associated with silver-smithing techniques.

HOLLOWING AND BLOCKING

Dish shapes in sheet metal may be produced by hollowing or blocking. As the metals generally used are soft, these operations are carried out with either a highly polished dome-ended hammer or a pear-shaped boxwood mallet.

The metal is held at an angle to a wooden block which has a hollow cut in the end grain. (Fig. 4.12.)

The hammer or mallet should strike the metal beyond its point of contact with the hollowing block.

Hollowing is carried out by working from the outside edge of the required dish in circles towards the centre.

Hollowing and blocking tend to reduce the circumference of the original disc, and so the metal is compressed into itself and becomes thicker.

SINKING

When the blows are started at the centre of the dish and continue to the edge in concentric circles, the metal at the centre is stretched and thinned. This process is called sinking.

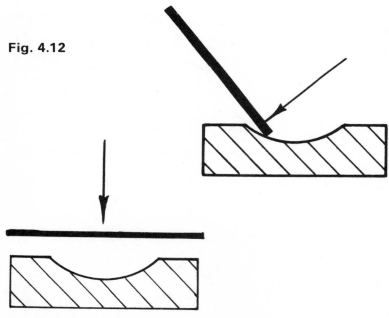

Fig. 4.12

Fig. 4.13

RAISING

Deep vessels may be made by raising them from the sheet. A disc is cut and hollowed. The hollowing is continued until the sides can no longer be brought up.

A circle of the size required for the base of the vessel is drawn with a pencil compass at the centre of the underside of the disc. The dish is held at a slight angle to the face of a raising stake with the pencil line at the point of contact with the end. A raising hammer or mallet is used to knock the metal onto the stake.

The work is rotated a little and the blows are repeated until one revolution has been made. A ridge will have been made round the dish. The workpiece is moved slightly towards the worker and with the ridge still resting on the end of the stake, the procedure is repeated.

Fig. 4.14

The process continues until the edge of the metal is reached. The final knocking down of the rim onto the stake is carried out with a mallet, to prevent the edge from thinning. At this stage the work has to be annealed as it will have become work hardened. Additional courses of raising may have to be done in order to reduce the diameter of the vessel and increase its height.

To determine the approximate diameter of the disc needed for raising, the average height is added to the average diameter thus:

height = 80 mm
average diameter = 65 mm
Therefore diameter of disc = 80 + 65 = 145 mm

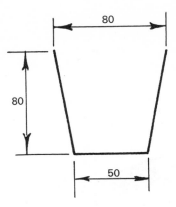

Fig. 4.15

However, if the vessel is to have square (upright) sides, add approximately 4 mm to the diameter and, if it is to be oversquare, then a further 4 mm should be added.

CAULKING
The rim of the vessel may be thickened by hammering the edge of the metal into itself with a raising hammer. This process is termed caulking and is carried out after each course of raising and before annealing, to prevent the edge splitting as the circumference is reduced.

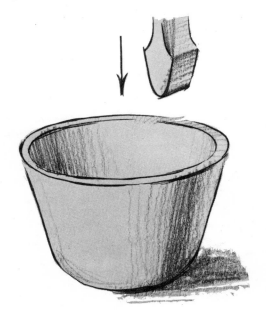

Fig. 4.16

PLANISHING
The shape of a vessel may be obtained by means of hollowing, blocking, sinking, or raising, but as heavy blows are used in each case to move the metal into shape, the surface finish is not always very good. The metal appears dented and uneven and the process of planishing is carried out to: true the surface of the vessel (to remove ripples or undulations on the surface and make it regular); true the final shape of the vessel; and to harden the metal, although often it will be softened again when soldering takes place.

A light-weight hammer with a highly-polished face is used to tap the metal onto a highly polished stake. The hammer face should be flat for domed work and domed for flat or straight-sided vessels. The stake should be of a very slightly smaller curvature than the work, and the work must be held firmly onto it. Planishing is commenced at the centre of the work in the case of bowls and at the base of flat-bottomed vessels. The planishing hammer blows must overlap one another. Use an even, rhythmic action with the hammer falling from about 30 mm above the surface of the metal. Pencilled guide lines help to keep the planishing even.

SPINNING
Another method of producing vessels from sheet metal is to spin them on a lathe. This process is used extensively in industry and requires special and expensive equipment, as tremendous end thrust is exerted on the lathe spindle. In schools, the very malleable and ductile metals such as aluminium and copper may be spun into small vessels on a robust centre lathe. A former—more correctly known as a chuck or a pattern—of the required vessel is turned on the lathe backplate or faceplate. This former may be made from hardwood, metal or a hard plastic, such as epoxy resin. The disc of metal to be spun is annealed and held very firmly between the former and a follower or pressure pad, more correctly known as a tail block, which is supported by a revolving centre in the tail stock of the lathe. The disc must be mounted true to the axis of the lathe. (See Fig. 4.17 overleaf.)

It is advisable to sweat a small pellet in the centre of copper discs to register in a recess in the follower, and to trap aluminium between a boss on the former and cavity

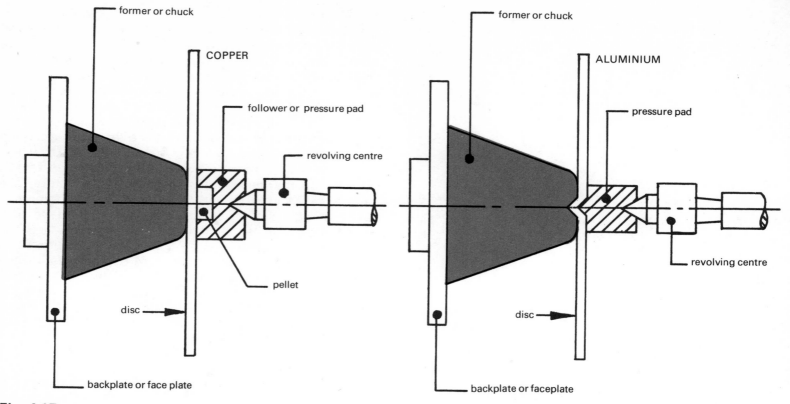

former or chuck

COPPER

former or chuck

ALUMINIUM

follower or pressure pad

pressure pad

revolving centre

pellet

disc

disc

revolving centre

backplate or face plate

backplate or faceplate

Fig. 4.17

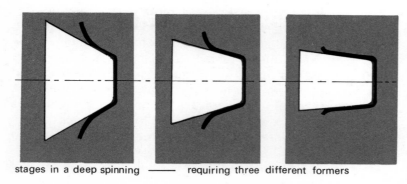

stages in a deep spinning ——— requiring three different formers

Fig. 4.18

in the follower. The pellet on the copper may be unsoldered and the pip on the aluminium may be planished down after spinning.

With the disc rotating, the metal is burnished or rubbed down onto the former with a long tool resting against pegs in a bar in the tool rest.

The tool is made of highly-polished tempered steel, about 12 mm in diameter. A wooden tool may be used on aluminium. The surface of the metal is lubricated with grease to reduce friction. The spinning is commenced at the follower and the metal is forced right down to the former from the beginning.

SEAMED VESSELS

Cylindrical and conical vessels may be made from developments cut from flat sheet (Fig 4.19).

The metal is malletted round a suitably-shaped stake with a rawhide mallet. The shaping is started at the edges which form the seam. The seam is then prepared and soldered with the appropriate grade of silver solder. The joint is held together with soft iron binding wire. (See the section on solders, p. 48.) The vessel may then be trued-up by planishing it. Seamed vessels may also be raised in or flared out by raising, before the final planishing.

SCORED JOINTS

Rectangular or polygonal sectioned vessels may be made up by scoring the corner joints and soldering up when bent into shape in order to strengthen the corners. (See section on cutting, p. 112.)

COLD FORGING

Section such as heavy wire, rod and strip of the malleable, non-ferrous metals may be cold forged on suitable stakes, using raising and collet hammers to perform the initial shaping and a planishing hammer to finish the work.

The metal may have to be annealed frequently as it work hardens very quickly.

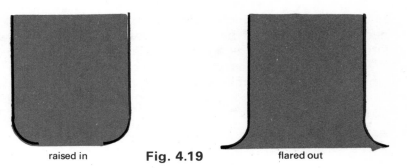

raised in   **Fig. 4.19**   flared out

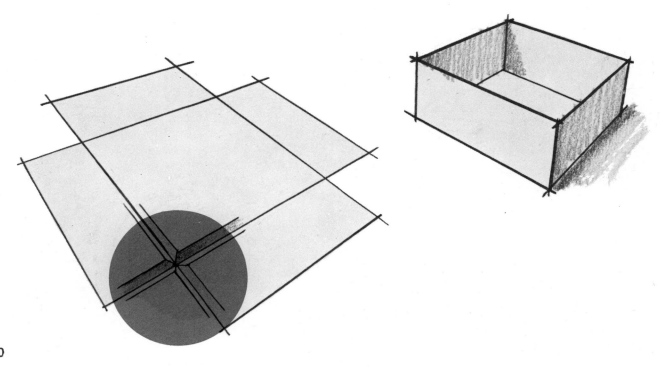

Fig. 4.20

PROBLEMS

Possibly the most natural shape to create by dishing is circular, as the tension throughout the metal is more or less uniform. The truing-up of such a shape is much easier than shapes where the cross-section varies. Oval shapes and shapes where the curves change direction are much more difficult to produce accurately.

Therefore the first problem in this section concerns a simple dished form which is circular in plan, but you must decide first what can be done to make it visually more interesting. The basic shape may be made more exciting if you add to it (but this can become complex unless you limit yourselves very strictly to simple shapes), remove an area, and/or replace the removed piece in a different position.

1 Using the last two suggestions, design and make a small abstract, based on a 100 mm diameter dished form. Work to a scale of half-size throughout the planning stage.

(A) Cut a number of circles from thin coloured card. These circles are to be cut into two pieces as described in Fig. 4.21. The two pieces are to be arranged and pasted onto a sheet of black or white paper showing the systematic development of the shapes and arrangements. At first the circles should be divided using a single straight line cut. Select a division which is visually interesting and thoughtfully arrange the pieces in a variety of ways. Further circles may be divided into two pieces by using two straight line cuts.

Continue throughout this planning to arrange the two pieces of each circle and paste them on your design sheet.

The form from which the shape is to be cut eventually is dished, or curved. You may think that curved cuts would be more appropriate. Experiment first by dividing circles by one curved cut, and then, possibly, by two curved cuts. Finally, try a combination of one curved and one straight cut.

(B) From your design sheet, select what you think is the most pleasing shape and arrangement. Try to visualise how this will look when made in metal.

(C) What metal would be most suitable? Consider the ease of working, that is the malleability of the metal, its gauge, the suitable methods of joining and the colour of the metal.

(D) How will the dished form of the metal be cut? What tool would be used for a straight cut, and what tool for a curved cut?

(E) If you make one in stainless steel and one in copper, would you use the same gauge metal for each?

(F) The two pieces shown in Fig. 4.28 are joined on the edge. Do you think soft solder would be adequate? If silver solder is used, does it create additional problems?

(G) How would you fasten the pieces together?

(H) Consider possible surface treatments—see Appendix A.

(I) How would you mount such an article to show its shape and form to the best advantage?

(J) Could you now develop this idea on a very small scale to produce jewellery shapes?

Single pieces like those planned in answer to Problem 4 (p. 44) are easy to adapt for brooches, pendants, earrings, cuff links, tie pins, lapel badges, as shown in Fig. 4.29, but necklaces, bangles and bracelets may demand a different treatment as it may be necessary to repeat the unit several times, as seen in Fig. 4.30.

2 As a possible jewellery form, plan a unit based on a circular dished shape which forms an interesting visual link when the unit is repeated. This should be planned as before using cut out card shapes.

Methods of joining each adjacent link: is there a problem in joining curved pieces? Is there a practical advantage in having a straight edge anywhere? If a large number of units are required how are these to be made? (See section 4, pp. 71 and 74.) Having decided on a form

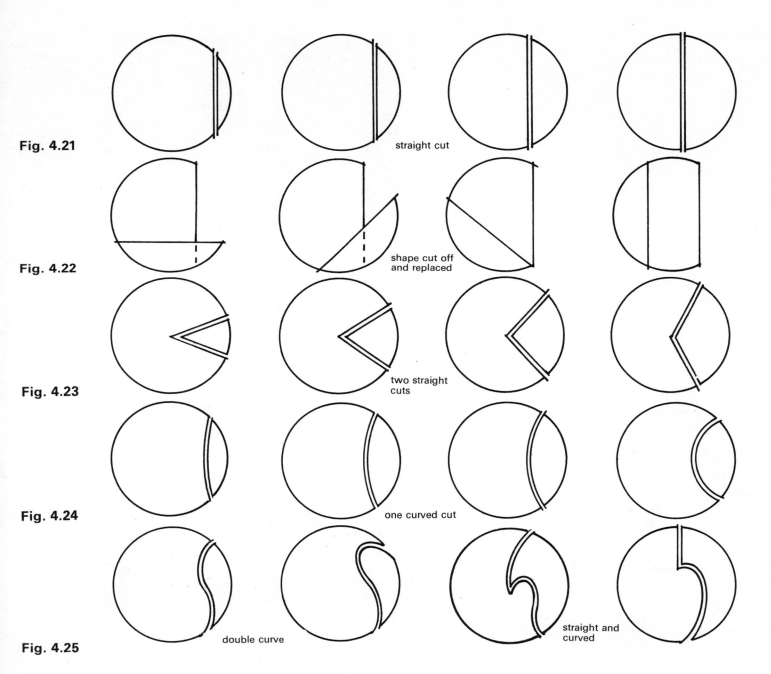

Fig. 4.21

Fig. 4.22

Fig. 4.23

Fig. 4.24

Fig. 4.25

straight cut

shape cut off
and replaced

two straight
cuts

one curved cut

double curve

straight and
curved

Fig. 4.26

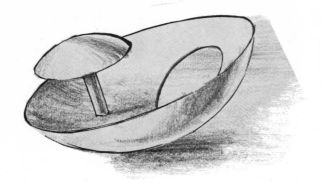

Fig. 4.27

Fig. 4.29

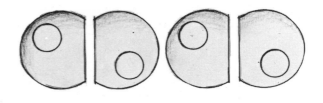

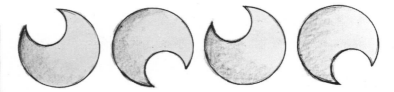

Fig. 4.28

Fig. 4.30

Fig. 4.31(a)

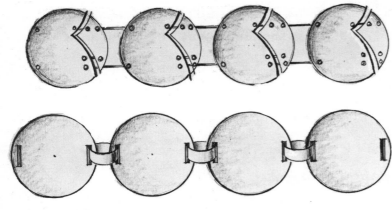

Fig. 4.31(b)

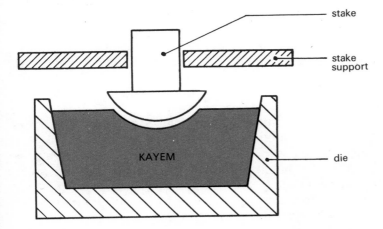

Fig. 4.32

how will the two ends be fastened when in use? (See pp. 135–7.)

The dishing of these small shapes may be done either as described on p. 64, or by forcing a selected stake head into a die made of (a) hardwood, carved to fit the stake, (b) Kayem, cast around stake head, as in Fig. 4.32, (c) hard rubber or polyurethene such as Flexane 95L or Avothane (see p. 74).

MALLEABILITY—INDUSTRIAL METHODS

You have seen that sheet metal may be shaped into vessels by supporting it over a hollow and hammering the metal into the depression. In industry, this method of shaping has been modified and mechanized.

Several industrial processes may be simplified for use in school workshops, and three of these possibilities will be outlined, namely cupping or drawing, press forming and forming with a rubber die.

CUPPING or DRAWING

The sheet metal, or **blank,** is shaped by a punch—taking the place of the hammer—forced into a die, which in turn replaces the sandbag or hollowing block.

The punch is made to the required inside shape of the vessel. To allow the blank metal to bend and flow into the right shape, the die must be larger than the punch by at least the thickness of the metal all the way round.

To prevent the blank being cut and to aid the flow of the metal, the leading edge of the punch and the opening of the die are rounded and highly polished. (See Fig. 4.33.)

The punch and the die aperture, and the surfaces of the blank should be liberally lubricated with a medium grease to assist the slippage of the metal during the drawing operation. To restrict the puckering, pleating, and crinkling of the blank, a pressure pad is used to hold the blank firmly to the die face, while still allowing it to slide into the die opening. Pressure may be applied to the punch in a variety of ways: engineer's vice, arbor press, toggle press or fly press, or even a sledge hammer if skilfully used.

As with the silversmithing process the shaping operation will be easier (less pressure will be needed for a shorter time) if the blank metal is in the fully annealed state.

When using ductile materials, a reduction of between twenty and forty per cent of the blank diameter may be

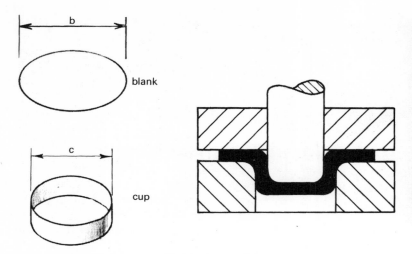

Fig. 4.33 diameter 'c' may be between 20% and 40% of diameter 'b'

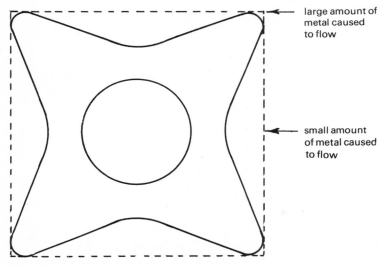

Fig. 4.34

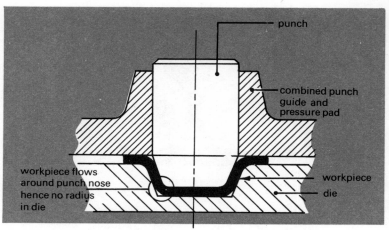

Fig. 4.35 cross section lay-out of tool for press forming

attempted successfully in a single drawing operation. When a circular cup is required, and if a circular blank is used, the contraction of the metal is evenly disposed around its circumference as the cup is drawn. When a square or rectangular blank is used, the contraction is unevenly disposed around its periphery. Due to the larger amount of metal at the corners, it is more difficult for the metal to flow. Excessive work hardening of the blank may result and the metal could be thinned or split.

PRESS FORMING

In this type of shaping operation, the sheet metal is formed between a male **punch**, the shape of the inside of the vessel, and a female **die,** which is shaped to the external contours of the vessel. So generally, the die dimensions are larger all round than those of the punch by an amount equal to the thickness of the blank metal (see Fig. 4.35).

The working or forming surfaces are highly polished and sometimes even case hardened (see p. 109). The punch and die are usually made of bright mild steel but other materials may be used. For example:

(a) tool steel; heat treated (pp. 106–8) has long life, good for quantity production but expensive,

(b) zinc based alloy, Kayem; easily cast, low melting point, good for batch production, expensive *but* reusable,

(c) aluminium alloy, e.g. LM4; easily cast, high melting point compared with zinc, usable for small numbers only, cheaper than zinc and also reusable,

(d) wood; hardwood necessary with close grain, working

done into end grain only, use as a die only, possible for very small numbers only, prevention from splitting is a problem, but it is easily shaped with carving gouges.

Obviously, these materials may be used in a variety of combinations, but there are many factors which determine the choice of the material for the punch and die. Invariably in school work, the blank metal must be in the fully annealed condition (see p. 108).

The basic principles relating to the punch and die radii, pressure pads, location of blank, lubrication of blank, alignment of punch and die, removal of completed workpiece, etc. are as for drawing and cupping.

D.A.T.—M.—D

This process may be used when the sides of the vessel are other than cylindrical (as in the drawing and cupping method mentioned earlier). As the punch presses the workpiece material against the side of the die, any wrinkles will tend to be squashed or ironed out. Internal radii of the die are not always necessary if the blank is shaped by the punch.

Some vessel shapes would allow the die to be cast round the punch and used without further shaping, after polishing and the forming of the die radius. Other vessel shapes would necessitate further work on the punch or die after casting in order to produce the clearance needed between the punch and die to accept the thickness of the metal blank.

FORMING WITH A RUBBER DIE

In concept this is perhaps the simplest way of the three forming processes considered, yet the size of workpiece possible in the school workshop is strictly governed by the pressure available.

The workpiece is shaped by squashing it between a hard rigid former and a flexible, supporting matrix. The former is usually a punch shaped to the inside contour and dimensions of the desired workpiece, although it may sometimes be the die (shaped to the outside contour and dimensions of the workpiece). (Fig. 4.36.)

For this explanation, it is assumed that the punch is hard and rigid.

The softer, pliable former — the die — is of a hard, usually synthetic, rubber. Often a polyurethane rubber is used. Commercially available types are Avothane and Flexane 95L.

As the punch is forced onto the blank, the rubber of the die is displaced, but, if it is enclosed in a strong container, the rubber will resist the displacement and wrap the blank round the punch. When a large force is used, the workpiece will be wrinkle free.

This forming method has the advantage that only the punch has to be made, the rubber die being reusable for quantity production and for a range of punch shapes and sizes.

As this technique of forming metals is usually associated with functional objects only, the relevant design problem

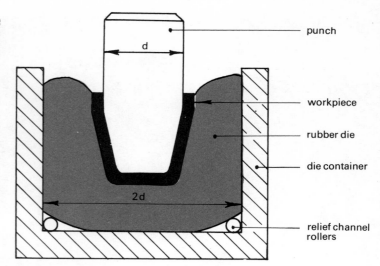

Fig. 4.36

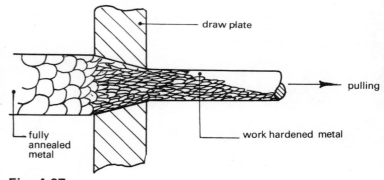

Fig. 4.37

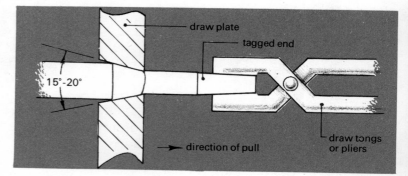

Fig. 4.38

has been delayed until you have read Chapter 5 which deals more fully with designing methods.

DUCTILITY

This section concerns the working of metal rod by pulling it through a hardened steel die which changes the section to that of the hole in the die plate. The effect of this process on the crystal grain structure of the metal is shown in Fig. 4.37.

Both wires and tubes may be drawn to either smaller cross-sectional dimensions, or into different shapes, such as squares, D-section, hexagonal, oval or rectangular. The hole in the draw or die plate is tapered. The sides of the hole are polished and the sharp edge at the small end is rounded off to leave a good surface finish on the drawn metal. (Fig. 4.38.)

For silversmithing work, the draw plate has a series of holes graded evenly in size.

The metal to be drawn is filed or hammered to a taper at one end so that it will pass through a hole and project sufficiently to be gripped by draw tongs or pliers. The metal should be annealed. Wire may be coiled up to ensure even heating. The metal should be lubricated with soap or petroleum jelly to reduce friction and make the draw easy.

The metal is then pulled through the hole, so reducing it in cross-sectional size or changing its shape. The process is repeated for the next smaller size hole and continued until the desired size and shape is achieved.

The metal may have to be annealed between draws.

To prevent the walls of tubes from being crushed when drawing, a series of rods is used inside the tubes. The rods must be lubricated to aid their removal from the tube.

Tubes may be made from flat strip. The width of the strip is calculated from the diameter of tube required. It is best to make the strip a little wider than calculated. The end of the strip is filed or cut to a taper and the strip is hammered to a U-shape along its length. A suitable lubricated rod is placed in the U and the U is closed with a mallet. The rough tube is then drawn through successively smaller die holes until the tube is formed and reduced to the required size.

Wire and tube drawing may also be carried out on a draw-bench. The draw tongs hook into a ring which is in turn hooked into a link on an endless chain or belt on the bench. The chain is moved by a sprocket rotated by a handle or wheel.

Experiment by drawing twisted wires, of various sections, through a die.

Experiment further with several wires twisted together as a rope, and draw them.

PROBLEMS

The design work that follows, introduces you to more complex problems concerning the arrangement and organization of space. They involve consideration of both positive and negative forms and are arranged so that you will be able to explore the metallurgical property of ductility for yourself whilst solving them.

Experiment by taking a small rectangle of card and removing an area from it. You will realize, if you now put this against a dark background, that although you still have basically only one form, the shape which surrounds it also adds to its interest. (Fig. 4.39.)

Experiment further by replacing the smaller area in a different position on the original rectangle to create a second form. Explore this idea thoroughly to find several possible arrangements. (Fig. 4.40.)

Continue the experiment by re-creating these two shapes in thin wire. You will see that it produces more shapes, because it is possible to see through the figures as well as seeing around them.

In Fig. 4.41 the wires themselves make the positive forms, but some of the most interesting shapes are the negative shapes contained within the wire framework.

For future design use, record the planning of these shapes in your design folder. Draw them accurately, full size and in Indian ink. From these drawings, select one, showing the two shapes in what you consider to be a reasonable position. Then experiment with the addition of a third rectangle as before.

The addition of this shape may mean that you have to reconsider the positions of the first two shapes again, since—as with all design—any addition, no matter how large or small, changes the whole concept.

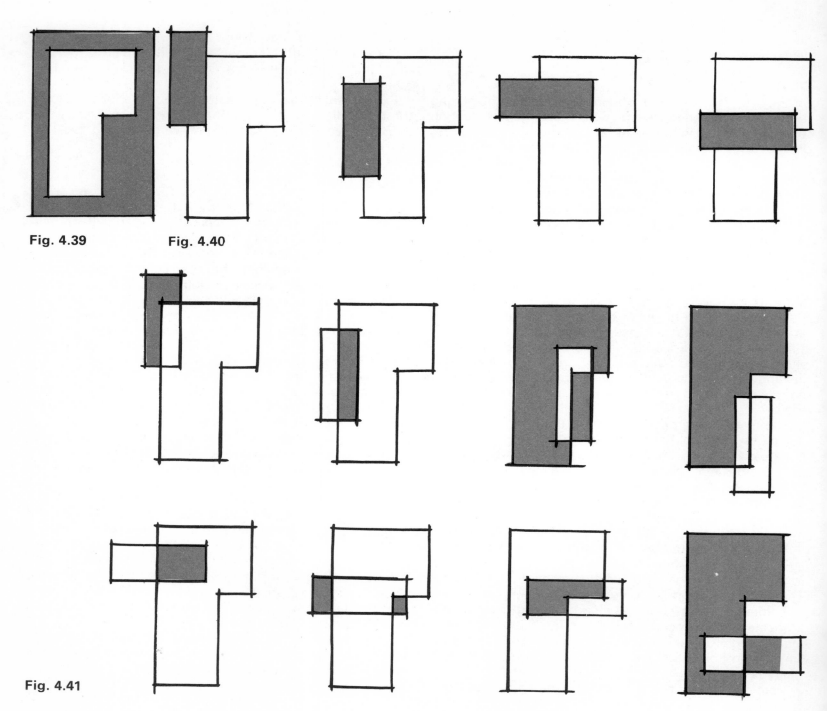

Fig. 4.39   Fig. 4.40

Fig. 4.41

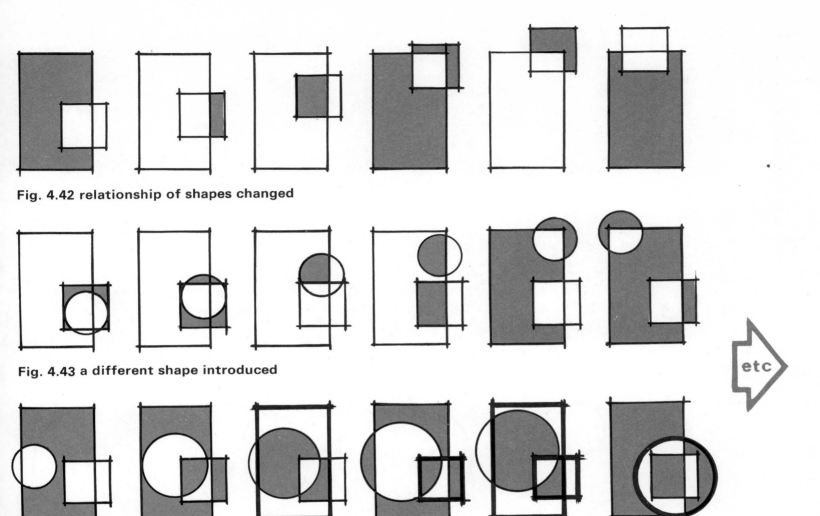

Fig. 4.42 relationship of shapes changed

Fig. 4.43 a different shape introduced

etc

Fig. 4.44 change of scale of one shape

weight of line changed

1 Using this idea of positive and negative forms, design and make a piece of jewellery in the form of a pendant or a small brooch.

(A) For the first stage, work with a rectangle 40 mm x 25 mm and a 25 mm square. Arrange these in a variety of positions as described earlier. Record each shape in your design folder. (Fig. 4.42.)

(B) Add to these a third shape of your own choice and possibly change the scale. (Figs. 4.43, 4.44.)

(C) Select several of these shapes which appeal to you most and re-draw each, varying the weight of line for each shape as shown. Notice how it alters the overall appearance.

77

(D) From these, select your final shape and decide details for fixing or hanging, and the construction.

(E) From a length of 3 mm square section copper wire, draw down three pieces to different thickness and/or sections to coincide with your design. Use the heaviest section to make the main rectangle. Mark it out carefully, and join as you think best.

(F) Form the square, using the second size wire and the third shape, using the lightest wire.

(G) Join together, add fittings and finish.

(H) Could the scale be altered to make earrings, or a mural panel for your bedroom wall?

2 This time, using positive and negative circular forms, design and make a tie clip, hair slide, cuff links or a pendant.

(A) As the size for each of these articles may differ, it is suggested that you begin planning with three circles,

one of 30 mm diameter and two of 20 mm diameter. Your final design can be scaled accordingly.

(B) Plan as before, first with two inner circles.

(C) Then add a third. You will notice that the negative forms then become very different.

(D) Vary some of the inner diameters and weights of line. When the tube is drawn, the smaller the diameter, the thicker will be the wall of the tube.

(E) Choose your final design, scale accordingly, plan construction as before and complete.

(F) Sketch these arrangements in your folder and describe what you see or feel about these shapes, for example, their qualities of movement and tension (see p. 14).

It is essential that you become aware of negative forms, because every positive shape created has a negative counterpart and this negative is just as important as the positive form. This applies whether the object being considered is a chair or a piece of abstract sculpture.

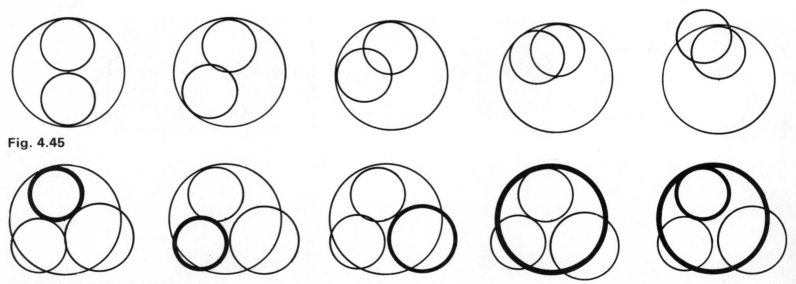

Fig. 4.45

Fig. 4.46 one circle thickened　　　　　　　　**two circles thickened**

A Monstrance, in silver and wrought iron—based on circular forms.

Chapter 5

A FULLER DESIGN PROCESS

Design problems become much more demanding when functional objects rather than abstracts are involved. Functional objects must be visually interesting and must also fulfil the purposes for which they are intended. In such cases the planning stage is even more important and therefore demands a fuller design process.

The overall problem is first broken down into smaller sub-problems, so that the detailed planning necessary can be directed in the first instance to small parts. From here, each design is probably worked differently, for design cannot be thought of as a series of separate steps, but rather as a whole process. Nevertheless, a logical approach towards a solution will demand a certain procedure such as that shown opposite.

For your guidance in this book this process has been summarized into the four stages shown on the right of the page which are now explained in detail by means of a worked example. You will notice how every subsequent stage depends entirely upon the analysis for its success and also how impossible it is to consider any other stage of the design process separately without continually referring back and associating it with the original design analysis.

1 Clear understanding of the problem.	Identification	Statement of problem
2 Specify exact demands.	Specification	
3 Collection of relevant facts and data.	}	Analysis
4 Examination of problems in the light of these facts.		
5 Ideas leading to a possible solution are considered and experimented with. Restrictions of material, time, tools, etc. are considered here.	Synthesis	
6 Possible solutions are developed and checked against the original specification and a final choice made; detailing of construction size, etc. A scale model is made to show the solution in three dimensions before continuing.	Development	Synthesis
7 An answer is made up. The first one is called a prototype.		Solution
8 Evaluation of the answer against the problem to decide modifications that may be needed.		Evaluation

1 STATEMENT OF A PROBLEM

This is sometimes referred to as the specification or design brief. Here, the problem must be very clearly defined and stated by asking such questions as: what is it for, why it will be used, where it will be used, by whom it will be used, by how many different people it will be used and when it will be used.

For example, suppose the problem is to design and make a device for keeping divested clothes from the dirty floor in a school metalwork shop during a practical lesson. The problem must first be clearly defined as shown before, using questions such as those stated, and any others that you think relevant. Answers to these questions provide us with an initial specification.

It is essential that all the relevant answers to these questions and any other resulting information is recorded by writing, drawings, photographs or any method which seems appropriate. It cannot be overstressed that this is the basis of good designing technique, and each following stage should be checked carefully against this statement to ensure that any outcome does not conflict with this original specification.

2 ANALYSIS

This is the stage where you should look more closely at the problem and break it down into the sub-problems mentioned earlier. It entails collecting all known facts before any attempt is made to solve the problem. Appropriate answers to the sub-problems can also be supplied where these are known, but they should still be written at this stage where possible. To carry the example a stage further:

Problem	Specification	Analysis
		The school has a uniform including blazers, caps and coats. The coats will be left in the main cloakroom.
(a) What is it for?	It is necessary to store clothes, etc., in the school workshop during a metalwork lesson.	The most likely clothes are jackets and caps and possibly, scarves. Jackets have loops by which to hang them. Only problem with scarves is to allow enough height above the floor for them to drape. Material used must be naturally clean and easily wiped clean when not in use, i.e. it should not rust or corrode.
(b) Why will it be used?	To protect clothes, to keep them from the dirty floor and oily surfaces, for tidiness, to keep cap and coat together so cap is not misplaced.	In order to avoid damage to clothes, it should not have rough surfaces, e.g. splinters or burrs. As it will be made in the metalwork room, metal will be used in this example.
(c) Where will it be used?	On the wall near entrance, easily accessible.	On a wall, so find out what is best height for a boy to reach (Fig. 5.1). To be fixed to a brick wall.
(d) By whom will it be used?	Boys between the ages of 11 and 18 years.	Therefore space must accommodate various sizes.
(e) By how many people will it be used?	Approximately 20.	Maximum 20. Boys will file in together so it is essential that the clothes can be stored quickly.
(f) When will it be used?	All the year through, but only during lessons, so for only two hours at a time.	Therefore possibility of wet garments, moisture must not adversely affect the finish of the metal.
		Add to this as your information grows.

Fig. 5.1

To arrive at an analysis of the problem, it may be necessary to refer to books or other sources of information with the sole aim of clarifying the problem but *never* with the idea of copying someone else's solution. Merely to reproduce a previous solution would suggest that you do not understand the problem sufficiently well to formulate your own conclusions. You can ensure against this at the analysis stage and this is why its importance is stressed.

3 SYNTHESIS—BUILDING TOWARDS A SOLUTION

This is the stage where all the known facts are brought together and possible solutions explored. These will involve sketches, diagrams, and models, and methods of construction and likely materials will be tested. No idea, however tentative, should be ignored and no information dismissed without careful consideration. An open and receptive mind is essential and, at this early stage, time should not be wasted on one idea only, but all possibilities should be considered whether they prove suitable or not for further development. (See Figs. 5.2—7.)

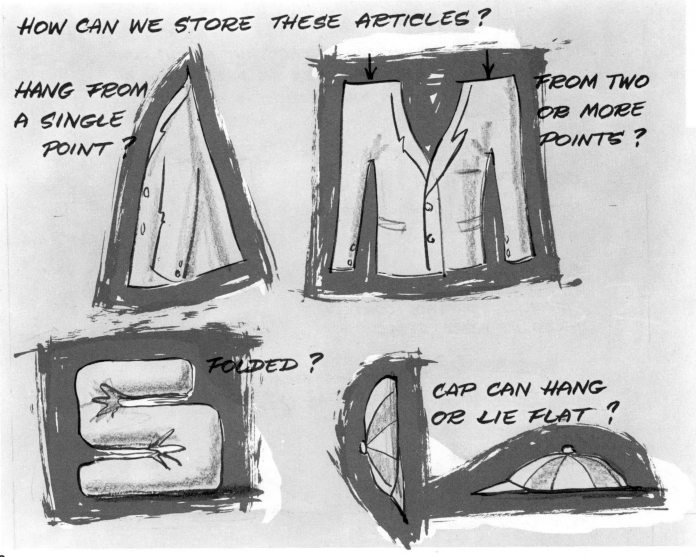

Fig. 5.2

GOOD POINTS
QUICK AND EASY TO USE
TAKES UP LITTLE ROOM

PULLS COAT AT BACK, BUT AS THE COAT
IS ONLY HUNG FOR THE DURATION OF A
LESSON THE EFFECT IS MINIMISED.

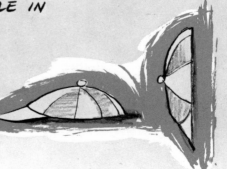

GOOD POINTS
STORES COATS IN GOOD ORDER

BAD POINTS

DIFFICULT TO PLACE COAT ON
TAKES UP MORE SPACE.

THIS METHOD SEEMS
TO HAVE LITTLE IN
ITS FAVOUR

THE CAP COULD HANG OR LIE
FLAT WITH EQUAL EASE.

Fig. 5.3

TO HANG FROM ONE POINT APPEARS TO FIT THE PROBLEM BEST. SPACE IS LIMITED SO CLOTHES MUST HANG NEAR THE WALL THEREFORE A PROJECTION FROM THE WALL SEEMS THE SIMPLEST SOLUTION. THE PROJECTION MUST SLOPE UPWARDS TO PREVENT THE COATS SLIPPING OFF.

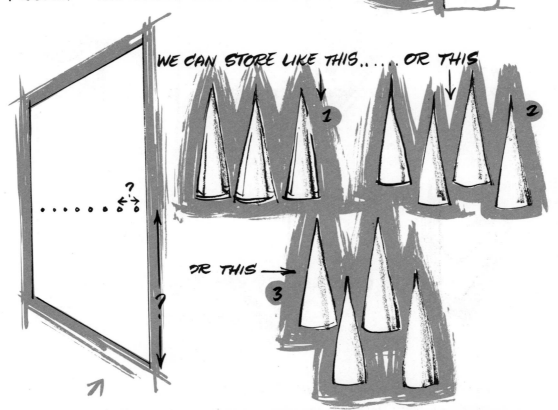

WE CAN STORE LIKE THIS..... OR THIS

1

2

OR THIS →

3

AS WE HAVE SPACE ON THE WALL FOR N.º 1, NO REAL ADVANTAGE APPEARS TO BE GAINED BY N.º 2 OR N.º 3.

WE REQUIRE A PROJECTION WHICH IS SMOOTH AND
ANGLED SO THE CLOTHES CANNOT FALL OFF.
ALSO WE REQUIRE SOME PROVISION FOR HOLDING A CAP.
EXPERIMENT WITH POSSIBLE SOLUTIONS AND
METHODS OF FIXING TO WALL.

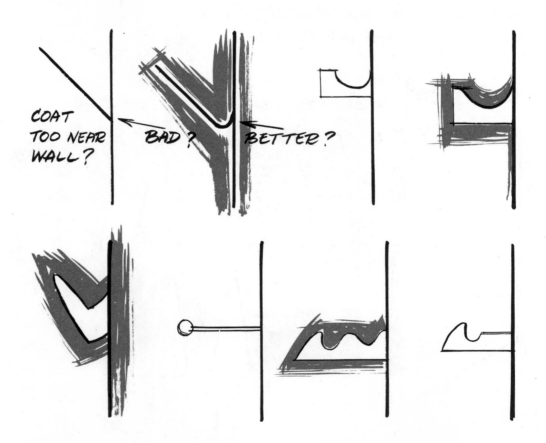

EXPERIMENT WITH OTHER POSSIBILITIES

Fig. 5.5

IF THIS ARM IS LONG ENOUGH THE CAP CAN ALSO FIT, BUT THE COAT HAS TO BE FED ON AND OFF. POSSIBLY A SEPARATE HANGER WOULD BE BETTER. THERE IS NOT ROOM AT THE SIDE OF THE COAT SO THE CAP MUST HANG ABOVE.

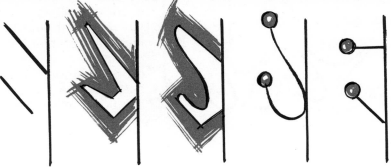

FIXING TO THE WALL IS PERMANENT AND MUST BE STRONG. RESEARCH INTO WALL FITTINGS.

ALL THE ABOVE SKETCHES SHOW ONLY SIDE ELEVATION. WHAT ABOUT OTHER VIEWS?

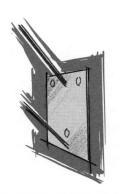

THE FIXING MUST BE STABLE.

Fig. 5.6

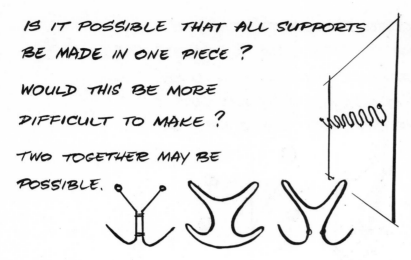

IS IT POSSIBLE THAT ALL SUPPORTS
BE MADE IN ONE PIECE ?

WOULD THIS BE MORE

DIFFICULT TO MAKE ?

TWO TOGETHER MAY BE

POSSIBLE.

Fig. 5.7

Development
By carefully checking all the possible solutions against the original 'Statement of the Problem' and the resulting specification, and making the appropriate tests mentioned, one solution will prove to be more suitable than others. This stage, therefore, involves the development, modification and refining of this particular idea. All possible faults and shortcomings should be eliminated before the final solution is reached, and this will probably demand the making of a scale model and, in some cases, full-sized mock-ups will be necessary. Testing equipment may have to be made to prove the effectiveness of the suggested design.

Solution
At this stage, some positive means of recording is essential so that the final solution to the problem can be constructed. Usually, this takes the form of a working drawing and notes, which will show sizes, methods of construction, materials, finish, methods of fixing, etc. Such information should give clear and concise information for the construction of this

solution. Very often, it is only when the object can be seen full-size that something which needs alteration becomes apparent.

Because of this, it is advisable to leave the final working drawing until the model has been made and possibly even modified further, for it is a good idea to regard this first answer only as a prototype.

4 EVALUATION
No design should be thought of as *the* solution to that particular problem, but as an idea that is in itself capable of further development and as just a part of this design process. Architects, town planners, bridge builders, aircraft designers, all use this method of approaching their solutions, even though they may not set them out in this way.

This procedure, although set out in separate stages is, in fact, a whole process. Once the specification has been clearly stated, the designer must always refer back to this throughout his explorations so that he can test the validity of his ideas against the demands of the original problem. Although you will move ahead a step at a time, designing is not a series of separate activities, for each step is a vital part of a fuller design process.

The design process is completed when the problems posed as a result of the design analysis have been gradually solved by sketches and written statements, and finally collected in the form of a working drawing and ultimately a model or prototype. This building up process is called synthesis. When the model is complete, the final design is then evaluated and if it proves satisfactory the solution is made up. Otherwise, necessary modifications are made first.

You yourself are now asked to carry this process through on a problem which incorporates all the design and technology covered so far in this book. You will be taken through the initial steps of this first functional design problem from the written statement, to the full analysis, then to the beginnings of the synthesis stage, when you will be left to collect and assemble your own thoughts before making a model of your solution. From this, you will evaluate its success and make any final modifications thought necessary before making up your answer.

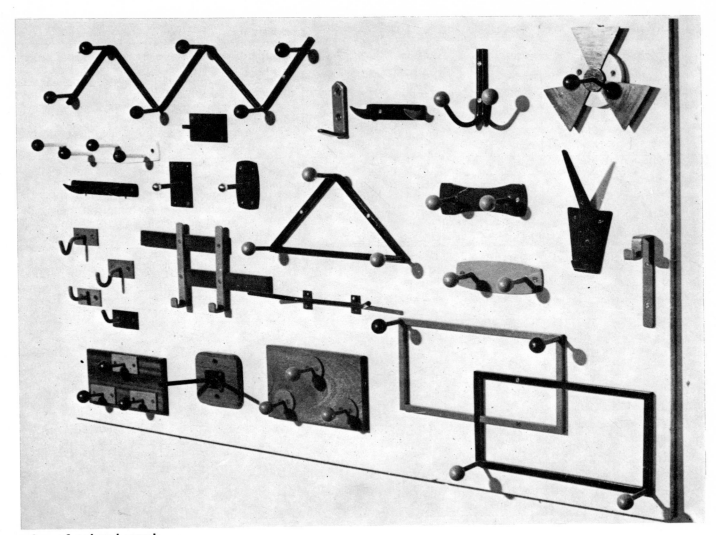

Fig. 5.8. Examples of school work

PROBLEMS

1 If a pot of tea is made by pouring boiling water onto loose tea leaves, there is a tendency for these tea leaves to be transferred to the cup when the tea is poured. Design and make a device to prevent this from happening, which will be suitable for normal domestic use.

Planning. Before starting to think about the form the device will take, it is necessary to find out exactly what the problem involves. (See design analysis on p. 90). To help you with your statement of the problem and resulting analysis, a beginning is made here from which you should work. It is not intended to be complete in any way but serves only to direct your thoughts at this important stage. Read it carefully before proceeding. You may not agree with it all, in which case you can make your own statements in your analysis.

Problem	Specification	Analysis
(a) What is it for?	To filter the tea whilst pouring it into a cup.	It must therefore have a perforated area to allow hot tea to pass through whilst retaining the tea leaves. The size of the perforation will depend on the size of hot, wet tea leaves. You will need to find this out. The perforated area could be of mesh, or have holes drilled into a base. The size of complete article will depend on the size of cups and mugs. Find out.
(b) Why will it be used?	To allow brands of tea that are not available in tea bags to be brewed in the teapot and when poured, to prevent the tea leaves from entering the cup.	As the tea is hot, will the device cool it on entry so that the cup of tea becomes cooled too early? Should heat be retained by the device? If it does retain heat, it will become hot itself and therefore difficult to handle. So it must be made from materials that will withstand boiling water and yet not get too hot to handle.
(c) How often will it be used?	Many times daily.	If used only once a day, it might need to be different from one used every few minutes, for regular washing-up might lessen the need to consider ease of cleaning when deciding on the material to use. Even so, limited daily use should minimise any effects of tarnishing.
(d) Where will it be used?	In the home.	Might be in the kitchen at normal working height, and/or in the dining room at normal working height but from a sitting position, or in a lounge from a sitting position onto a lower-than-average working surface. It might be made to go into a particular home. Would it need to be different if considered for Buckingham Palace?
(e) By whom will it be used?	Any member of a household.	Therefore it must be very simple to use as children and old people will use it. It must be designed for both right- and left-handed people. *This may affect the shape.*
(f) By how many people will it be used?	Any number, but only one at a time.	If used at the tea-table, it could be passed from one person to another. *This may affect the shape.*

Problem	Specification	Analysis
(g) When will it be used?	Any time of the day.	This should make no difference to the design—or will it?
(h) Where will it be kept when not in use?	Unknown—could be in a drawer, cupboard or hung on the wall.	One kept in a drawer *may* be different from one to hang on a hook. Consider this when deciding shape.
(i) The speed of pouring must be considered.	Tea must pass through or past the device as fast as it leaves the teapot.	Tea may be dammed back a little as the trapped tea leaves clog the perforations in the base area, therefore a retainer, or cup or bowl must be included to stop the tea spilling over if poured too quickly. *This will affect the shape.*
(j) How will it be stored between pourings?	Unknown.	Being wet underneath, it will either drip onto, or wet, the table top unless some provision is made for it—it may need a special stand to accommodate it.
(k) How often will it be handled?	Often.	Therefore it must not be too hot to touch—it may be dropped suddenly onto the crockery. See (b). Some insulation may be needed, *which may affect appearance.* It should be light to pick up.
(l) Will cleaning be necessary?	Essential, as it will be used in the context of food.	It must not rust, corrode, or tarnish appreciably. See (c).
(m) Add to this list as ideas and thoughts occur to you.		*It must be pleasant to look at as it will be used on different occasions in the home.*

Synthesis

The twelve points which follow, show a possible design synthesis in progress.

When all decisions have been made, model your proposed solution in thin card or wood, and make any modifications thought necessary before starting work on the real thing.

If you have decided to press your prototype from one piece of metal the necessary press forming tool must be designed and made when the size and shape of the 'cup' part of the article is known.

As before, you will be taken through this first engineering design problem carefully, stage by stage, up to the point of synthesis when you will be left to complete the final design solution yourself.

Keep all the design sheets relevant to both these items together in your design folder as one project, and include either a photograph or a pictorial sketch of the final piece, together with working drawings.

1 YOU SHOULD HAVE MEASURED SEVERAL CUPS AND KNOW THE SIZE FOR WHICH YOU ARE DESIGNING.

DETERMINE THE LARGEST AREA OF MESH WHICH WILL CONVENIENTLY FIT THE CUP.

2 TO PREVENT TEA LEAVES SPILLING. SEE *i*

3 SOME MEANS OF HOLDING SEEMS NECESSARY. SEE *k*

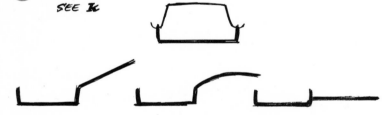

4 HANDLE HERE COULD ACT AS A STEADY

5 EXTRA SUPPORT.

6 BOWL TOO DEEP?

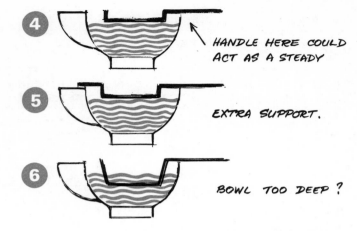

AT THIS STAGE WE ARE THINKING ALONG THESE LINES.

UNSTABLE?

IS THIS BETTER?

OR THESE?

7 WHAT MATERIAL CAN WE USE?
IN THIS EXERCISE WE ARE LIMITED TO
METAL, WHAT INFORMATION HAVE WE GOT?
SEE *a.b.c.d.k.l.m.*

COMPILE A LIST OF POSSIBLE METALS
AND GAUGES.
CONSIDER SURFACE TREATMENTS, SEE APPENDIX Ⓐ

8 MESH WILL BE DIFFICULT TO SHAPE AND
ATTACH. HOLES MAY BE MORE SUITABLE.

9 IF WE ASSUME THE USE OF A PRESS TOOL
LET US EXAMINE OUR CONCLUSIONS AGAIN.

HARD TO MAKE?
HARD TO CLEAN?
?
← TOO DEEP?
?

10 IF WE ACCEPT ONE OF THESE BOWLS   HOW CAN WE
HOLD IT OVER THE CUP.

← IN THE WAY?

THESE TWO   COULD BE MADE FROM A SINGLE
SHEET?

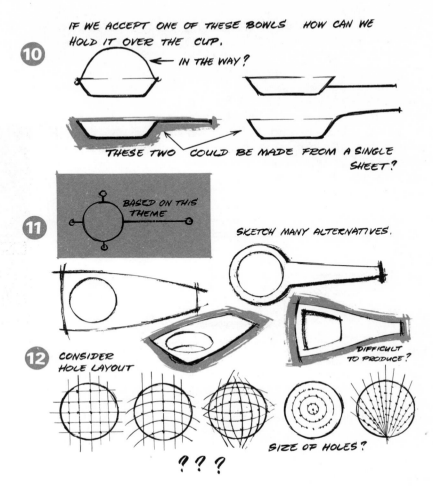

BASED ON THIS
THEME

11 SKETCH MANY ALTERNATIVES.

DIFFICULT
TO PRODUCE?

12 CONSIDER
HOLE LAYOUT

? ? ?

SIZE OF HOLES?

Design Analysis for the cupping tool, or press tool

Before analysing the problem in detail, it will be helpful to remind yourselves of the technical process involved and to understand this thoroughly before attempting to follow the design process through. Fig. 5.9 shows the general principle of drawing, that of forcing a punch into a piece of sheet metal—the blank—held over a die. To prevent cockling, it is held against the die by a pressure plate. To ensure that the punch is located co-axially with the die, it has a guide and it can be seen that this one component fulfils a dual function; as a guide for the punch and also as a pressure plate.

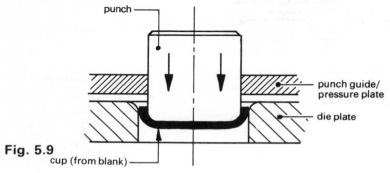

Fig. 5.9

This is obviously only a diagrammatic representation and before such a tool can be made, a number of sub-problems have to be identified and solved. The solutions to these will lead you to the synthesis stage of the design process.

As this project is directly related to the tea-strainer, Problem 1, we can begin with certain known dimensions of the bowl and hence of the punch, as the inside contour of the cup is that of the punch nose. Analyse the problem as follows:

The Punch

(a) What diameter? Take data from tea-strainer, assuming it to be cylindrical.

(b) What working length should it be? Data from tea-strainer.

(c) What radius on the punch face?

Note. If it has no radius, it may cut the metal. The radius helps the blank metal to flow round the punch. There is a certain minimum radius—see Fig. 4.33, p. 72.

(d) How is it to be positioned centrally over the die?

(e) How is it to be guided square to the die?

(f) Why should it be guided square to the die?

(g) If the solution to (d) and (e) is in the form of a punch guide as shown in Figs 4.35 and 5.10 then how thick should this be?

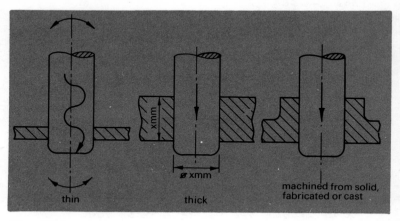

Fig. 5.10

(h) Does the answer to (g) alter the answer to (b)?

(i) What material could be used for the punch?

(j) What finish should the punch have—on the punch face, on the radius, and along its cylindrical length?—so that the blank is not marked, so that the blank metal flows as freely as possible, and so that the punch slides in its guide as smoothly as possible.

(k) Will the punch material require heat treatment? If so, what? (See p. 106).

(l) How will pressure be applied to the other end of the punch? Which of the following ways are available in the workshop?

a large engineer's vice,

an arbor press,

a toggle, eccentric or cam press,

a fly press,

a sledge hammer (have you the skill to use it in this situation?),

a drop hammer.

(m) Does the answer to (l) determine the shape of the other end of the punch?

The Die

(a) What diameter for the hole? Fig. 5.9 shows that the die diameter is larger than the punch diameter, by at least the thickness of the blank metal *all round*, but as mentioned earlier, as the metal flows into the die, the metal of the blank surrounding the die hole has to be displaced. This displacement can be made to produce a cup of constant wall thickness, or the metal can be encouraged to flow into itself and thicken the wall relative to the base.

(This is a similar situation to that found when raising a vessel from the sheet in silversmithing.)

(b) What depth of die-hole?

Note. A flat-faced punch will form a flat-bottomed cup, hence the die hole need not be the depth of the tea-strainer bowl, but the travel—depth of stroke—of the punch will have to be accommodated.

(c) What is the radius on the rim of the die hole? (See note (c) for the punch.) This radius allows the blank metal to flow into the die hole.

(d) Will the size of the radius on the edge of the die make it necessary to modify the solution to (b) above?

(e) What material could be used for the die?

(f) What finish should the die have in its bore, on the radius, and on the surface of the die over which the blank will slip?

(g) Will the die material require heat treatment? If so, what? (See Fig. 5.10.)

Punch Guide—Pressure Plate and Die Plate

(a) What length of guide will be necessary to guide the punch square onto the blank? (See note (f) for the punch.)

(b) Need the pressure plate be this thickness everywhere? (See Fig. 5.10.)

(c) How are the punch guide/pressure plate and die plate to be assembled so that the punch will be co-axial with the die hole? Can guides or dowels be used? If so, how many and of what length and cross section should they be? Why should you not use machine screws or bolts? (Figs. 5.11 and 8.14.)

(d) Should the guides or dowels be fixed to one or other plate? If so, to which and how?

(e) As the pressure plate is to prevent the blank buckling, it will have to be held at a distance from the die plate approximately equal to the thickness of the blank. It should nip the blank. Will the pressure required during cupping need to be kept constant, increased or decreased?

(f) If the answer to (e) is 'I don't know', could you devise a simple way of applying pressure to the blank which can be adjusted during cupping or when cupping test pieces?

(g) Will this pressure-applying device foul the means of applying pressure to the punch?
If so, what modifications can be made to avoid this?

(h) From what material could the punch guide/pressure plate be made?

(i) What surface finish should the bore of the punch guide have? What surface finish should be given to the face of the pressure plate which comes into contact with the blank?

(j) What diameter of blank will have to be used to form the cup? This may be obtained by trial and error, but a guide will be found on p. 72. This information will control the placing and spacing of the guides or dowels, screws, etc.

(k) What margin of metal will be needed for strength and to guide the blank around the hole and around the punch? Will this margin be large enough to accommodate the guides or dowels, screws, studs, etc?

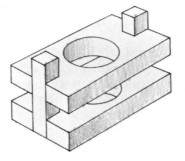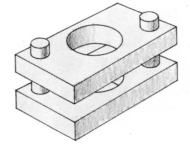

Fig. 5.11

General

(a) When the cup has been drawn it may form a tight fit on the end of the punch. As the blank and tool surfaces will be lubricated, will this make it easier or more difficult to remove the cup from the punch?

It may be helpful to drill a hole through the punch on its axis.

If the punch can be pulled back through the punch guide/pressure plate, the cup will be stripped from the punch. Could the punch be fixed to one jaw and the die to the other jaw of an engineer's vice?

The punch, of course, need not be pushed into the die so far that the cup has straight sides. A flange could be left on the cup as shown in Fig. 5.12.

(b) How can the blank disc be held in the correct position when the tool is assembled for cupping or drawing?

You may well find other questions to add to these that will need answering as you approach your final solution.

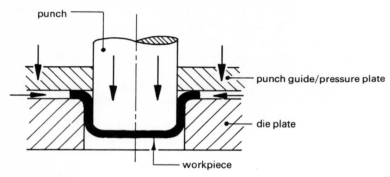

punch

punch guide/pressure plate

die plate

workpiece

Fig. 5.12

Synthesis or Building towards a solution

Work through each of these sections methodically, sketching as many possible solutions to each question as possible. Always refer back to the other questions as a more positive solution emerges, to see if it also fits in with other requirements or if it will need still further modification before fulfilling every need.

As you gradually work from stage to stage, collect your final solution of each part and put them together in the form of working sketches. When these seem satisfactory, proceed either to a model in a suitable material, or a working drawing.

Even with a thorough approach like this, minor modifications may still be necessary as you make up the tool. Be sure to note these on your final drawings for future reference if necessary.

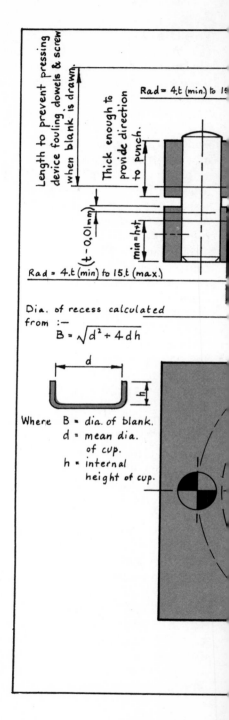

Length to prevent pressing device fouling dowels & screw when blank is drawn.

Thick enough to provide direction to punch.

Rad = 4.t (min.) to 15.

$(t - 0.01mm)$

min = h+t

Rad = 4.t (min.) to 15.t (max.)

Dia. of recess calculated from :—

$$B = \sqrt{d^2 + 4dh}$$

d

h

Where   B = dia. of blank.

d = mean dia. of cup.

h = internal height of cup.

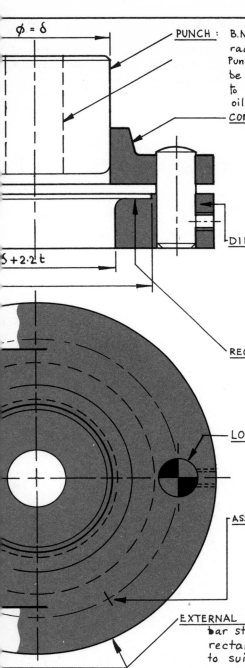

φ = δ

S + 2·2t

PUNCH : B.M.S. V. fine turned finish. Form turn radius at end. Polish.
Punch bored through to permit bar to be used to push off cap (?) Allows air to help separate (suction of lubricating oil.

COMBINED PUNCH GUIDE & PRESSURE PAD: B.M.S. Fine turned finish for sliding fit of punch. Could be of cast L.M.4 (see alternative shapes on L.H. & R.H. sides.) This would reduce weight, length of location dowels & clamping screws. Screws to be recessed below bottom limit of punch top when blank is drawn.

DIE : B.M.S. or KAYEM 1. Thickness to allow for threading for clamping screws & to clamp dowels. Thickness equals sum of recess for blank + die radius + external height of cup. Die could be supported on parallels for deeper cups to be drawn. Finish as for punch.

RECESS : Allows blank to be located centrally under punch / over die hole. Depth of recess smaller than thickness of blank so that blank may be "nipped" by pressure pad. This stops cockling of blank.

LOCATION DOWELS: to locate axis of punch on axis of die. Two only req^d. spaced diametrically opposite. To be of substantial diameter. φ 10 m.m. or φ 12 m.m. ? Silver steel to fit drilled & reamed holes.

ASSEMBLY CLAMPING SCREWS : 3 or 4 studs & wing nuts or machine screws equally spaced. Clearance through pressure pad and threaded in die. Screws positioned to allow clamping pressure to extend as near blank as possible M8?

EXTERNAL FORM OF TOOL : May be of round bar stock or from flat stock – square or rectangular. Position dowels & screws to suit.

Various shapes of punch possible – different shapes of cup.
SPRINGS : transfer pressure to pressure pad when drawing & strip cup from punch afterwards (use hard rubber instead of springs ?) (Shallow cups only.)

Could be spring or hard rubber loaded.

BOTTOM PRESSURE PAD : Acts as a stripper – of cup from die hole. Also helps to keep bottom of cup flat.

LOCATION METHOD ? PUNCH to be coaxial with DIE. BLANK over DIE hole.

A recess could restrict the use of the tool to the making of cups of one height / depth Other methods of locating blanks could be used, eg.,
a. Three pins project above die surface by less than thickness of blank. May be removed & repositioned.
b. A tinplate or card template could be fitted over dowels. Provide holes for screws.

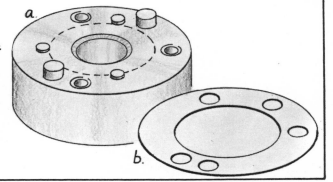

a.

b.

The drawing on page 97 shows a design for a press tool taken from a designer's folder. The drawings which follow on pages 99, 100 and 101 show sheets from a designer's folder as he works from a written design analysis to the solution of a problem.

PROBLEM. To devise a means of storing plastic tape boxes. What type of boxes : Phillips library boxes made in plastic. ? Provision for spare spool. Box sizes 5", 5¼", 7" (NB. Spool sizes quoted). Although plastic boxes it might be helpful to keep dust out. Need to be able to see box labels.

Cases are plastic so mustn't scratch. Should provisions be made for anything else? eg. Leader tape and splicing equipment.

PROBLEM RESTATED : Devise a means of storing/ stack 3 different sizes of plastic tape boxes such that any single one can be removed and the tape number or title easily seen.

METHODS OF STORING : ① Band round them ② open ended sleeve ③ series of pockets ④ tilted bookstand type ⑤ one side of cube removed. ⑥ Chest of drawers construction. ⑦ Carousel ⑧ Open storage

One requirement that stems from the analysis is that provision should be made for additional storage. ie duplicate units should interlock. Most of the design use too much material.

Type ④ may be further reduced.

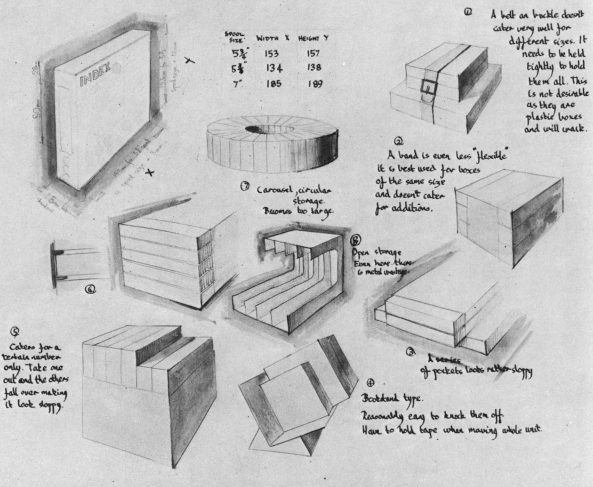

SPOOL SIZE	WIDTH X	HEIGHT Y
5¾"	153	157
5¼"	134	138
7"	185	189

⑦ Carousel, circular storage. Becomes too large.

⑤ Caters for a certain number only. Take one out and the others fall over making it look sloppy.

⑧ Open storage Even here there is metal wastage.

④ Bookstand type. Reasonably easy to knock them off Have to hold tape when moving whole unit.

③ A series of pockets looks rather sloppy

② A band is even less "flexible" it is best used for boxes of the same size and doesn't cater for additions.

① A belt an buckle doesn't cater very well for different sizes. It needs to be held tightly to hold them all. This is not desirable as they are plastic boxes and will crack.

It has been concluded that the rack need only be a small structure, as much of the material is superfluous in the designs previously investigated. As all the faces of the tape box are parallel and do not taper a structure holding just the bottom of the box would hold them. There would be no risk of them falling out. The rack therefore need only hold 1 side and a part of another. The most convenient sides are the bottom and the back. If support is given along the whole length of the bottom only part of the back is needed. The simplest form would therefore be a triangular shape. This is however rather harsh and when it is empty doesn't have any interest on its own. Curved lines would be out of place for such a rectilinear article as the tape box. The length should be decided for the smallest size as the larger sizes will be easily held in the same size. It might be found that 7" is too big to incorporate in the same size.

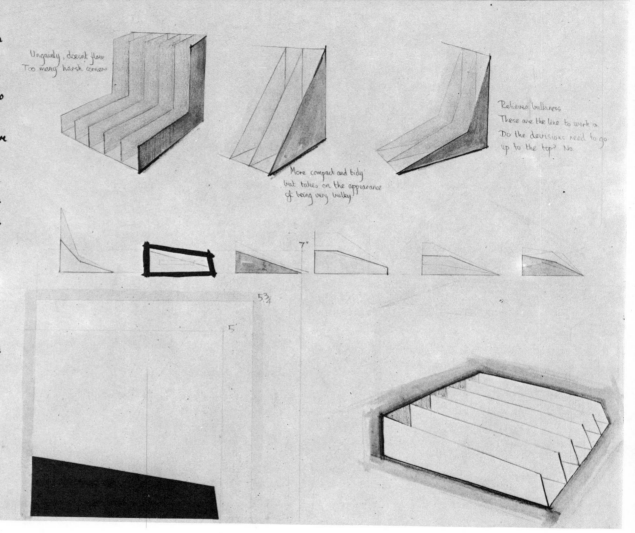

Ungainly, doesn't flow
Too many harsh corners

More compact and tidy but takes on the appearance of being very bulky

Relieves bulkiness
These are the lines to work on
Do the divisions need to go up to the top? No

7"

5¾"

5"

The problem, it has been decided, is to be solved by a mainly bottom holding device which is made up of a number of shaped strips. The problem is how to join them and does it need visual lightening. In the final conclusion provision should be made for increasing the number of boxes. This will be free standing as a tape recorder is a portable piece of equipment so I think provisions for wall fixture are unnecessary. Being free standing it should have a little weight to it although the tapes themselves give a good deal of weight. Being made of metal there is a good chance of it scratching the plastic boxes. To overcome this adhesive felt can be put on the surfaces in sliding contact with the boxes. The give in this will hold the boxes firmly. The material : Aluminium too easily bent unless in thick section. Bright Mild Steel would rust - could be sprayed. Brass too expensive. Aluminium best, sprayed steel comes second.

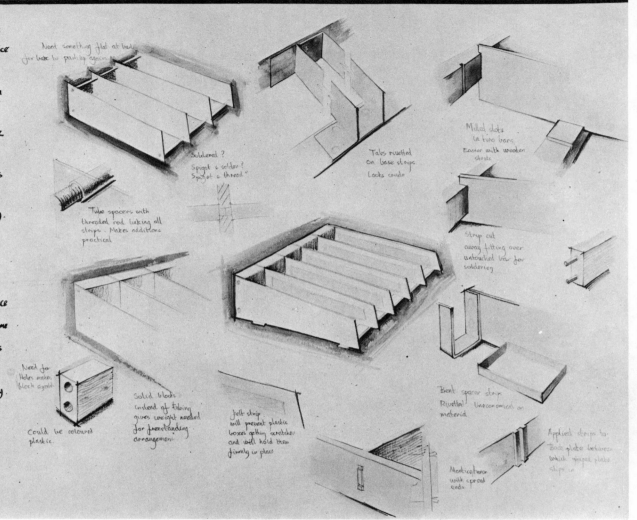

Need something flat at base for base to push up against

Soldered?
Spigot & solder?
Spigot & thread?

Tube spacers with threaded rod linking all strips. Makes additions practical

Tabs rivetted on base strips. Looks crude

Milled slots in two bars. Easier with wooden slots

Strip cut away fitting over untouched bar for soldering

Need for holes make block signid

Could be coloured plastic

Solid blocks instead of tubing gives weight needed for freestanding arrangement

Felt strip will prevent plastic boxes getting scratched and will hold them firmly in place

Bent spacer strip Rivetted. Uneconomical on material

Applied strips to back plate between which shaped plates slip in

Medicatenia with spread ends

101

Chapter 6

HARDNESS

You will know from your practical work that some metals are harder than others and in previous sections we have referred to the property of work hardening. To study this property of hardness in more detail, it is first necessary to define it and later to design methods of testing and comparing the hardness of different metals. This knowledge will help in your selection of the most suitable metals for use when designing solutions to certain problems.

Hardness is best defined as the ability of one metal to scratch, dent or cut another. You know that a steel knife blade can cut lead so steel must be harder than lead, but a similar comparison between all metals is not so easy and requires a more scientific method of testing.

The metals most likely to be used in a school workshop include mild steel, lead, gilding metal and brass, aluminium, tool steel, copper, nickel silver, zinc base alloy, stainless steel and cast iron. List these metals in your folder in what you consider to be their order of hardness, starting with the hardest and ending with the softest. How can you make sure that the order in which you placed the metals is correct?

TESTS

Firstly, you can scratch or mark a specimen of each metal. Before attempting to set up such a test you must ask the following questions:

1 With what can I scratch the metals?
2 Can I scratch the hardest metal?
3 How can I actually do the scratching?
4 How can I compare or measure the amount of scratching?
5 Can I be sure that the effort I use to scratch one metal is the same as that used for another, in fact for all metals?

If you can answer these questions satisfactorily, you can carry out tests and check that your original list is correct, or amend it if necessary.

Possible answers may include:
1 (a) Diamond, e.g. old glass cutter or grindstone wheel dresser.
(b) Tungsten carbide, e.g. old masonry drill tip or tile cutter.
(c) Coarse emery-cloth, e.g. corundum or aloxite grit. In each case the specimens must be held or mounted in some way.
2 Yes, all with the above.
3 Drag the scratching tool across the surface of the specimen.
4 Visually, the scratches on soft metals will be deeper than on hard metals.
5 You cannot rely on holding the scratching tool in your hand. But you can devise a piece of apparatus similar

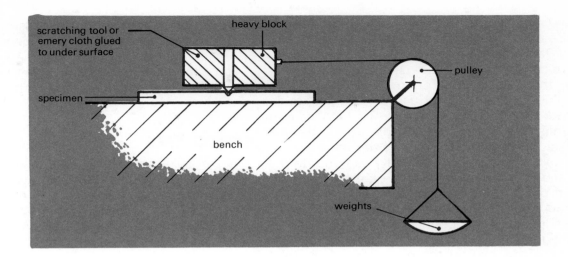

scratching tool or emery cloth glued to under surface

heavy block

pulley

specimen

bench

weights

Fig. 6.1

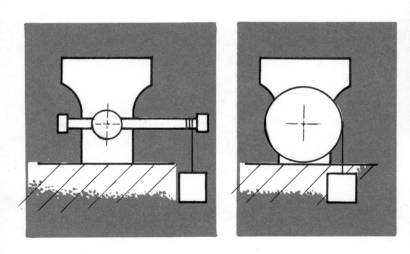

Fig. 6.2

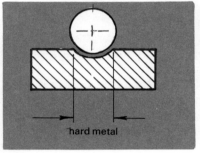

hard metal

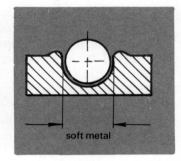

soft metal

Fig. 6.3

to that used in physics to measure friction (Fig. 6.1).

The biggest problem with this test is in comparing the depth or width of the scratches on the specimens. Some scratches may be so fine that they can hardly be compared. Therefore, is it possible to devise tests involving the cutting or denting of metal in which it will be easier to compare one specimen with another?

Such tests will only help you to place the metals in rank order of hardness or softness. They will not really tell you how much harder or softer one metal is than another unless you can *measure* the depth or width of the scratches, or the effort used to cut or form the dent.

Can you devise a method whereby you can measure the difference in, say, the depth of the dents? Some of the questions you must answer in solving this problem will include:

1 With what can I dent even the hardest metal specimen?
2 How can I do the actual denting?
3 How can I be sure that the effort used to dent is the same for all specimens?
4 How can I measure the size or depth of the dents?

The following are possible answers to these questions but they raise other questions still to be answered:
1 (a) As for the scratching test.
   (b) A hard ball-bearing, e.g. tungsten carbide.
2 (a) Drop the denting tool on to the surface of the specimen. You would have to use a weighted tool in order to mark the hardest specimens. The tool must be dropped from the same height for each specimen. Is it convenient just to drop the tool, or should you control it so that it falls in a given place? How can you do this? Could you slide the tool down a tube or allow it to swing from a given position like a pendulum?

If you drop a golf ball on grass, on carpet, on wood, or on concrete, the ball will bounce. What do you notice about the height of the bounce? Does the ball bounce as high when it is dropped on the grass as it does on the concrete? Can you measure the height of bounce as a measure of the hardness of the ground or floor? Would a similar test be possible with metals?

(b) Squeeze the denting tool into the metal specimen. This could be done by applying a heavy weight or by squeezing the specimen in an engineer's vice.
3 By conducting the tests under the same conditions for all specimens, i.e. by using the same denting tool, the same weight, the same height, and the same amount of squeeze or effort on the tommy bar of the vice. This last effort is called **torque.** How can you be sure that the torque used is the same for all specimens? How can the amount of torque used to produce a dent be measured?

You could, perhaps, add a weight to the tommy bar of the vice, but you must be sure that the tommy bar is in the same position for all specimens and preferably horizontal. Why? (Fig. 6.2.)

If you use a standard thickness for the specimens and a small ball-bearing, the test will be fairly accurate. Greater accuracy will be gained if you can either substitute a wheel for the tommy bar, or turn the vice screw with a torque wrench which will measure the amount of torque used.
4 If you use a ball-bearing for the test can you rely on measuring the diameter of the dent? Is the diameter of the dent really directly proportional to the force used? What should you measure if you cannot use the diameter of the dent? How can you do the measuring?(Fig. 6.3.)

You will have noticed that metals can be placed in a simple order of hardness, and that, with a little ingenuity, you can measure the hardness of metals so that you can say that one metal is so much harder or softer than another.

PROBLEMS

1 Devise a suitable method of testing the hardness of metals from the suggestions given and plot your results on a simple graph: hardness to metal.

Interesting results can be obtained if these tests for hardness are applied to metals which have been heat treated (see later sections of this chapter). For instance, what difference in hardness is there between bright drawn mild steel as cut from stock and that quenched from a range of temperatures between 100°C and 800°C? If a carbide point is used, it may be possible to note the hardness differences between silver steel specimens which have been tempered to different temperatures.

Alloys can easily be made from lead and tin. Differing amounts of either metal will produce alloys of differing hardness.

2 Make such a series of lead and tin alloys using a small refractory crucible as on p. 18 and determine the answers to the following questions:
(a) How is the hardness altered by varying the proportions of lead and tin?
(b) What are the melting and freezing temperatures of each alloy?
(c) Does the metal change from liquid to solid instantaneously and at one specific temperature, or does it take some time to solidify while the temperature falls?
(d) Does the metal go directly from liquid to solid, or is there a 'pasty' stage in between?

Most of these questions can be answered by plotting a simple graph: temperature to alloy.

Simple apparatus can also be designed to test and measure other physical properties of metals, e.g. tensile, bending (p. 126) and shear strength (p. 128), elasticity, ductility and malleability.

More elaborate tests for hardness are carried out in industry. These are standardized tests using universally accepted scales of hardness:

Brinell hardness testing is done by pressing a ball into the piece of metal. The Brinell hardness number is calculated thus:

$$\frac{\text{Load on ball in kilogrammes}}{\text{Spherical surface area of impression in square mm}}$$

Tables are published giving the hardness number when the diameter of the impression has been measured. Standard loads are used.

Vickers Pyramid hardness testing is done by pressing a square, pyramid-shaped diamond onto the surface of the specimen. The Vickers Pyramid hardness number is calculated from the load used and the length of the diagonal of the square dent made.

Rockwell hardness number is found by using a steel ball or a diamond cone. The depth of the dent is used to give the hardness number.

The *Shore Scleroscope* uses the height of the first bounce to give the hardness number, when a diamond-pointed tool is dropped down a glass tube.

The *Izod* test gives a hardness value found by recording the angle of swing of a pendulum hammer past a specimen clamped in a vice. The pendulum fractures the specimen as it falls. Harder metals absorb more kinetic energy when fractured and therefore prevent the pendulum from swinging very far past the point of impact.

The *Charpy* test is similar to the Izod, but the pendulum hits a cutting tool which cuts the specimen.

The Izod and the Charpy tests really involve the toughness as well as the hardness of the metal specimens (see p. 126).

You will notice from the results of your experiments, that increased hardness has been given to pure metals by alloying them with others. This simple example should remind you that, unlike a natural material such as wood, metals can be made increasingly versatile by careful alloying. Once a metallurgist can analyse the exact requirements of a metal in terms of fusibility, ductility, malleability, hardness, etc, he can experiment with alloying techniques until he produces a metal which meets these requirements. New alloys are being introduced regularly as a result of great technological projects such as supersonic flight and space travel which demand even greater strength and reliability from metals.

Although these projects appear to have little to do with individual people, their everyday lives benefit tremendously from the results of the research involved, as these alloys are gradually used in wider ranges of industry to produce goods at lower costs for their use and consumption.

In earlier sections, you learnt how sufficient heat allows metals to dissolve into each other to form alloys and also, how lesser heating energizes and re-arranges the atoms within a metal so that on cooling, it becomes annealed (softened), see p. 108. From this it will be realized that heat, in varying amounts and in different ways, is mainly responsible for the hardness of metals.

The hardest metal used in your previous tests and the one in greatest use throughout the world is the ferrous alloy we call steel. It is necessary now to examine this metal in closer detail to understand the variety of grades of steel that are available to the designer and how the hardness of each can be altered by heating and cooling in different ways, a process known as heat treatment.

Steel is fundamentally an alloy of iron (ferrite) and iron carbide (cementite). As ferrite is soft and cementite extremely hard, the hardness of the steel increases with the amount of cementite added. This is explained in Fig. 6.4 which shows in pictorial form the relationship between ferrite, cementite and pearlite (grains consisting of alternate layers of ferrite and cementite) for each of the alloys concerned.

This arrangement of the different constituents applies at temperatures below 200°C. After this, the heat energy supplied causes more iron carbide to go into solution with the iron, producing greater areas of this harder material. If it is allowed to cool normally, the metal changes back to its original structure, but if it is cooled very suddenly from the temperature which causes the change to take place, the hard structure produced by the heating is retained. Thus steel is hardened.

Such a hardening process is possible only with steel

having between 0.4 and 1.3 per cent carbon content. With less than 0.4 per cent, there is insufficient carbon to form enough iron carbide and more than 1.3 per cent carbon will not go into solution with the iron as Fig. 6.4 shows.

This further alloying takes place at different temperatures according to the carbon content of each specimen of steel. The process is shown in Fig. 6.5. A specimen from within this given range is heated until a point is reached when continued heating does not result in an increased temperature for a while. Then, suddenly, the temperature continues to rise as before. It is during this pause in temperature rise that the change in structure takes place. If heating is continued, a second pause takes place and from then on no further change occurs before melting.

If the specimen is allowed to cool naturally, the cooling curve also shows the two arrests but these occur at a lower temperature in each case—as shown by the dotted line.

Fig. 6.6(a) shows the heating and cooling curves for the specimens concerned and Fig. 6.6(b) shows a simplified graph where a mean line has been drawn between the arrest points in each case. It is from such a chart that the craftsman works when hardening steel, and when effecting any of the other five heat treatments possible. Each are now explained in detail and reference should be made to Fig. 6.6(b) in each case.

Hardening

Any chosen specimen should be heated above its upper critical point—into the austenitic range—and soaked, or retained, at that temperature long enough for the whole mass of metal to change into austenite. Then the metal

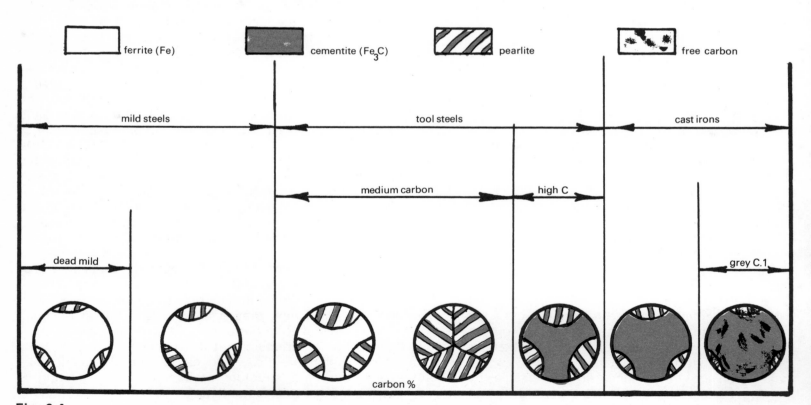

Fig. 6.4

should be quenched immediately so that the structural change on cooling takes place in the critical range resulting in either ferrite and cementite (in the case of specimens between 0.4 per cent and 0.87 per cent carbon content), or cementite and pearlite (if between 0.87 per cent and 1.3 per cent carbon), either of which is very hard indeed. *Heating* should be done either in a muffle furnace to control the temperature and ensure uniform heating, or by a normal gas/air torch.

When heated, the metal will oxidize and a scale will be formed on the surface. The depth of the scale will be reduced if the heating is done quickly, but it must be remembered that the metal has to be heated throughout its thickness.

is safer to quench in thin sperm oil if in any doubt. Care should be taken to ensure that there is sufficient oil to prevent its resulting rise in temperature from reaching flash point (Fig. 6.7).

Although such heating and quenching of tool steel results in a very *hard* structure, the grain size so produced is needle-like which makes the metal extremely *brittle*. This brittleness makes it impossible to use the metal unless it is removed by a gentle annealing at a low temperature. Such a process is called tempering and, because it re-

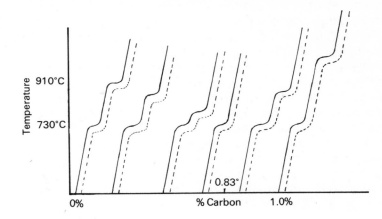

Fig. 6.6(a)

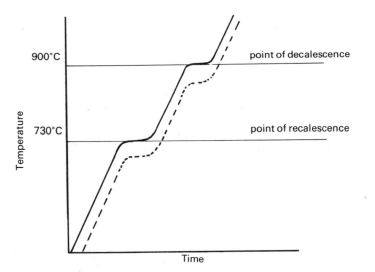

Fig. 6.5

Quenching should be done in water—preferably running water—if under 12 mm in cross-section, and the specimen should be vigorously swished in the coolant to prevent a jacket of hot steam from surrounding it and delaying the cooling effect. If the specimen is greater than 12 mm in section, the outer edges may cool and contract before the centre of the mass which would result in cracking. A thin layer of oil on top of the water prevents this if the specimen is only just in excess of 12 mm in section, but it

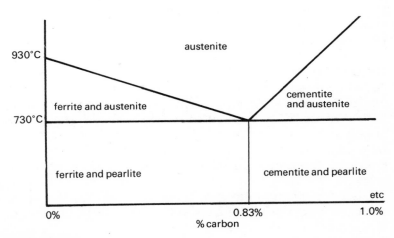

Fig. 6.6(b)

moves the brittleness, it makes the hardened metal very tough.

Tempering

The temperature range for tempering is between 200°C and 300°C depending on what the specimen is to be used for when finished. The higher the temperature used, the greater the toughness but the lesser the hardness, and the lower the temperature used, the harder the final metal but it remains slightly brittle. Consequently, tools which are to be used for cutting, and therefore need a very hard, sharp edge, are tempered at the lower end of this range, and springs, etc. which need to be hard but very tough, are tempered at the higher end. (Fig. 6.9).

Heating should be done in a temperature-controlled oven, so that the exact temperature required can be used. This prevents the metal getting too hot and makes quenching unnecessary. If such an oven is not available, great care has to be taken to ensure that the correct temperature is reached with a gas/air torch and that the work is quenched immediately to prevent it over-heating.

Fortunately, at different temperatures within this range, the oxides are thicker and therefore burn at different colours. If the metal is cleaned to brightness after hardening, these colours can be seen when tempering and used as an accurate guide for the craftsman, but the work *must* be quenched when the correct colour reaches the desired point to prevent overheating by conduction. Fig. 6.8 shows the recommended temperatures and colours for tempering various commodities.

Annealing

As with other metals mentioned earlier, steel can be annealed to counteract work hardening, and reduced to its softest possible condition if heated above the upper critical point, soaked at that heat for a few moments and then cooled. The cooling should be done as slowly as possible, by switching off the current and leaving the work in the oven for twenty-four hours—or by turning off the forced draught to the fire and leaving the work in the burning coke (if the forge fire was used), or burying in sand or lime (if a gas/air torch was used).

On *steels* only, to recrystallize after work hardening,

without reducing to the softest possible condition, a process known as normalising can be employed.

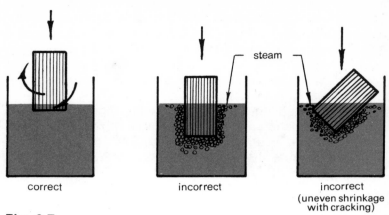

correct   incorrect   incorrect (uneven shrinkage with cracking)

Fig. 6.7

Article	Temperature °C	Colour
turning tools, scribers	230	pale straw
drills, milling cutters	240	dark straw
taps, scoring tools	250	brown
punches, reamers	260	brown to purple
press tools	270	purple
cold chisels	280	dark purple
springs	300	blue

Fig. 6.8

Normalising

This entails heating the specimen to a point above the upper critical point and then leaving it to cool naturally. This will allow recrystallization without seriously affecting the balance of the alloying constituents. (Fig. 6.9.)

The final heat treatment that is possible on steels is to enrich the carbon content on the surface of the steels in the mild steel range, turning the skin into a tool steel which can then be hardened and tempered for use thereafter. Such a process is called case hardening.

Case Hardening
This is done by packing the specimen in a box filled with a carbon-rich compound, sealing the lid to prevent oxidization, and heating and soaking above the upper critical point of 950°C, for a determined period. The longer it is soaked, the thicker the resulting hard case. This part of the process is called carburizing. When the right amount of carburization has been achieved, the work can be hardened—by heating and quenching as before— then tempered in the normal way.

Superficial hardening, which merely produces a hard skin, can be done with a gas/air torch. The specimen is heated to a bright red heat, dipped in a carbon-rich material such as Kasenit, then re-heated and dipped two or three times. Finally it is re-heated to bright red and quenched in water, which hardens the new skin.

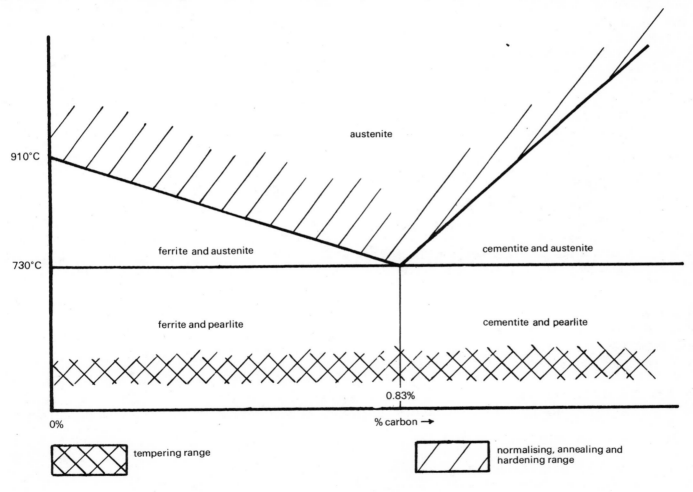

Fig. 6.9

109

Case hardening is usually done where a component is to take a lot of hard wear on the outside but needs a soft inner matrix to cushion the effect of sudden blows. A good example is the gudgeon pin that holds a piston on to a connecting rod. It must stand up to continuous wear and withstand the shock of each explosion within the cylinder head.

STEEL—INDUSTRIAL METHODS

In the engineering industries, steel is frequently required to perform exacting tasks. The composition of each type of steel is very carefully worked out. The type of heat treatment to be used must be chosen with equal care to bring out the useful characteristics of each metal.

Furnace

Whatever heat treatment is to be given it is usual to heat the steel in a furnace in which the temperature is very accurately, thermostatically controlled. Furnaces may be heated by coal, gas, electricity or oil and may have inert gas pumped through them so that the metal will not oxidise.

Sometimes articles are heated in molten salts, such as sodium cyanide. The salts melt at known temperatures and when molten, they exclude air. The liquid also helps to heat the article uniformly. This is known as the salt bath process. Other baths may contain sand or even low-melting-point metal.

Temperature

The temperature of the furnaces or the articles may be measured in several ways:
(a) for low temperatures a mercury-in-glass thermometer may be used,
(b) higher temperatures are measured with pyrometers of which there are two types, (i) thermo-electric-thermo-couple and (ii) optical—disappearing filament. Both types of pyrometers have scales reading in degrees centigrade.

There are other ways in which temperatures may be indicated—Seger cones are made to collapse at prescribed temperatures and special coloured paints and crayons change colour when they reach specific temperatures.

Quenching

The quenching of components must be done with care to avoid uneven cooling which may cause areas of hardness, distortion or perhaps cracking. Quenching media include water, brine, soluble oil, special oils, and also a blast of cold air.

Case Hardening

In industry, the pack method of carburising is carried out on a much larger scale. It is usual to use steels of between 0.15 and 2.0 per cent carbon. When these metals are subjected to high temperatures for prolonged periods, the cores of the articles develop a coarse grain structure. This is refined by reheating the article to about 900°C and quenching it in oil. The case, although of a coarse grain structure, is refined when hardening is carried out.

Carburizing is another hardening process which can be done by immersing components in a salt bath containing carburizing salts. These salts are usually of a cyanide compound and are very poisonous.

A further method of case hardening is by the nitriding process whereby the components are placed in a box which is heated to 500°C and through which ammonia gas is passed. Special steel alloys which are suitable for nitriding are used and the resulting nitrides are very hard. This method does not require quenching.

PROBLEMS

1 Design and make a simple device for opening a crown-capped bottle—for use on picnics.

Decide first of all if it is to be hand operated. Then ask yourself all the relevant questions as shown on p. 81, and record your answers to these on your design sheet so that you can refer back to them as you start exploring possible answers in sketch form.

2 Design and make a screwdriver for fitting 13 amp plugs to electrical leads.

Begin with a design analysis as before. Consider the

width and length of blade, insulation, and the type of grip required of the handle. Consider every possible answer to questions like these *before* sketching solutions.

ALLOY STEELS

The property of hardness in steels may also be obtained by alloying them with other metals such as chromium, tungsten, nickel and vanadium. These steels overcome the limitations of plain carbon steels which tend to corrode, to lose their hardness at high temperatures and large, heated specimens need quenching when they are being hardened which creates the risk of distortion or cracking.

The most significant alloy steels for your present studies are stainless steels and high speed steels.

Stainless Steel

Stainless steels contain at least 12 per cent chromium. The chromium in the steel produces a very thin oxide film on the surface of the metal which prevents further corrosion and gives the steel its stainless properties. There are three groups of stainless steels:

martensitic—hardenable and magnetic, used for tools and the knives of cutlery sets;

ferritic—non-hardenable;

austenitic—has high ductility, is non-magnetic, used for cold forming such as flatware and kitchen sinks.

The most widely used stainless steels are in the austenitic group (of which En 58E is the most suitable for school work). General details are given below, in Fig. 6.10.

High Speed Steel

There are a number of high speed steels, details of which are also given in Fig. 6.10.

Alloy steel	Alloying elements	Properties	Uses
Austenitic stainless steel	18% chromium 8% nickel	Corrosion resistant. Good mechanical properties up to 1100°C.	Particularly suitable for domestic and decorative purposes.
High speed steel	4% chromium 18% tungsten 1.5% vanadium	Great hardness, resists softening at high temperatures, therefore faster cutting speeds.	Lathe tools, milling cutters, drills, reamers, etc.

Fig. 6.10

Chapter 7

METAL CUTTING

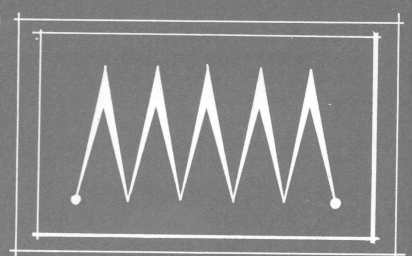

You have seen that metal may be shaped by a variety of processes:

(a) by casting, which utilizes the fluidity of the metal or alloy when molten,

(b) by cold and hot working, i.e. pressing, rolling, forging, extruding, and drawing, which utilizes the properties of ductility, malleability and plasticity.

(c) by joining, i.e. soldering, brazing, welding, rivetting, threading, folding and the use of adhesives.

(d) by wastage, or metal removal by cutting with hand or machine tools, to produce a component from a larger piece of stock. Although this is wasteful it is still one of the major—if not *the* major—metal shaping processes. Metallurgists, designers and production engineers are constantly investigating ways in which components can be made with the minimum amount of metal wastage.

From the sections dealing with the grain structure of metals it will be seen that a component produced by cutting may be weaker, size for size, than one produced by casting or forging as shown in Fig. 7.1, yet the characteristics of the metals used for casting, forging and cutting may well reduce this difference in strength.

The ability to cut metal depends on its properties of hardness, brittleness, ductility, malleability, plasticity, toughness and its shear strength.

Industrial methods of shaping also include electro-forming, electromachining and sintering or powder metallurgy.* (See p. 158 for a definition of sintering.)

Although the process of cutting is mentioned only in (d) above—where the process is of primary importance, it is also essential in the other shaping methods and very few articles can be made without the metal being cut at one stage or another.

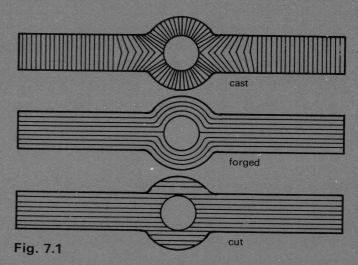

Fig. 7.1

* You may like to read about these methods in *New Ways of Shaping Metal*, by Fishlock & Hards (Newnes, 1965).

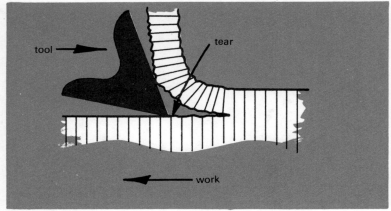

Fig. 7.2

The tools generally used are the cold chisel, scoring tool, file, saw, lathe tool, shaper tool, twist drill, reamer, tap, die, milling cutter, scraper, grinding wheel, and the shears. If you examine them you will find that they are all based on the same principles, although the shape of the cutting tooth or edge differs slightly from one to another depending on how it is used and what material it is intended to cut.

Obviously, the cutting tool must be of a harder material than the metal being cut, but the degree of hardness depends upon the amount of cutting required of the tool. All the cutting tools likely to be used in the school workshop are made of metal alloys, but in industry other hard materials like diamonds and ceramics are used as well. Whatever the material, however, the one common feature which all cutting tools *must* have is a leading cutting edge.

CUTTING ACTION

Basically, when a cutting tool acts on metal, the bulk of the chip is *torn* away from the workpiece in front of the cutting edge and the actual cutting edge then cleans up the torn surface (see Fig. 7.2). The shape of the cutting tool depends on the work it has to do and on the metals it has to cut.

The cutting angle is reduced from a right angle because:
(a) the tool must not merely rub the metal as this would cause unnecessary friction and heat,
(b) the tool must *cut* as much as possible rather than

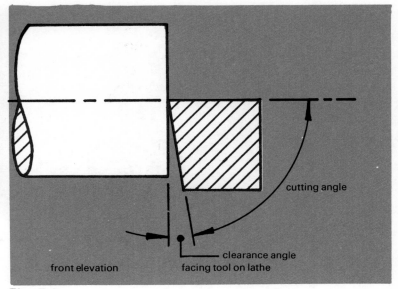

front elevation   facing tool on lathe

Fig. 7.3

merely tear the metal (see Fig. 7.3).

Therefore, the first angle formed in shaping the cutting tool is called the **clearance angle.** A secondary clearance angle may be given to a tool to prevent any possible interference between the tool and the work during cutting.

The second angle is formed with respect to (b) above, and is called the **rake angle.** It is especially important as it allows the chip to slide away from the face of the cutting edge as shown in Figs 7.4 and 7.5.

These two fundamental features are shown in relation to some basic tools in Fig. 7.6.

Some tools are given side rake, side cutting angle and side clearance depending on the direction in which they are fed against the metal.

The size of the rake and clearance angles, and hence the cutting angle, depends on factors such as:
(a) the angle at which the tool is held to the workpiece (e.g. lathe tool-bit holder or cold chisel),
(b) whether the work, or tool rotates to produce a flat, conical or cylindrical surface or helical groove,
(c) the nature of the metal being cut.*

* See *Know Your Lathe* (publ.—Boxford Machine Tools Ltd., Heckmondwike, Yorks.).

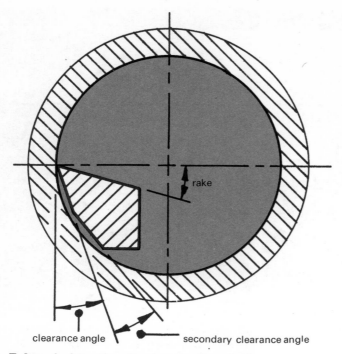

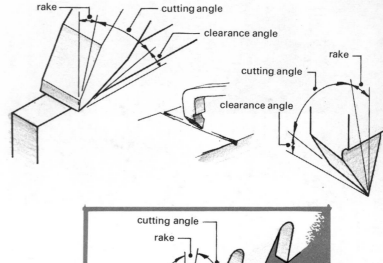

rake — cutting angle — clearance angle

cutting angle — rake — clearance angle

clearance angle — secondary clearance angle

Fig. 7.4 end elevation boring tool on lathe

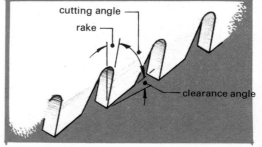

cutting angle — rake — clearance angle

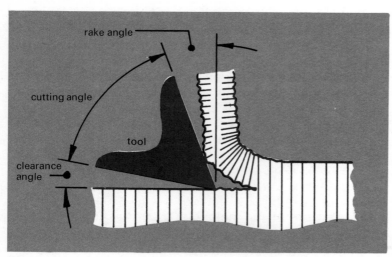

rake angle

cutting angle

tool

clearance angle

Fig. 7.5

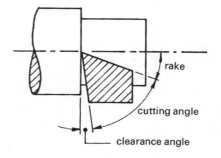

Fig. 7.6

rake — cutting angle — clearance angle

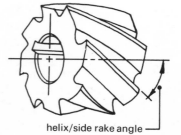

helix/side rake angle

Fig. 7.7

114

The shape of the space, or throat, and the distance (pitch) between the cutting edges are regulated to accommodate the swarf produced during cutting so that the tool does not get clogged with swarf and jammed in the workpiece.

Fig. 7.8(a)

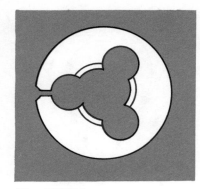

Fig. 7.8(b)

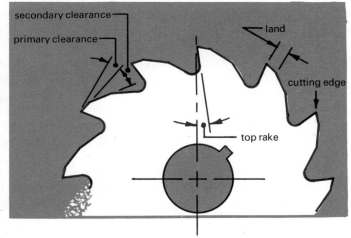

Fig. 7.8(c)

CUTTING SPEEDS

The cutting speed is the speed of the tool passing through the work, or the speed of the work passing the tool.

Cutting speed is expressed in metres per minute and metals are cut at different speeds. In practice, the speed at which a metal is cut depends on a variety of factors, even though a theoretical speed is stated for each metal.

These factors include:

(a) *The metal of the tool itself*. Tool steel, or carbon steel (C.S.) is used at a slower speed than high speed steel (H.S.S.) whereas stellite and sintered carbide-tipped tools are used at even higher speeds.

(b) *The width and depth of the cut*. This involves the volume of metal removed per cutting edge per minute, or the loading on the tool and its edge.

(c) *The rigidity of the tool*, its size and the way it is supported.

(d) *The rigidity of the work*, its bulk and manner in which it is held.

(e) *The use of cutting fluid*, which reduces friction between the work and the tool, and between the swarf and the tool face. Cutting fluid also cools the work and the tool, and washes the swarf away from the cutting edge. Different cutting fluids are used on different metals.

(f) *The metal being cut*. As a general rule, soft and ductile metals are cut at high speeds while hard and brittle metals are cut at low speeds. *This is the most important factor* controlling cutting speeds.

To calculate the speed in rpm of the cutting tool, or the work, the formula below may be used.

$$N = \frac{1000 \times S}{d \times \pi}$$

where N = rpm of the work or tool
S = cutting speed of metal expressed in metres per minute
d = diameter of work or tool measured in millimetres

A guide for selecting the ram strokes per minute of a shaping machine is to use the formula:

$$Rst = \frac{1000 \times S}{2L}$$

where Rst = ram strokes per minute
S = cutting speed of metal in metres per minute
L = length of stroke in millimetres

For a shaping machine, the cutting speed of metals may be taken as half the lower value for turning.

A table of cutting speeds of metals and basic plastics in metres per minute is given in Fig. 7.9.

Materials to be cut	Cutting speed in metres per minute using a H.S.S. tool
Dead mild steel and mild steel below 0.4% carbon.	24 to 30
Carbon steel 0.4% to 0.7% carbon.	18 to 24
High carbon or tool steel 0.7% carbon and above	12 to 18
Stainless steels— martensitic (heat treatable, used for cutlery)	12 to 18
austenitic (work hardening rate high, press work, suitable for schools).	6 to 12
Grey cast iron	24 to 30
Alloyed cast iron	15 to 21
Aluminium	30 to 60
Brass, gilding metal, nickel silver	30 to 60
Brass leaded	45 to 75
Bronze	30 to 60
Copper	30 to 60
Zinc based alloys, Kayem	45 to 75
Plastics—general	300—or as fast as possible, use a very sharp tool, take shallow cuts and ensure a full flow of lubricant.

Fig. 7.9

USE OF CUTTING TOOLS

A cutting tool will perform most efficiently when it acts with an even, steady pressure against the workpiece. The cutting edge will be damaged if it is overloaded because the cutting speed is too high, the depth of cut is too great or the feed rate is too fast.

Generally when the cutting edge of a tool is in continuous contact with the workpiece it will be evenly loaded,

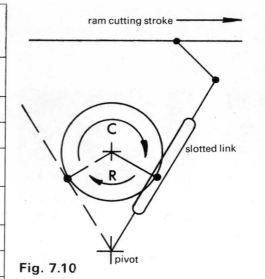

ram cutting stroke ⟶

C = cutting stroke

R = return stroke

the cutting speed takes place at a slower speed than the return stroke

slotted link

pivot

Fig. 7.10

e.g. scoring tool, lathe tool, twist drill, reamer, hand or bench shears. When using other tools, especially ones with multiple cutting edges, it is advisable to ensure that at least two edges, or teeth, are in contact with and cutting the metal, at any given moment. Such tools will include files, saws and milling cutters and their teeth are said to be in intermittent contact with the workpiece. A cutting stroke, or pass, should be commenced slowly and lightly, and the speed and feed increased when the cutting action is spread over several teeth.

The cutting stroke of the single point shaping machine tool begins at rest, increases to a maximum and slows to rest before commencing its return stroke. This is shown in Fig. 7.10, but see also Fig. 9.30(a), p. 148.

The length and position of the cutting stroke should be arranged to allow the tool to enter the workpiece at a slow speed, and *not* to hit it at high speed. The force of the impact may break the tool or cause it to bend into the workpiece and take a deeper cut than is intended. This is illustrated in Fig. 7.11(a).

Similarly, when a lathe tool is fed across or into a non-cylindrical workpiece, uneven loading is imposed on the tool (Fig. 7.11(b)).

You can now consider the application of cutting in the

design context, beginning in the first instance with hand tools and then considering each of the principal machine tools in turn.

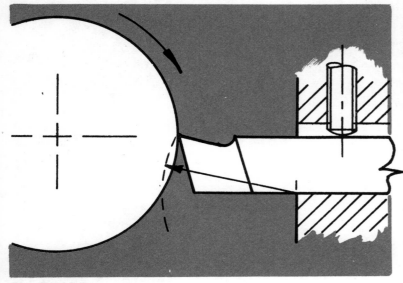

Fig. 7.11(a)

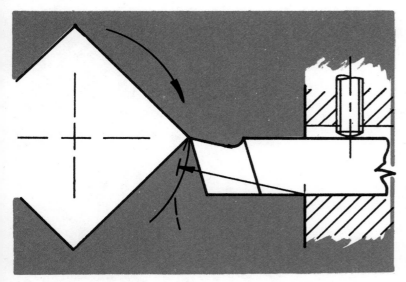

Fig. 7.11(b) effect of work/tool cutting pressure when turning

PROBLEMS

1 For this first problem you are advised to explore the properties of shaping sheet metals by simply cutting and folding as one might with paper. Prepare several squares of paper measuring 100 mm x 100 mm and draw a centre line on each. Cutting symmetrically either side of the centre line with square cuts, inclined cuts or curved cuts as suggested in Fig. 7.12, experiment to discover what shapes you can produce by folding the paper about these cuts. Any resulting shape in paper can be similarly produced in metal.

2 Based on the experiments carried out for the last exercise, design and make from 20 S.W.G. (Standard Wire Gauge) gilding metal or 24 S.W.G. stainless steel, a holder to support six pieces of toast. Begin, as always, by thoroughly analysing the problem and finding the sub-problems that must be resolved in the final design, e.g. size of average round of toast, ease of loading and unloading toast, passing the holder at the table and cleaning.

From your written analysis, work through preliminary design sketches until a final form emerges. Before commencing work in metal, make a model of your holder in stiff paper so that minor alterations can be made if necessary before the real thing is attempted (see Fig. 7.13).

TEXTURING

It is generally expected that the surface of any piece of machined metal will be smooth and of regular shape, whether it is flat, helical, curved, cylindrical, or conical, and a rough surface is regarded as a poor finish.

Perhaps the most common textured surface produced by a machine is **knurling.** This is normally limited to external cylindrical surfaces and generally to work carried out on a lathe. A variety of standard textures and patterns can be produced by knurling tools: diamond (L.H. and R.H. spiral), straight and checkered (inverted diamond).

A machined surface should be smooth, from good tool finish so you must create a texture by interrupting the surface with smooth cuts made by cutting tools such as

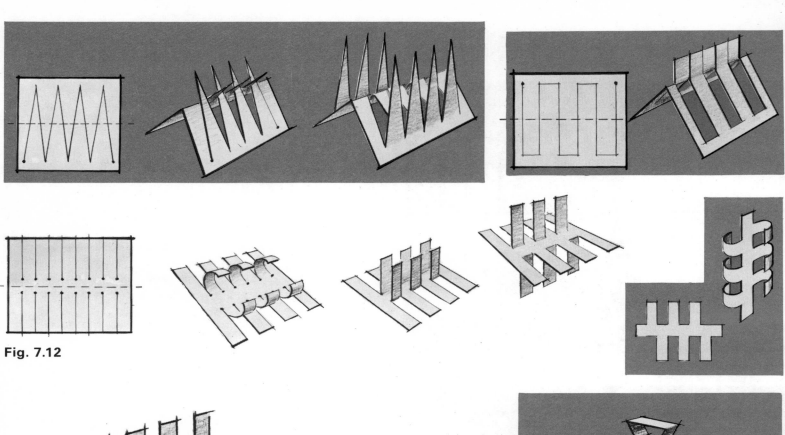

Fig. 7.12

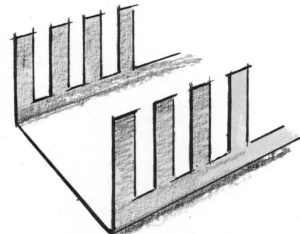

Fig. 7.13

the twist drill, lathe tool, shaping tool and milling cutter.

The following problems concern the cutting of textures using the principal machines in a workshop, as a form of controlled and planned decoration. Preceding each will be simple guide notes relevant to the machine in question.

THE LATHE

The workpiece, according to its shape, may be held by the conventional methods, i.e. collet chuck, three-jaw self-centring and four-jaw independent chucks, face plate, between centres or between chuck and tailstock centre. Remember that some of these methods permit the workpiece to be rotated on the lathe spindle axis, whilst others allow the workpiece to be off-set. Regular and irregularly shaped pieces may be held.

The cutting tool, held in the tool post, may be fed onto the workpiece in a variety of directions:
(a) parallel to the spindle axis, by means of the carriage feed,
(b) perpendicular to the spindle axis, by means of the cross-slide feed, and
(c) inclined to the spindle axis, by means of the compound/top slide feed. On sliding, surfacing and screw-cutting lathes, automatic feed is provided on the carriage and cross slide feeds only.

A helical groove may be cut when the lathe is set up for screwcutting. A cutting tool held in the tailstock may be fed into the rotating workpiece on the lathe spindle axis.

Less conventional workpiece-holding methods are possible and extend the versatility of the lathe. The workpiece may be clamped:
(a) directly in the toolpost,
(b) on an angleplate, fixed on the compound slide in place of the toolpost,
(c) on a milling attachment (vertical slide) in place of the compound slide.
In these cases, the work is fed to the cutting tool by means of the machine movements because the cutting tool must be made to rotate. The tool is usually held in either a collet chuck, four-jaw independent chuck or between centres.

The range of cutting tools which may be used on a lathe include the standard profile turning and boring tools, specially ground profile (form) tools, centre drills, twist drills, reamers, slot drills, end mills, form milling cutters and fly cutters.

Remember that when form tools with wide cutting edges are used with slow speeds and feeds to avoid tool chatter, the tool must still *cut* and not *rub* the metal.

The lathe may be used as a shaping machine. The workpiece is held rigidly and the tool is traversed over its surface. Work held on the spindle may be indexed by means of the chuck jaws or the gear train. Make sketches in your design folder to show how this shaping and indexing can be done.

PROBLEMS

1 Experiment with the different textures and patterns you can cut on a lathe, by machining each face of a 35 mm cube of duralumin in a different way, using a different cutter on each face. Keep this cube, or a full photographic record of it, in your folder for future reference when designing.

2 Design and make a lady's bracelet from six panels of 2 mm or 3 mm metal each measuring approximately 25 mm x 30 mm. Each panel is to be textured by concentric circles around *two* different centres.

Begin by working on paper marking two centres for each panel and drawing three circles 5 mm apart around them. Then move the centres and repeat. Experiment now by varying the width between the rings and possibly introducing a third centre. See p. 135 for methods of linkage.

When each panel has been finally designed, use soft solder to mount it centrally on a piece of square brass rod so that you can set it up in a four-jaw chuck for turning about each marked centre (see Fig. 7.14). Cut the texture, as circles or part circles, with a form tool. Remove chucking piece and apply linkage. Design and add clasp if necessary.

THE SHAPING MACHINE

The workpiece may be held in a variety of ways:

Fig. 7.14

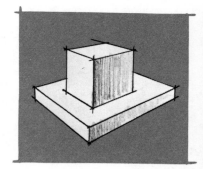

(a) directly on the worktable (workbox), on the top or slide face,

(b) on an angle plate mounted on the worktable.

(c) in a machine vice, with or without a swivel base, mounted on the worktable. The worktable of some machines may be made to swivel on its cross slide,

(d) using a dividing head.

The movements of the shaping machine restrict the tool to a simple to and fro movement over the workpiece. The tool slide is used to apply depth of cut and may be used to feed the tool vertically, or at an angle, through the work when the depth of cut is applied by means of the worktable movement.

The angular/radial position of the tool in the tool post and the direction in which the tool or the workpiece is fed to take the cut, controls the rake, cutting and clearance angles of the tool. The direction of tool or workpiece feed also controls the hand of the tool (the direction of rake angle). (See Fig. 7.15.)

When the tool returns after its cutting stroke, it is allowed,

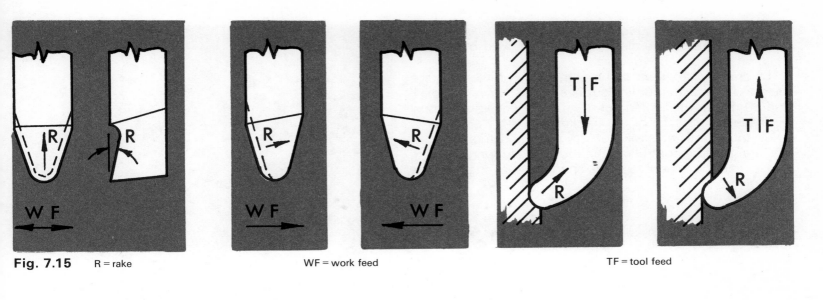

Fig. 7.15   R = rake   WF = work feed   TF = tool feed

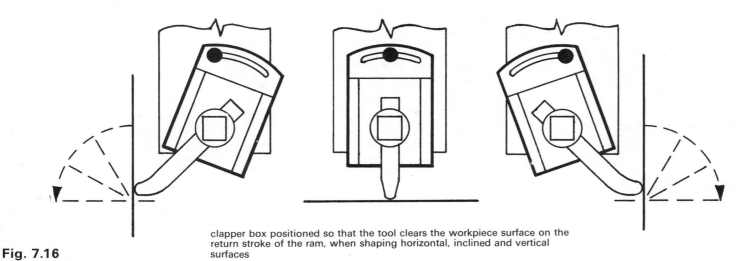

clapper box positioned so that the tool clears the workpiece surface on the return stroke of the ram, when shaping horizontal, inclined and vertical surfaces

Fig. 7.16

by the construction of the clapper box, to lift clear of the workpiece and ride over the uncut surface. This reduces wear on the tool and permits the workpiece to be fed beneath it, or the depth of cut to be increased for the subsequent cutting stroke. To facilitate this movement, the clapper box may be swivelled on the tool slide (Fig. 7.16).

The worktable may be traversed on a cross slide under the tool in a horizontal plane parallel to the tool ram traverse, but at right angles to it. The table feed may be manually or automatically controlled. The position of the workpiece may be set by using the vertical slide, but this *must not* be used for feeding the workpiece onto the cutter. So the

D.A.T.–M.–F

surfaces normally produced by the shaping machine are generated, that is, the plane surface is created by a combination of tool and work feed.

To create a textured surface, the tool profile must be used to form a straight line surface or cut, however small, and a number of regularly or irregularly spaced cuts must be made on the face of the workpiece.

As the length of stroke of the ram (and tool) and its position may be controlled, the tool in its forward, cutting stroke can be made to stop short of the edge of the workpiece.

PROBLEMS

1 Design and make a chess piece from a block of duralumin approximately 30 mm x 30 mm x 50 mm. The piece can be any of the major pieces, i.e. castle, knight, bishop, queen or king.

Begin by cutting coloured card to the required proportions and remove areas systematically at right angles. Make a pictorial sketch at each stage of how the article will look.

When you have finalised your shape on paper, make a block of plaster of Paris to the size of the chess piece and carve the shape you have planned. Do not be afraid to modify at this stage if it does not appear quite right in three dimensions, but when the design is finally complete, make a working drawing to assist you when machining the piece. See Figs. 7.17(a) and 7.17(b).

The Milling Machine

The process of milling consists of passing the workpiece against a suitably shaped revolving cutter.

There are basically two types of milling machine, one which carries cutters on an arbor in the *horizontal* plane and parallel to the worktable and the other which carries cutters in the end of a spindle which is normally in the *vertical* plane and perpendicular to the worktable. A large variety of sizes and shapes of cutters may be used on these machines.

The workpiece may be held in a number of ways:
(a) directly on the worktable,
(b) on an angle plate mounted on the worktable,

(c) in a machine vice, with or without a swivel base, mounted on the worktable,
(d) using a dividing head,
(e) on a rotary table.

The work may be moved in three directions, vertically, transversely and longitudinally on the machine. Normally only the longitudinal traverse is operated when taking a cut, the other two movements being locked to increase the rigidity of the workpiece.

When using the *horizontal milling machine* the workpiece, whenever possible, is fed against the rotation of the cutter. This action is called up-cutting, as shown in Fig. 7.18. The advantage of this method is that the cutter tends to push the workpiece away and to cut against the backlash of the worktable screw. A disadvantage is that the cutting action tends to lift the work from the machine worktable, necessitating adequately clamped work.

A similar principle applies to the position and direction of the workpiece feed in relation to the rotating cutter of the *vertical milling machine*, although frequently the cutters are used to machine slots and grooves causing the cutter to make part of its cut on its trailing edge.

Fig. 7.17(a)

Fig. 7.17(b)

Fig. 7.18

PROBLEMS

1 Experiment with the different textures you can cut on a milling machine, by machining each face of a 35 mm cube of duralumin in a different way using a different cutter on each face. Unlike the turning exercise, this can be partly pre-planned by pressing wood or metal shapes into Plasticene (Fig. 7.19). Keep this cube also for future reference when designing.

Fig. 7.19

2 From your answer to the last question, select a prefered texture and make a paper-weight from another 35 mm cube.

3 Design and make a cigarette box from a piece of duralumin tubing, 80 mm diameter and approximately 6 mm thick. As before, begin by analysing the main problem to find the sub-problems that must be resolved in the final design, e.g. length of a cigarette, how the lid will fit, how the base will be made, etc. and then sketch possible solutions.

If the tubing is not available, it can be cast from ingots of LM4 quite satisfactorily.

Design and make any of the following items, using any suitable surface texture for decoration:

4 Candle holder.

5 Desk clock case.

6 Table lighter.

7 A rectangular cigarette box.

8 Desk calendar.

9 Table lamp base.

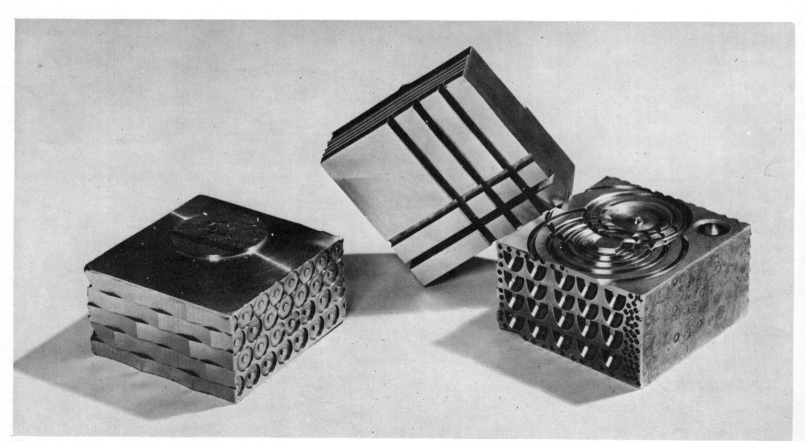

Fig. 7.20

124

Fig. 7.21

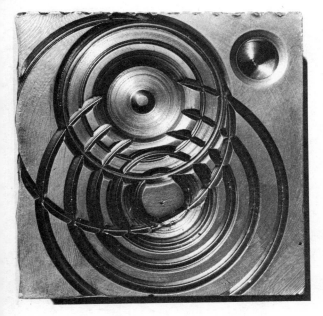

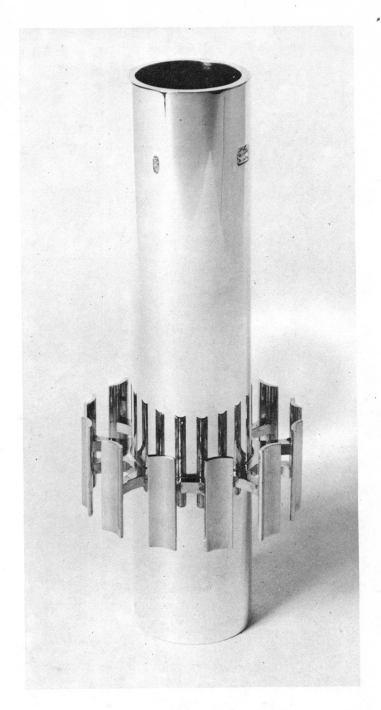

Chapter 8

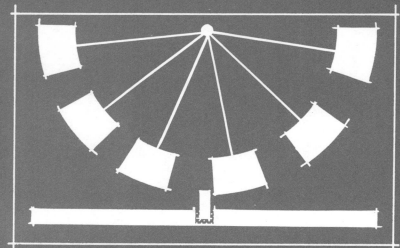

TOUGHNESS

Toughness is a difficult property to explain in metalworking terms. It is not the same as hardness.

Simply, toughness refers to the ability of a metal to withstanding bending or shear loading, as shown in Fig. 8.1, without fracturing. Unlike a clean edge formed when cutting, a component that has been sheared shows distortion at the edges of the shear. Brittleness is the opposite of toughness.

From this definition it will be seen that copper is extremely tough whereas cast iron is not. Toughness must *not* be confused with either strength or hardness.

As with the properties of malleability and ductility, toughness cannot be expressed in simple numerical terms. It is necessary to devise tests which will allow a comparison between the toughness of different metals. Tests of this kind should make it possible to draw up a personal set of specifications on which to base future design work.

TESTS

From the given definition of toughness you can devise your own tests for a range of metals available in the school workshop (see Chapter 6 on Hardness, and the list of metals on p. 60).

As with the other tests, the specimens must be of the same size, cross-section, etc., in order to standardize the results of the tests.

(1) The first problem is to devise a means of bending a series of test pieces and to measure the force required to do the bending.

If you place a specimen vertically in the jaws of an engineer's vice and strike the protruding end to bend the piece to a right angle, you can count the number of blows needed to perform the operation. There are many obvious inaccuracies involved in this method.

(2) Another way to measure the toughness of specimens, providing their size is convenient, would be to bend them forwards and backwards through the same angle until they break. The number of movements (forwards and backwards past the neutral position is two movements) is then a measure of the toughness of the material. This method involves work hardening the metal beyond its fatigue point.

(3) To conduct more accurate tests you can, of course, design a completely independent piece of equipment, or you can adapt something you already have. For example, you can design and make a simple piece of apparatus which can be used in place of the existing jaws of an engineer's vice so that a specimen is bent when the vice is tightened. The remaining problem would be to measure the force needed to tighten the vice. See Fig. 8.2.

One solution to this sub-problem may be to use a torque wrench. The torque—during movement—required to

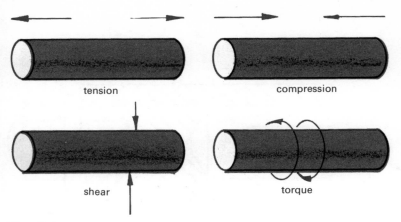

tension

compression

shear

torque

Fig. 8.1

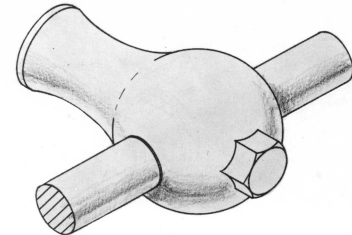

Fig. 8.3

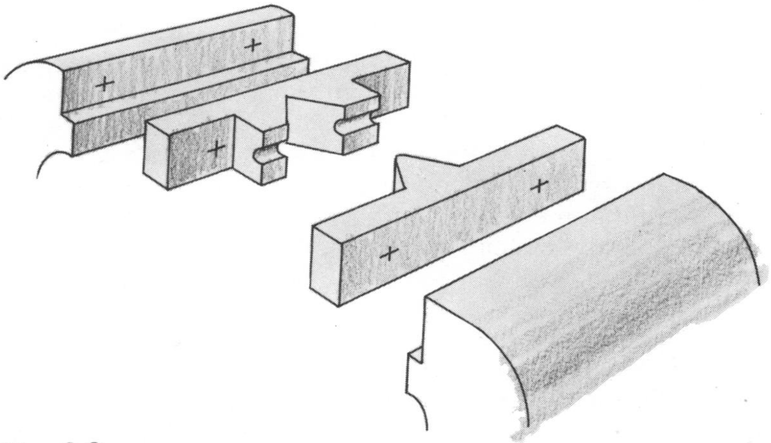

Fig. 8.2

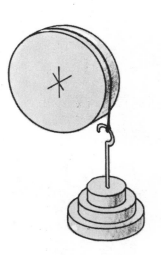

Fig. 8.4

bend each specimen to the same angle may be taken as a measure of the toughness of the material. A means of fixing the torque wrench to the vice screw would have to be devised—a possible solution is shown in Fig. 8.3.

A second solution could be to fix a pulleywheel or disc to the vice screw and suspend weights from the periphery of the wheel. The weight required to bend each specimen to the same angle may then be taken as a measure of the material's toughness (see Fig. 8.4.)

In these two tests you will have bent the specimens to the same angle by using different forces or weights. You could, of course, use a standard force or weight and then take the angle as an indication of toughness.

(4) From this last suggestion, we can lead on to another idea by exploiting the use of a shear pin. A shear pin is frequently used as a key, locking together two gear wheels on a shaft in the gear train of a lathe, so that if an excessive load is placed on the leadscrew or feedshaft, the pin

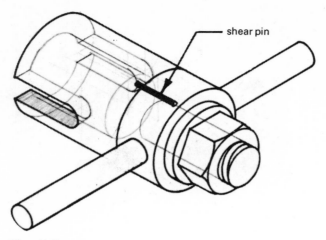

shear pin

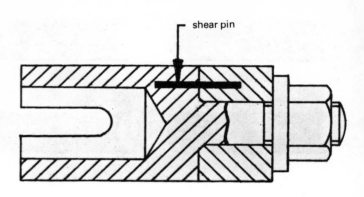

shear pin

Fig. 8.5

Fig. 8.6

shears (is broken) before damage is done to the shaft, bearings, gear teeth, etc. See Fig. 8.6.

The shear strength of a piece of metal of uniform thickness may be assumed to be constant. The shear pins used in the device shown in Fig. 8.5 should be cut from the same length of stock for all specimens in the same series of tests. The vice is tightened until the load on the pin cannot prevent the two parts from rotating and the shear pin gives way. This should occur when the same moment of force is applied in each test, hence the force exerted on each specimen will be the same. The specimen will be bent but it will be noticed that the angles to which specimens of other metals are bent are not the same. The angles of bend of the specimens are then used as a measure of their toughness.

(5) A more direct way of using shearing to measure the toughness of a metal is to adopt a technique similar to the Izod or Charpy method. Another description of toughness is to refer to the amount of energy a material can absorb before it fractures. In the Izod test (see Fig. 8.7) a notched specimen is held in a vice so that the notch is at vice jaw level.

The vice is situated at the bottom dead centre of the swing of a pendulum of known length and weight. The pendulum is allowed to fall freely from a set height and swings in comparatively frictionless bearings. The weight of the pendulum carries a hard steel striker which hits the specimen just above the notch and fractures it. Energy is absorbed by the specimen when it is fractured and so, although the pendulum continues its swing, the length of arc is smaller than that through which it descended.

The amount of energy absorbed is indicated in Newtons (m/kg) by a pointer on the dial.

PROBLEMS

1 Work from any one of these five suggestions (or a modification of any of them) to design and make your own apparatus for testing the shear strength of metals and alloys. Begin, as always, by analysing the problem thoroughly to find all the less obvious sub-problems. Then build towards a systematic solution to these through sketch designs, and, from the final sketched solution, make an accurate working drawing to assist you in the making stage.

2 Using the apparatus you have designed in answer to Problem 1, compile a table to show the comparative shear strength of the common metals. Be sure to test them in different stages of heat treatment also (see Chapter 6).

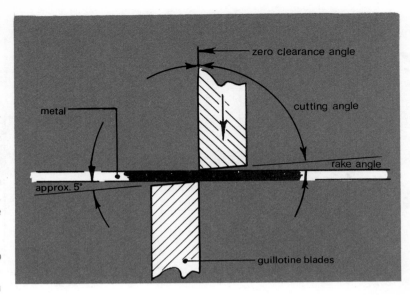

Fig. 8.8

Fig. 8.7

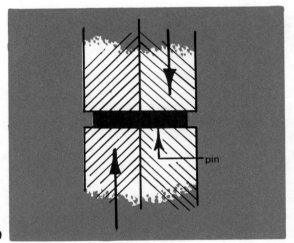

Fig. 8.9

BLANKING AND PIERCING

Your work in this chapter has used the fact that metals will fail when subjected to shear loads.

Normally, shearing means cutting sheet metal with hand shears: tinman's snips or bench shears or guillotine. The shearing action is of the scissor type, in which one

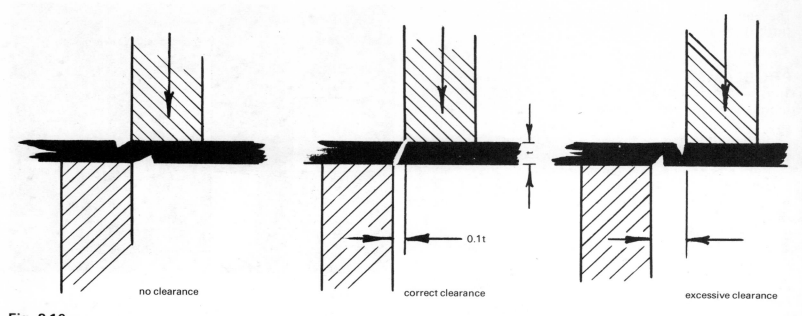

no clearance

0.1t

correct clearance

excessive clearance

Fig. 8.10

blade passes another. The shearing process in this case
follows the outline of the shape to be cut (Fig. 8.8).

In the fourth method of testing shear strength on p. 127,
the forces acting on the shear pins were acting at right
angles to the axis of the pin. In such a case, the cutting is
carried out by the edges of the holes in which the pin is
located. It will be seen from Fig. 8.9 that the cutting angle
is 90°, resulting in nil rake and clearance angles.

This is an idealistic situation and assumes that everything
behaves with 100 per cent efficiency. In fact, in order to
make a clean cut, there should be a very small gap between
the two cutting edges as they pass. The size of this gap
(or clearance) is related to the thickness of metal being
cut and has a value of approximately 0.1t, or 10 per cent
of the metal thickness (t). The effects of an incorrect
clearance are shown in Fig. 8.10.

It is a very demanding and tedious task to mark out and
cut from sheet metal a large number of workpieces identical
in size and shape. It is difficult enough, in a school work-

Fig. 8.11

130

shop, to make two identical workpieces! In industry, the problems are overcome by the use of blanking and piercing tools. These tools are used to stamp shapes from, and punch holes in, sheet metal. Sheet metal—or stock strip as it is called—is passed between a flat-faced punch, of the required size and shape, and a matching hole, the die hole. The punch is then forced through the stock strip, shearing the metal on the edges of the die.

Unlike the process of hand shearing, the cutting action in blanking and piercing is generally made to occur instantly along the whole outline of the shape. In other words, the whole shape is pressed from the parent stock strip of metal in one movement. To do this, heavy pressure is required for a short time, whereas with hand shears a lighter pressure is used for a longer time to do the same work.

If you look at the edges of a mass produced washer which has been made by piercing and blanking (see Fig. 8.11) you will notice that there are two quite distinct textures. The bright, fairly smooth, cut-looking part is produced by the metal being sheared, and the rougher texture is produced when the load on the metal being cut has become so great that it is torn from the surrounding metal.

In the school workshop it is possible to make a very simple form of blanking or piercing tool which may be used to make a number of identical units. Such a tool may be operated in an engineer's vice. The basic form of the blanking or piercing tool is shown in Figs. 8.12 and 8.13.

When working in schools, the clearance between the punch and the die may be disregarded.

PROBLEMS

1 Use the information supplied in these sketches and your solutions to the problems posed below to design your own tool.

Work logically through the problems, but do not hesitate to modify the solutions at which you arrive, especially the earlier ones. Think of as many solutions to each problem as possible, and record them on your design sheets. Make brief notes on the advantages and disadvantages of each solution. Finally, note the reasons for your final choice. Remember that the problems are interrelated because the parts of the whole tool are interdependent.

The size and shape of the unit to be blanked will have an influence on the solutions to the problems outlined below.

Die plate/bolster

(a) How thick ought it to be to withstand the pressure of blanking in the vice?
(b) How thick ought it to be to hold the dowels upright?
(c) How are the dowels to be held in the die plate/bolster?
(d) what material should be used?

Guide dowels

(a) What diameter should these be to withstand bending in use?
(b) How long should they be?
(c) What method should be used to hold them in the die plate?
(d) How many should there be? (See Fig. 8.14)
(e) How should they be arranged? (See Fig. 8.14).
(f) Could they be used to guide the stock strip as well?
(g) If your answer to (f) is 'No', how else can the stock strip be guided accurately under the punch?
(h) Will the dowels, or the method of fixing them, foul the vice when the tool is in use?
(i) What material should they be made from?

Punch Plate

(a) How thick should this be to withstand the necessary pressure?
(b) How thick, to allow the guide dowels to guide, and allow the punch plate to slide and keep parallel with the die plate without juddering and wobbling?
(c) Can the punch be fixed to it conveniently?
(d) From what material should it be made?

Punch

(a) What thickness is needed to blank the unit?
(b) How will it be fixed to the punch plate?
(c) What material should it be made from?

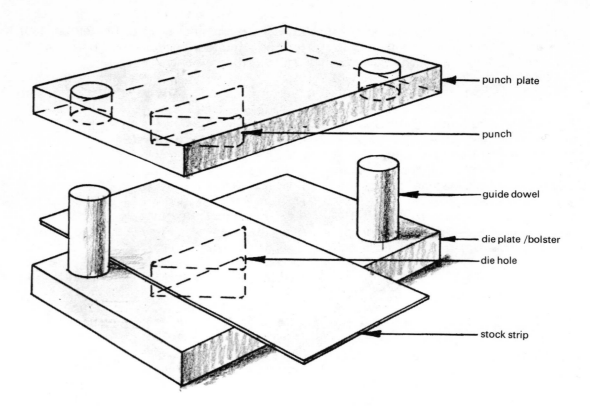

punch plate

punch

guide dowel

die plate /bolster

die hole

stock strip

Fig. 8.12

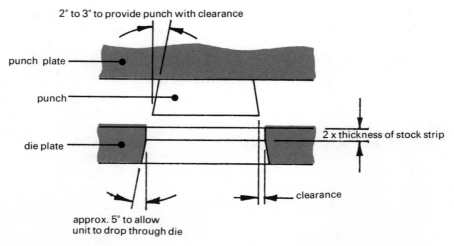

2° to 3° to provide punch with clearance

punch plate

punch

die plate

2 x thickness of stock strip

clearance

approx. 5° to allow
unit to drop through die

Fig. 8.13 scrap section of punch and die

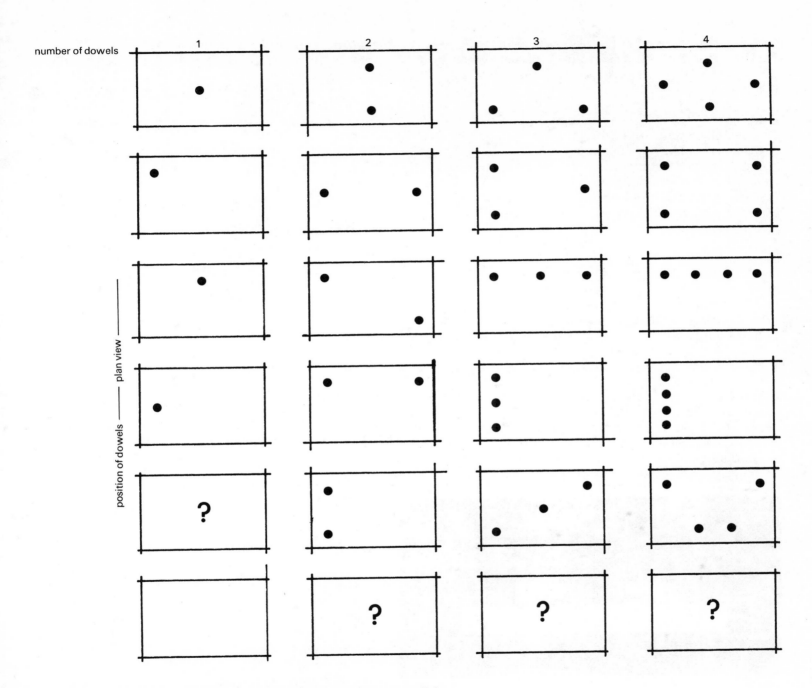

number of dowels

position of dowels — plan view

Fig. 8.14 think of as many solutions to each problem as possible

(d) What heat treatment is necessary—if any?

(e) Will the method of fixing foul the vice when in use?

(f) Will the method of fixing foul the stock strip when blanking?

General

The overall dimensions of the tool will be determined while the other problems are being solved.

Less obvious problems encountered in the use of the tool will include the following:

(a) How can the stock strip be prevented from jamming onto the punch when the punch has passed through it?

Two possible solutions are:

1 Surround the punch with hard rubber, e.g. the dense rubber used for soles of shoes. This will compress during blanking and expand and push the stock strip off the punch when the vice is undone.

2 Add stripper plates to the die plate. The stock strip runs in the groove which acts as a stock guide. The flange retains the stock strip as the punch is withdrawn. (Fig. 8. 15.)

(b) How can the stock strip be fed into the tool so that the stock is used economically?

(c) How can the blanking tool be fixed to, or put in the place of the jaws of the vice so that it does not have to be held? This frees one hand for other work, e.g. stock feed, and also facilitates the withdrawal of the punch from the die and stock strip.

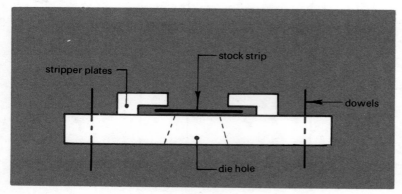

Fig. 8.15

Making the tool

Various practical problems arise in the making of the blanking tool.

(a) The punch plate must be a good sliding fit on the guide dowels.

(b) The punch must be accurately positioned over the die hole.

Continue like this, listing other problems before commencing the practical work.

When you have designed the blanking tool you must plan the logical sequence of operations needed to make the tool to ensure the necessary degree of accuracy. It is suggested that from your working drawing you make a procedure sheet using the following headings:

Part No.	Operation and sketches with notes	Tool	Speed	Feed	Remarks

2 Design a bracelet in which one unit is repeated several times and which can be produced on a press or blanking tool. What limitations are inherent in the problem?

(a) What section metal will the press tool accept?

(b) What type of metal will be suitable in the press tool?

(c) What gauge of metal will be suitable in the press tool?

(d) What limitations in size are there?

(e) What limitations of shape does the press impose?

(f) Are there any environmental considerations which are relevant?

(g) What kind of linkage can be used? (See p. 135.)

The linkage can influence the shape and the shape can influence the choice of linkage. For instance, if jump rings are used, four points of contact may be necessary and any cutaway must not affect these areas. The last type of linkage shown in Fig. 8.16 can be incorporated in the pressed shape.

You should have gained considerable skill and experience in developing shapes from geometric forms, and you can now set up your own problem for this project. But however you choose to design these links, they should be thought out systematically as previously suggested.

Many pieces of jewellery require two or more units which must be fastened together with a flexible joint. Some linkages allow movement in one direction and some in several directions but the latter is not always desirable. *Note.* Many fastenings can be bought (Fig. 8.20).

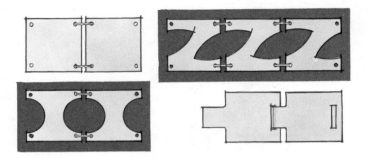

Fig. 8.16

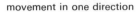
movement in one direction

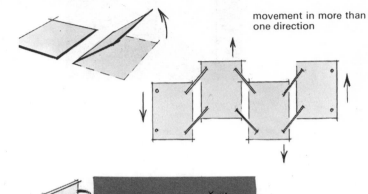

movement in more than one direction

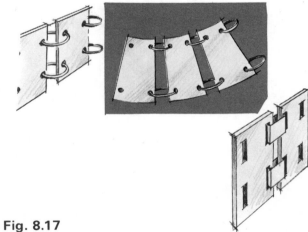

Fig. 8.17

135

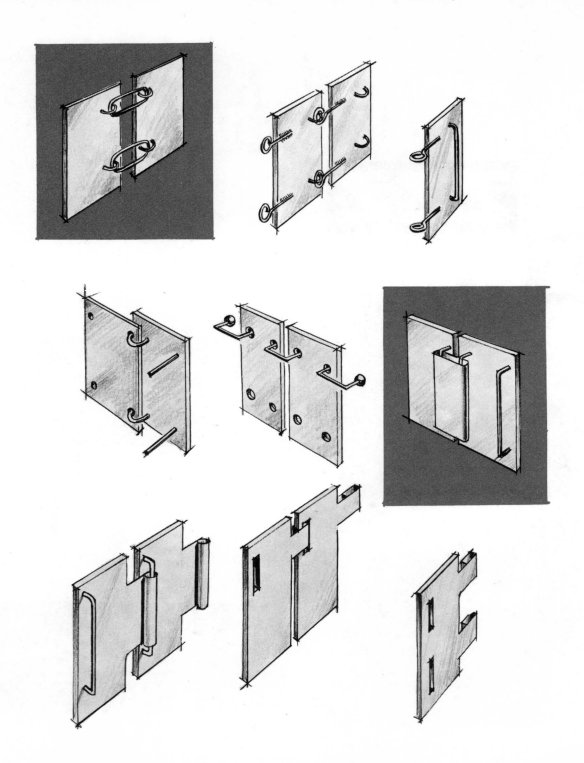

Fig. 8.18

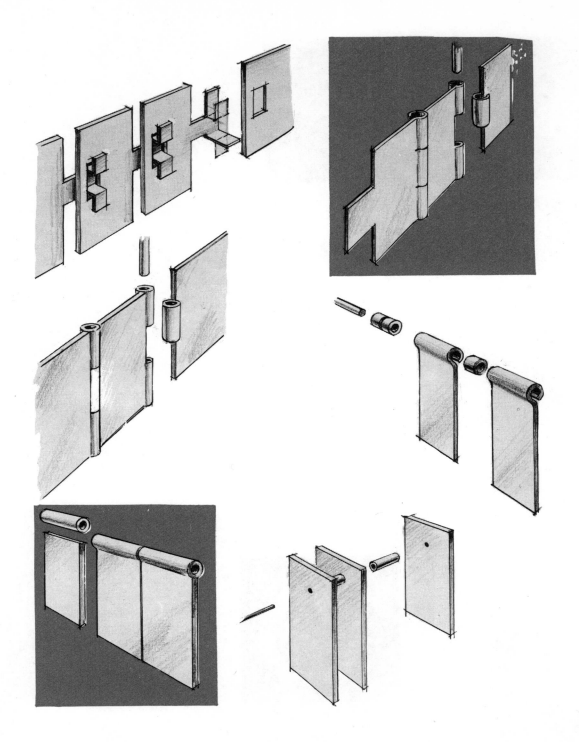

Fig. 8.19

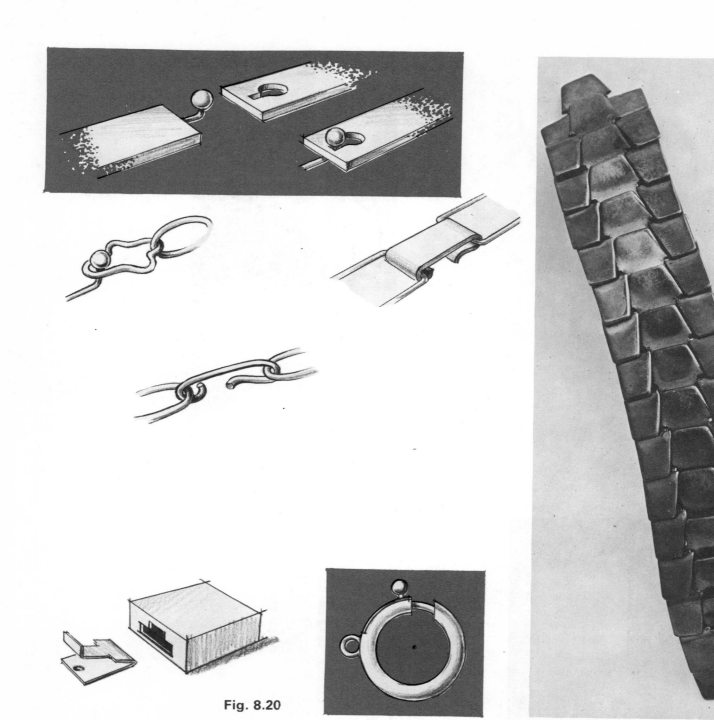

Fig. 8.20

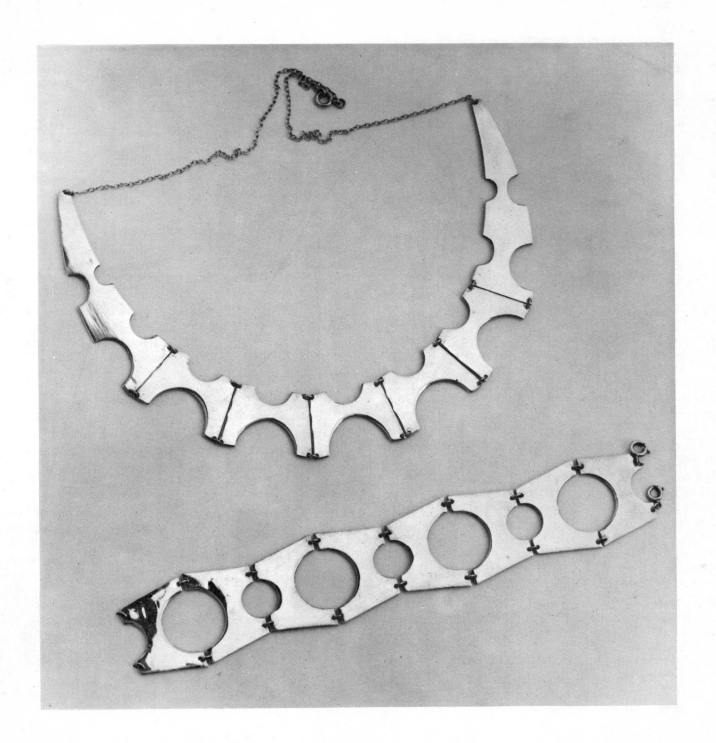

Chapter 9

MECHANISMS

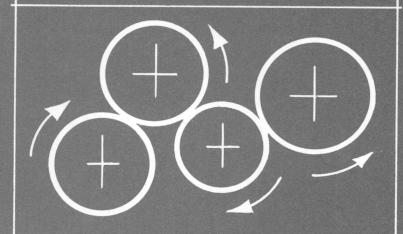

Very early in the story of primitive, prehistoric civilizations, we find that Man extended the powers of his body by using a stone to strike a flint, and by so doing produced a sharp edge with which he could cut. He developed his range of flint tools to include the knife, scraper, wedge, adze, saw and arrow-head. These tools, as you will see later, can be called machines. Primitive Man also discovered and developed more easily recognizable machines, such as the lever—a pole with which he prised stones from the ground or moved heavy loads—and the bow. The bow had two uses, firstly as the bow-drill, used to rotate flint-boring tools, and secondly to shoot arrows. In this second form, the bow was the first machine to be used to store energy.

Eventually ways were found of harnessing the energy of animals, the wind and water, and later on the mechanical energy of the raised weight and the wound spring were used.

Man has found that with the help of tools and machines he can achieve more than is possible with his bare hands and his own unaided physical strength:

(a) they enable him to exert less effort to perform a task,

(b) they make him capable of doing things which he could not otherwise attempt,

(c) they reduce the time taken to perform a given task, or enable him to complete more tasks in a given time,

(d) they may reduce the drudgery and fatigue produced by performing the task,

(e) they may lower the cost of performing the task,

(f) they can maintain or may increase the accuracy with which the task is performed.

You can possibly add to this list.

Although the first machines were made of wood, bone, stone and other natural materials, the discovery of metals speeded up and extended technological progress. Until recent years, the physical properties of metals placed them in a category superior to other natural and synthetic materials. By alloying and heat-treating, Man has been able to produce metals with certain desired physical properties capable of performing specific and demanding tasks.

Today machines are highly complex engineering devices, like typewriters, washing machines, cars and space vehicles. Without machines, life would be very different for they are used to produce food, build homes, give warmth, make clothes, help travel, aid education, provide work and leisure pursuits, and cure illnesses. However, all the complicated machines depend on the same functional principles as those discovered thousands of years ago and used in the earliest and most primitive machines. These basic machines are:

(a) the lever,
(b) the pulley,
(c) the wheel and axle, } modifications of the lever
(d) the inclined plane and the wedge,
(e) the screw, which is a modification of the inclined plane.

On the following pages some of the facts concerning these machines are outlined. Their variations and combinations are innumerable. All machines require energy (the ability to do work) before they can function. The law of the Conservation of Energy states that energy cannot be made and cannot be destroyed. However, for your purposes, you can say that energy can be wasted in that it may be used for doing work which is not useful. A machine can be defined as a device which transfers or transforms energy or force. Notice how each machine can change a force—change its direction, change its speed and change its position.

When it is necessary to move a load a certain distance, work has to be done. Work is calculated by multiplying the force acting on the load by the distance the load is moved. If, by using a machine, the resistance can be overcome, that is, the load moved, with an effort or force smaller than that acting on the load, a mechanical advantage has been achieved.

$$\text{mechanical advantage} = \frac{\text{load}}{\text{effort}}$$

As machines do not generate work, but merely transform it, the effort must be made over a greater distance than the load is moved, and the work put into a perfectly efficient machine is equal to the work done by it.

$$\text{work input} = \text{work output}$$

The **velocity ratio** is $\dfrac{\text{distance moved by the effort}}{\text{distance moved by the load}}$

With a perfect machine you can say that:

$$\text{efficiency} = \frac{\text{work done on the load}}{\text{work done by the effort}}$$

Unfortunately, no machine is ever 100 per cent efficient because friction is always present in its moving parts. Hence, in addition to the resistance of the load, the resistance due to the friction has to be overcome by the effort. So for practical purposes you will have to say that:

work input = work output + work lost overcoming friction

Hence:

$$\text{efficiency} = \frac{\text{work done on the load}}{\text{work done by the effort}}$$

LEVERS
A lever is a rigid beam able to rotate about a position, called the fulcrum, or pivot. The fulcrum may be an edge, or rivet or bearing. In the sketches, the fulcrum is shown by a ▲. There are three classes of levers.

First class Levers
The fulcrum is between the load and the effort.

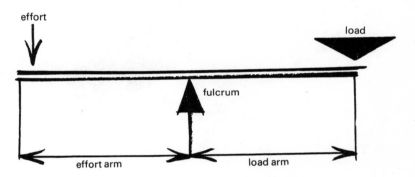

effort
load
fulcrum
effort arm
load arm

Fig. 9.1

Examples: seesaw (Fig. 9.1), oar (Fig. 9.2), beam balance (Fig. 9.3), crowbar (Fig. 9.4) and claw hammer (Fig. 9.5).

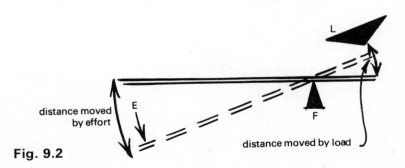

L
E
F
distance moved by effort
distance moved by load

Fig. 9.2

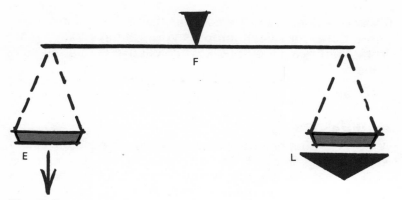

Fig. 9.3

Fig. 9.4

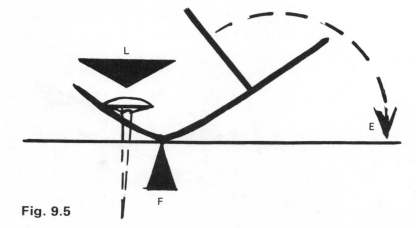

Fig. 9.5

Double levers
Two levers which work against each other (Fig. 9.6).
Examples: scissors, tinsnips, pliers, tongs.

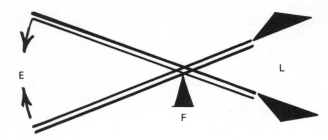

Fig. 9.6

Bell Crank levers
The fixed arms of the lever are at right angles (Fig. 9.7).

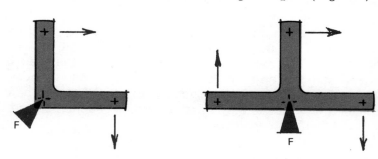

Fig. 9.7

Second class levers

The load is between the effort and the fulcrum (Fig. 9.8).

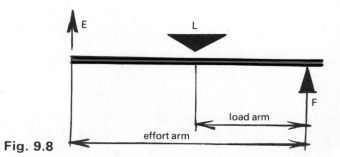

Fig. 9.8

Examples: wheelbarrow (Fig. 9.9) and crowbar (Fig. 9.10).

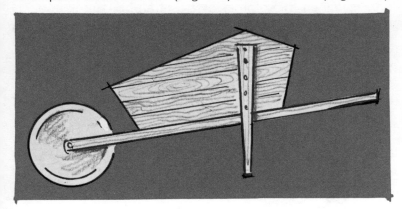

Fig. 9.9

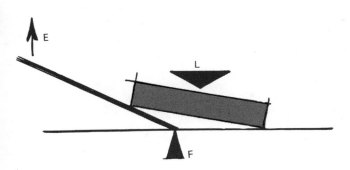

Fig. 9.10

Double levers
Example: nutcracker (Fig. 9.11).

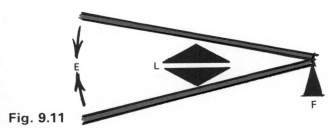

Fig. 9.11

Third class levers
The effort is between the load and the fulcrum (Fig. 9.12). Examples: shovel (Fig. 9.13), paddle, fishing-rod, claw hammer (Fig. 9.14).

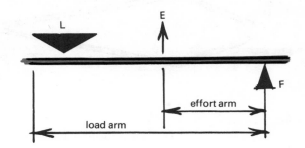

Fig. 9.12

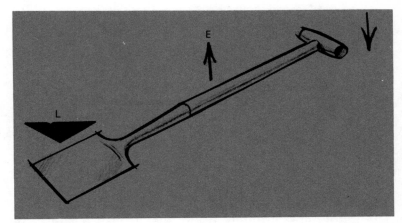

Fig. 9.13

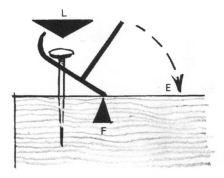

Fig. 9.14

Double levers

Example: tweezers (Fig. 9.15).

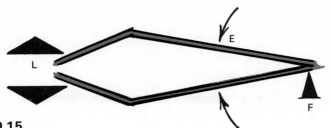

Fig. 9.15

Compound levers

A number of levers may be connected together in order to accentuate the change of force, direction, speed and position of a movement (Fig. 9.16).

Examples: typewriter keys and bench guillotine.

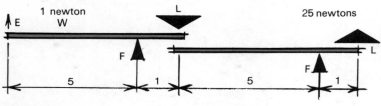

Fig. 9.16

Toggles

The toggle link is a very useful mechanism because the force between the links increases as the action brings the links into a straight line, when the force is at its maximum (Fig. 9.17).

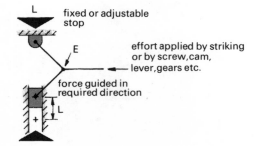

Fig. 9.17

This can be demonstrated by using the Triangle of Forces. When three forces acting at a point are in equilibrium, each force may be represented in direction and magnitude by the sides of a triangle taken in order. In Fig. 9.18, a known force, F_e, is applied in the direction a–o. Draw a_1–o_1 parallel to a–o to the scale of, say, 10 mm to 1 Nm^{-2}. Complete the triangle by drawing Fl_1 parallel to c–o and Fl_2 parallel to b–o. The values of forces Fl_1 and Fl_2 may be obtained by measurement.

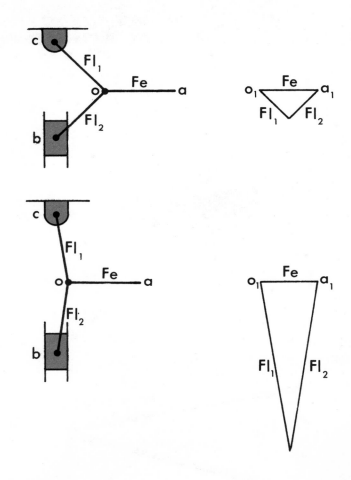

Fig. 9.18

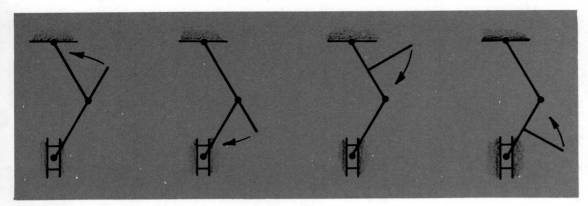

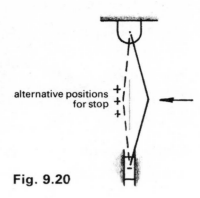

Fig. 9.20

Fig. 9.19

Effort forces may be applied in a variety of methods and directions (see Fig. 9.19).

When the force on the hinge, or pivot, pushes the links beyond the straight line, the force on the load is reduced (see Fig. 9.20). If a stop is positioned to prevent the links from moving very far out of alignment, considerable force (although not the maximum obtained), is still maintained and the mechanism is locked.

Examples: Mole wrench, floor board cramp (Fig. 9.21) and some sheet metal presses.

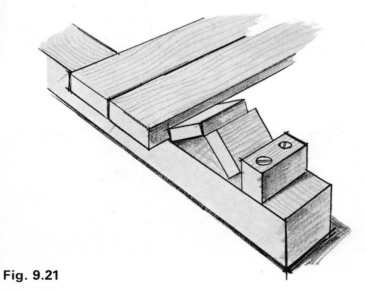

Fig. 9.21

PULLEYS

The pulley is a special kind of first class lever which acts continuously (Fig. 9.22).

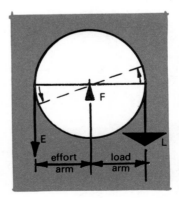

Fig. 9.22(a)

145

Single fixed pulley (see Fig. 9.23(a))

effort = load

effort distance = load distance

mechanical advantage is 1

velocity ratio is 1

Fig. 9.23(a)

Single movable pulley (see Fig. 9.23(b))

$$\text{effort} = \frac{\text{load}}{2}$$

$$\text{effort distance} = \frac{\text{load distance}}{2}$$

mechanical advantage is 2

velocity ratio is 2

Fig. 9.23(b)

Combined fixed and movable pulley (see Fig. 9.23(c))

$$\text{effort} = \frac{\text{load}}{2}$$

$$\text{effort distance} = \frac{\text{load distance}}{2}$$

mechanical advantage is 2

velocity ratio is 2

Fig. 9.23(c)

Two pulley wheels free to rotate on axle (see Fig. 9.23(d))

$$\text{effort} = \frac{\text{load}}{3}$$

$$\text{effort distance} = \frac{\text{load distance}}{3}$$

mechanical advantage is 3

velocity ratio is 3

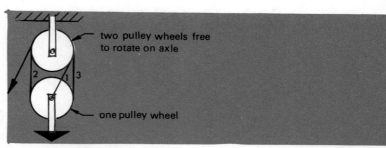

Fig. 9.23(d)

146

Differential motion (Fig. 9.24)

The differential principle depends on the difference in diameter between the two portions of the pulley or drum. The falling weight unwinds the rope from the larger drum, rotating it in a clockwise direction. The pulley is raised while the weight falls.

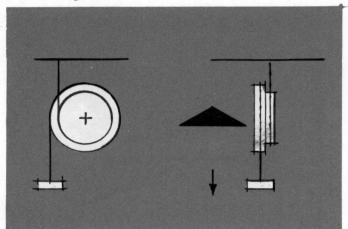

Fig. 9.24

Compound wheel and axle (Fig. 9.25)

This mechanism requires a long rope to raise the load a small distance. In one revolution the rope will wind onto the large drum by an amount πD, and at the same time the rope will unwind from the small drum by an amount πd. The total length of the rope is shortened by the amount

$$\pi D - \pi d$$
$$\text{or } \pi(D - d)$$

and the load is raised by $\dfrac{\pi(D - d)}{2}$

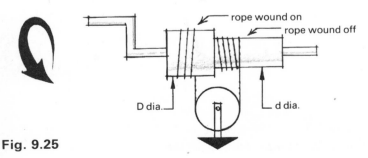

rope wound on
rope wound off
D dia.
d dia.

Fig. 9.25

Weston Differential Pulley Block (Fig. 9.26)

$$\text{velocity ratio} = \frac{\text{diameter A} \times 2}{\text{diameter A} - \text{diameter B}}$$

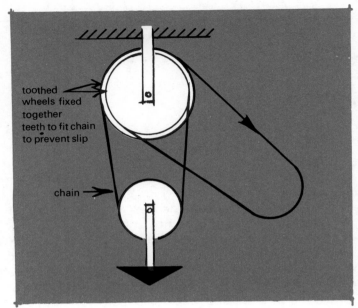

toothed wheels fixed together teeth to fit chain to prevent slip

chain →

Fig. 9.26

WHEEL AND AXLE (Fig. 9.27)

The wheel and axle is a device to provide a rolling action. When a load has to be moved it is easier to do so when it is on wheels or rollers, than it is to slide it along the ground. This is because rolling friction is less than sliding friction, hence the use of ball-bearings, roller and needle bearings.

A wheel and axle may also be regarded as a special kind of first class lever applied to rotating loads. The axle may be used to drive the wheel, or the wheel may drive the axle.

Examples: driving axle and road wheels of a car and the steering wheel of a car.

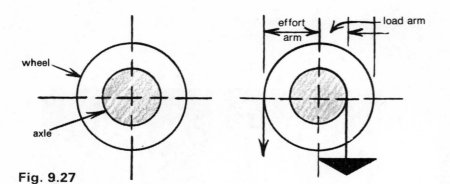

Fig. 9.27

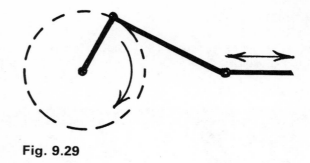

Fig. 9.29

The Crank

Two forms of crank are shown—the disc crank (Fig. 9.28(a)) and the bent crank (Fig. 9.28(b)). The arm of the bent crank may be regarded as a single spoke of a wheel (the spoke being turned by a handle).

Examples: car engine starting handle, mortise lock key and sardine tin opener.

With the addition of a connecting rod, the wheel and axle can convert rotary motion into straight-line, or reciprocating motion, and *vice versa* (see Fig. 9. 29).

Example: internal combustion engine (piston to crankshaft).

One crank used in the workshop is in the driving mechanism of the shaping machine (Fig. 9.30(a)). Rotary motion is converted into straight-line motion.

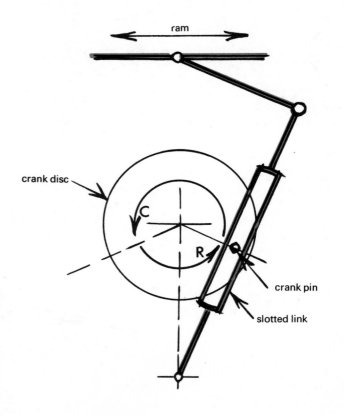

C=cutting stroke   R=return stroke

Fig. 9.30(a) slotted link system

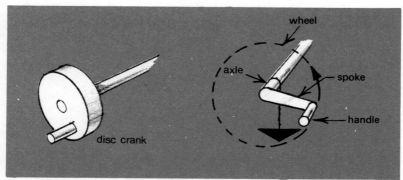

Fig. 9.28(a)   **Fig. 9.28(b)**

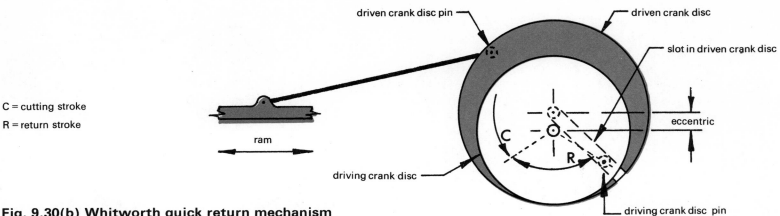

C = cutting stroke

R = return stroke

driven crank disc pin

driven crank disc

slot in driven crank disc

eccentric

ram

driving crank disc

driving crank disc pin

Fig. 9.30(b) Whitworth quick return mechanism

The driving crank pin rotates through a larger angle on the cutting stroke than on the return stroke. Hence, when the crank is rotating at a constant speed, the cutting stroke is slower than the return stroke. As the return stroke on the shaping machine is non-productive, it is advantageous that the tool is returned to its starting point quickly (Fig. 9.30(a)).

Cams and Eccentrics

A cam is a device, usually a disc or projection on a shaft or drum, for converting rotary into straight-line and other forms of motion. Fig. 9.31 shows various cam profiles.

The drum cam (Fig. 9.32) and the swash plate (Fig. 9.33) are two other forms of cam.

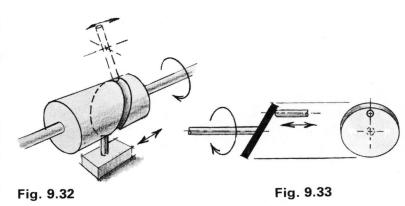

Fig. 9.32

Fig. 9.33

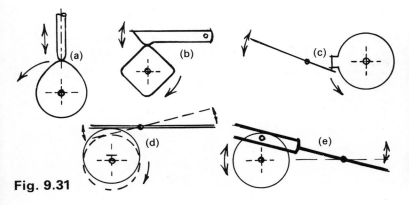

Fig. 9.31

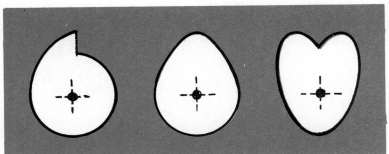

Belt and Chain Drive

Motion can be transmitted from one wheel to another by means of belting. These wheels are called pulley wheels. Some systems use flat section belts (Fig. 9.34(a)); some, V-section belts (b) and sometimes tooth belts (d) are used and engage in tooth wheels to prevent slipping. Chain is also used to transmit motion from one wheel to another and in this case a toothed wheel, called a sprocket wheel, is used.

Open belt (Fig. 9.35)
The wheels rotate in the same direction. The speed of the pulleys is found by using the formula:

r.p.m. of A × diameter A = r.p.m. of B × diameter B

Crossed belt (Fig. 9.36)
Wheels rotate in opposite directions.

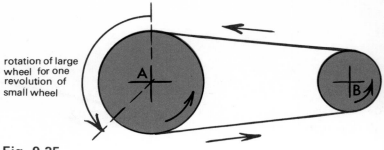

rotation of large wheel for one revolution of small wheel

Fig. 9.35

Fig. 9.36

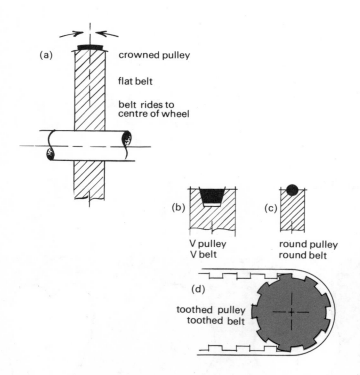

(a) crowned pulley

flat belt

belt rides to centre of wheel

(b) V pulley
V belt

(c) round pulley
round belt

(d) toothed pulley
toothed belt

Fig. 9.34(a) (b) (c) (d)

150

Gears

Motion and power may be transmitted by means of wheels joined by a belt and also by wheels which make direct contact with one another. This is perhaps the most common method of transmission. If the edges of the wheels are plain as in Fig. 9.37, motion and power can only be transmitted if there is friction between the wheels. Rubber and a variety of plastics can be used to provide the friction, as, for example, in the drive of a record player. Frequently, however, the resistance to the rotation of the driven wheel is greater than the frictional resistance between the driving and the driven wheels. When this is the case, the driving wheel will merely slip. To overcome this problem—to give a positive drive—the wheels are given teeth which mesh together as in Fig. 9.38. The teeth act as a quick succession of levers, the ends of which bear on one another.

The ratio of the revolutions of the gears is calculated from the diameters of the pitch circles. As only a definite number of teeth may be spaced on the circumference of the pitch circle of the wheel, the gear ratio is usually calculated from the number of the teeth on each wheel (see Fig. 9.39).

For two gear wheels to rotate in the same direction, a third gear wheel called an idler wheel, must be placed in the gear train (see Fig. 9.40).

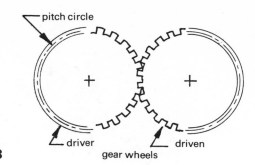

Fig. 9.38

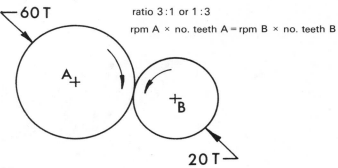

ratio 3 : 1 or 1 : 3

rpm A × no. teeth A = rpm B × no. teeth B

Fig. 9.39

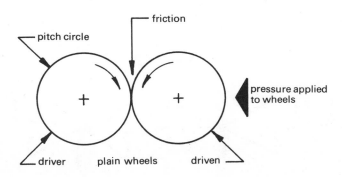

Fig. 9.37

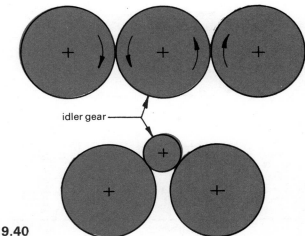

Fig. 9.40

151

Gears may connect shafts at angles to each other as in Fig. 9.41 (a) and (b).

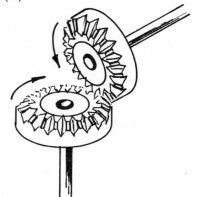

Fig. 9.41(a) bevel gear wheels

Fig. 9.41(b) spiral gear wheels

Gears may also be used to convert rotary motion into straight-line motion and *vice versa* (Fig. 9.42).

Fig. 9.42

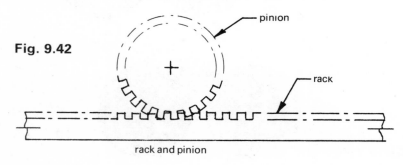

pinion

rack

rack and pinion

The shape of gear teeth, and the spaces between them are carefully designed so that friction between the wheels is reduced to a minimum. Maximum rotational power is then transmitted from one gear wheel to the next, and there is always contact between a tooth of one wheel and a tooth of the next (so that motion is as smooth as possible). The sides, or flanks, of the teeth are curved. The curves generally used are the involute, epicycloid and the hypocycloid. The gears in a gear train are kept as near the same size as possible for reasons of strength. This is one reason for the use of compound gear trains.

Gears are normally produced on specialized machines using very complex cutters. To cut gears accurately in the school workshop, an accurate means of indexing the gear blank is needed. Usually a dividing head is used, although indexing fixtures can be made or improvised using lathe change-wheels. Normally a milling cutter is used on a milling machine, but these cutters may also be used on a lathe equipped with milling attachments. Form tools may be used for shaping the spaces between the gear teeth when the blank is mounted in the lathe or on the shaping machine.

A variety of methods of producing less accurate gears can be employed. For example, wire spokes can be soldered to a boss or the boss may be cast about the inner ends of the spokes (Fig. 9.43(a) and (b)). Lantern wheels are often used for the pinions for this type of gear (Fig. 9.44). Wire pegs could be driven into holes in the circumference of a disc as in Fig. 9.45. Gears may be made from sheet material (Fig. 9.46) and small gears can be cast using the lost wax technique.

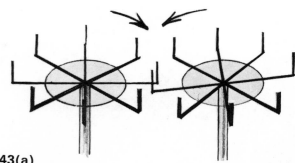

Fig. 9.43(a)

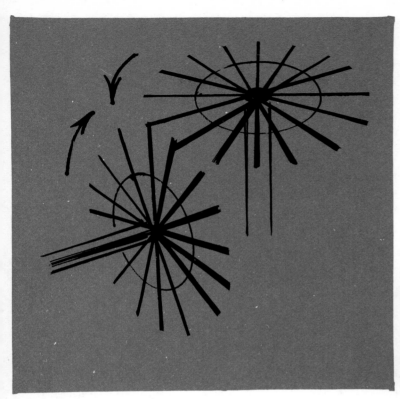

Fig. 9.43(b)

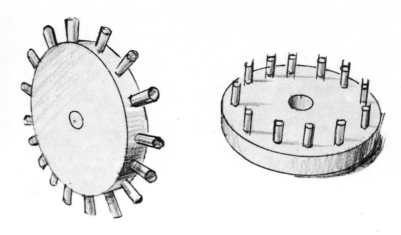

Fig. 9.45 'peg toothed gears'

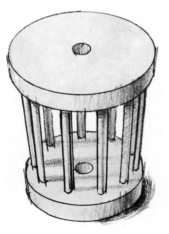

Fig. 9.44 lantern wheel

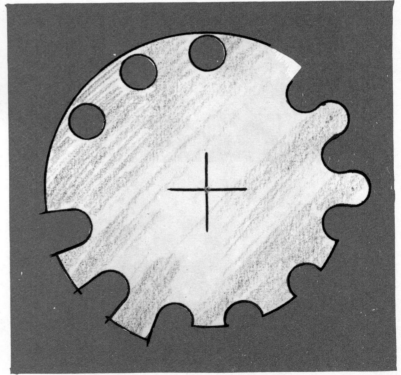

Fig. 9.46 'Knuckle wheels' Metal disc drilled or punched and filed, sawn or turned

THE INCLINED PLANE

Single (Fig. 9.47)

Examples: keys to fix gears, pulleys, wheels, collars, etc. to shafts (see Fig. 9.48).

Double—the wedge

The wedge is composed of two inclined planes fixed back to back (see Fig. 9.49).

Examples: knives, axes, lathe tools, etc.

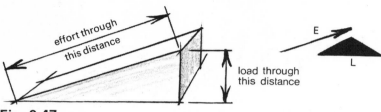

Fig. 9.47

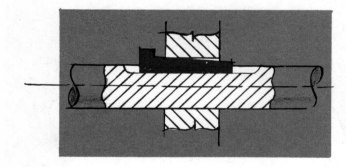

Fig. 9.48

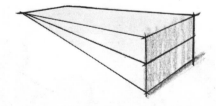

Fig. 9.49

The screw

The screw is a special kind of single inclined plane—one which is wrapped round a cylinder or axle (see Fig. 9.50). It is a spiral wedge. In practice, the thread is not put onto, but cut into the surface of the cylinder.

Screw threads are used to (a) *fasten*, for example, machine screws and torch bulbs, and (b) *transmit motion and force*, for example, lathe leadscrew and cross slide feed screws and car jacks. Note that the screw converts rotary motion into straight-line motion.

The **pitch** of a screw is the distance between the centre of one thread and the centre of the next thread. The **lead** of a screw is the distance between the centre of a thread and the centre of the same thread when it has made one complete turn. When a more rapid movement is required than is possible from a normal, single-start screw, a multi-screw is used (Fig. 9.51(a) and (b)), as in the cap of a fountain pen.

Thread form

There are many different sorts of sections of thread. These are generally classified into two groups: V and square. V-threads are used for fixing screws because of the friction between the inclined sides of the thread of the screw and of the nut. Square threads are usually used to transmit motion or force because the thrust of the thread face is parallel to the direction of motion.

Worm and worm wheel (Fig. 9.52(a) and (b))

For the worm wheel to make one revolution, if driven by a single-start worm, the worm must make as many revolutions as there are teeth on the worm wheel. Normally, the worm drives the worm wheel and not *vice versa*.

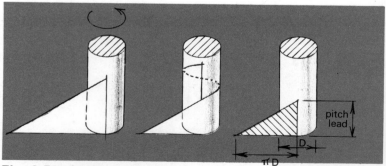

Fig. 9.50 single start thread

154

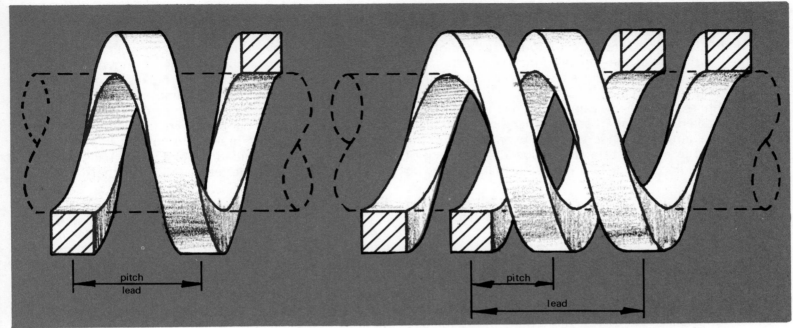

Fig. 9.51(a) single start thread

Fig. 9.51(b) multi-start thread (two start)

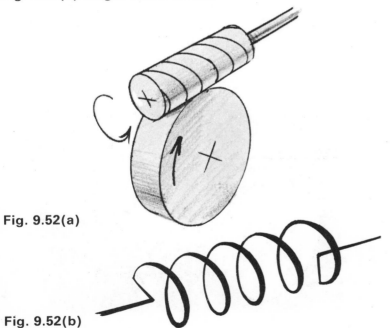

Fig. 9.52(a)

Fig. 9.52(b)

PROBLEMS

1 Examine the machines suggested below and for each list and state the function of the fundamental machines used, that is, whether they employ levers, pulleys, wheels and axles, etc.

Part	Fundamental Machine	Function

(a) wall-mounted can opener
(b) pillar drilling machine
(c) mortise lock key
(d) simple table-mounted, hand-operated mincing machine
(e) water tap
(f) crown cap bottle opener.

FRICTION

All mechanisms include moving parts. Surfaces cannot be made perfectly smooth, and when a rough surface of one part tries to slide over the rough surface of another, the minute projections on the surfaces rub on one another, so restricting the force of movement. The maximum force which resists the movement of one surface over another is called the force of static, or limiting, friction.

When one surface is made to move over the other, the force required to move it at a steady speed—the force of dynamic, or sliding friction—is less than that required to start it moving.

The ratio of the force of friction to the force pressing the surfaces together is called the **coefficient of friction.**

$$\mu = \frac{Ff}{Fp}$$

where μ = coefficient of friction
Ff = force of friction
Fp = force pressing surfaces together

In machines, a low value of the coefficient of friction between the surfaces of moving parts is generally required. Friction wastes energy and causes wear. This is evident in the heat generated and the noise the machine makes.

The designer, metallurgist and engineer try to reduce the effects of friction in the moving parts of a machine by selecting and developing the most efficient forms of bearing surfaces, by accurately machining and assembling them, and by correct lubrication.

Frequently, however, a high coefficient of friction is desirable between surfaces. This is shown in such instances as the clutch, tyres and brakes of a car. Without friction, motion could not be transmitted to the driving wheels and the wheels would not roll on the surface of the road to push the car along. Friction is used to stop the car moving when the brakes are applied.

Note. Vices and threaded fasteners and nails would not hold or cramp things together but for friction.

Bearing surfaces

Sliding surfaces. Because friction is independent of the area of contact, sliding surfaces are generally made as large as possible so that wear is spread and so that there is less chance of the oil or grease being squeezed out of the bearing under the load of the parts. This would cause surface-to-surface contact and increase friction.

Rolling surfaces. Rolling friction is less than sliding friction. Although wheels may roll, sliding friction is still present between the surfaces of the axle and bearing.

Rolling surfaces are provided by introducing wheels, or rollers, between the wheel and its axle, or between the axle and its bearing. These rollers may be in the form of cylinders, needles, or in the form of ball-bearings (Fig. 9.55).

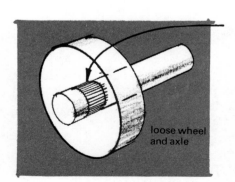

sliding surfaces

loose wheel and axle

Fig. 9.53

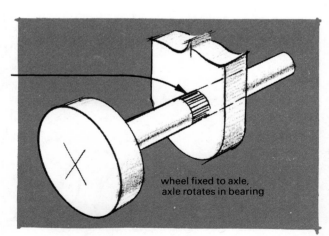

sliding surfaces

wheel fixed to axle, axle rotates in bearing

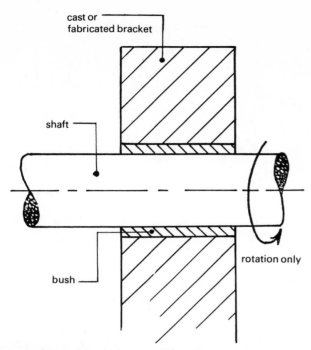

Fig. 9.54 plain bushed journal bearing

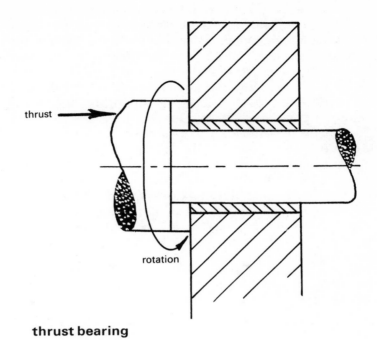

thrust bearing

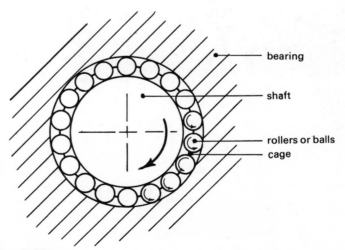

Fig. 9.55

Bearing Materials

With one exception, the two parts (moving and stationary) of a bearing are not made of the same type of metal. This is because the metals have an affinity for one another and tend to bind or seize. The exception is cast iron. Cast iron parts are used for the ram and guide ways of a shaping machine, and the top (compound) and cross slides, saddle and bed of lathe. The free graphite in the structure of cast iron acts as a lubricant.

Special purpose bearing metals have been developed. One group of alloys—the white metal and Babbit metals—form hard particles in a softer matrix when they solidify. See Fig. 9.56. The hard spots provide the required wear resistance whilst the soft matrix offers a cushioning effect under load and allows for self-alignment of the bearing. In use, the soft matrix wears away below the level of the hard spots, which makes provision for oil to get to the bearing surfaces.

The alloys most commonly used for bearings are shown in the table Fig. 9.57

Bearing Alloy	Constituents	Uses
Bronzes copper based Tin bronzes	10–15% Tin	
phosphor bronzes	0.3–1.0% phosphorous 9.0–13.0% tin	General use as bearing metals where load is heavy.
White metals tin based Babbit metal	89% tin 7.4% antimony 3.6% copper	Big-end bearings in car engines. High speeds, high loads.
lead based	13% antimony 80% lead 7% tin	Less severe conditions, light loads, low speeds.

Fig. 9.57

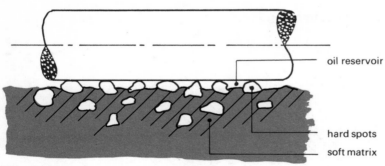

oil reservoir

hard spots

soft matrix

Fig. 9.56

Bronze bearings may be made by sintering as well as by machining. Metallic powder is compressed and then heated—sintered—to make the metal grains bind together and give the piece strength. These bearings are porous and allow oil to soak into them, so ensuring thorough lubrication. Sometimes powdered graphite is added to the bronze powder before compression. These bearings are often termed self-lubricating or oil-less bearings, as they do not require lubrication during the normal life of the machine.

Plastics

Several different types of plastics are used for engineering components. Nylon is perhaps the most widely used plastic for bearings and gears. It is easily shaped by machining from the solid and by moulding. Sintered nylon components contain additives to improve the material's physical properties. Nylon has a low coefficient of friction. It is tough, has high tensile strength, a high resistance to abrasion and is unaffected by most solvents. Nylon has a tendency to absorb moisture, and sintered nylon is porous.

Lubrication

Lubrication is achieved by the use of oils or greases—lubricants. Mechanisms are generally lubricated by fluids. The sliding surface is separated from the stationary surface by a continuous layer or film of lubricant. Within this layer the lubricant flows, or shears. The resistance to this flow is called viscosity. Generally viscous lubricants are thick, and they resist or cause drag on surfaces moving over them, just as golden syrup imposes more drag on a spoon as it is slipped into it, than when a spoon is put into single cream.

Lubricants

Oils are produced from mineral oil, vegetable stuffs, animals and fish. Mineral oils have better lasting properties than vegetable and animal oils, although these latter are more oily. Oils are often blended to improve their properties.

Greases originate from oils mixed with fats and/or soaps. Often the lubricating properties of greases are inferior to oils, but they are used because they are more convenient. For example, grease does not tend to run out of a bearing.

Additives. Various substances are added to oils and greases to extend their usefulness. Two examples of additives are:

Graphite, the crystal form of which is that of a very smooth flat plate. The crystals can slide easily over one another. Graphite also adheres well to metal surfaces.

Molybdenum disulphide, which has very similar lubricating properties—crystal form and adhesion—to graphite. Both these additives are useful for bearings running at high temperatures.

Properties of a lubricant should include:
(a) oiliness,
(b) lack of propensity to corrode the bearing surfaces,
(c) ability to conduct heat away from the moving surfaces,
(d) longevity; should not easily decompose into sludge,
(e) retention of viscosity at high temperatures,
(f) ability to withstand the loads of the bearing and not be squeezed out.

Air is sometimes used as a lubricant. Air, under pressure, is forced into a specially designed bearing and causes the sliding surfaces to separate. Air also acts as a lubricant under air cushion vehicles (A.C.V.) such as the hovercraft and hovertrain.

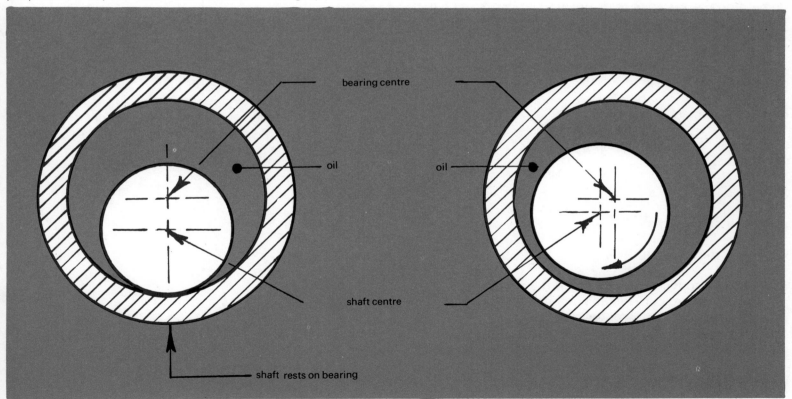

bearing centre

oil

oil

shaft centre

shaft rests on bearing

Fig. 9.58 stationary shaft   **rotating shaft**

MOTIVATION

The operation of all machines requires the application of a force through a certain distance in the direction of the force; there has to be an input of work. The ability to do work is called energy. There are many forms of energy. As mentioned before, energy cannot be created or destroyed; it can only be changed from one form to another. Prime movers convert a natural form of energy into another capable of producing motion. For example, a windmill converts the energy of wind into mechanical energy. Most forms of energy are ultimately dependent on the sun for their origin. A small part of the family tree of energy is shown in the diagram.

Two forms of energy are used primarily in the workshop. There is potential or stored energy (the energy which something has because of its position or state) and kinetic energy (the energy which something has because it is in motion).

The range of ways in which mechanisms can be energized includes the use of:

muscles—human or animal,

springs—tension, compression, coil,
pendulums,

flywheels,

wind—windmills, fans,

water—waterwheel, turbine,

expanding—convection currents, hot air engines
     gases—petroleum fueled combustion engines
    steam—piston engine, turbine,

electricity—rotational motors and linear motors, solenoids,

raised weight—falling (gravity),

elastic—tension, torsion (twisted).

PROBLEMS

1 Make sketch designs for each complete unit, in Figs. 9.59 and 9.60 to show how the changes of direction could be effected. Make any one of these up into a working model.

2 Design and make a simple device for removing the shells from edible nuts.

3 Design and make a device to spray water over a wide area of lawn during dry weather.

4 A musical toy is required for a local day nursery. Design and make a unit that will make simple musical sounds as a handle is turned.

5 Freshly ground pepper adds more to the flavour of a hot meal than pepper bought ready ground. Design and make a holder/grinder for peppercorns that can be used on a dining-table.

6 A collection of table-tennis balls is to be sorted into two boxes in such a way that each box contains an equal number of balls when the operation is complete. Design and make a piece of apparatus for doing this mechanically and as automatically as possible.

FAMILY TREE OF ENERGY

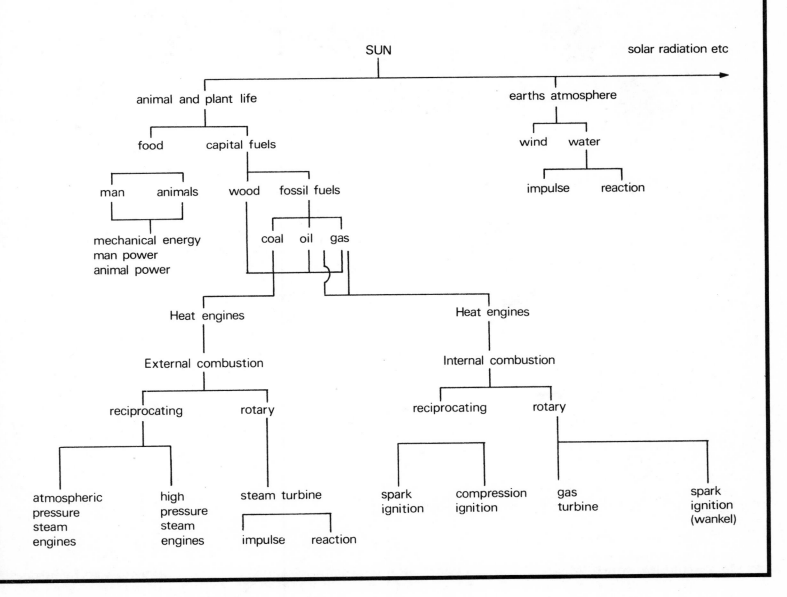

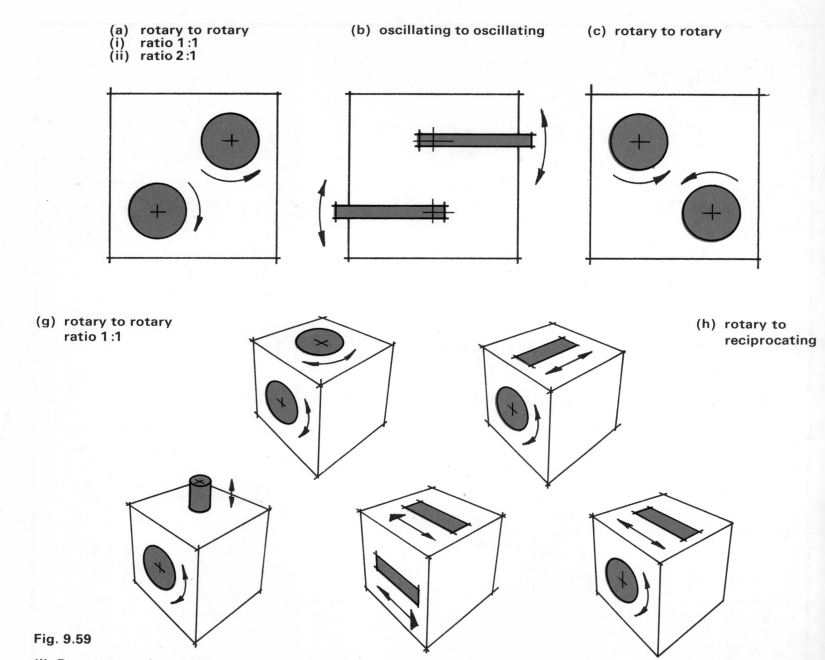

(a) rotary to rotary
(i) ratio 1 :1
(ii) ratio 2 :1

(b) oscillating to oscillating

(c) rotary to rotary

(g) rotary to rotary
ratio 1 :1

(h) rotary to reciprocating

Fig. 9.59

(i) Rotary to reciprocating
Slow lift quick return

(j) reciprocating to reciprocating

(k) rotary to reciprocating

(d) rotary to oscillating **(e) rotary to straight line co-axially** **(f) rotary to reciprocating**

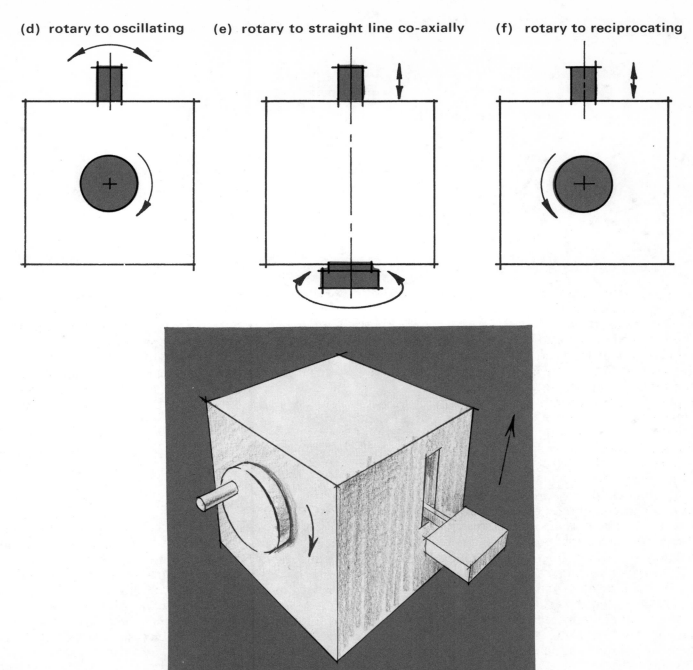

Fig. 9.60

Chapter 10
DESIGNING FROM NATURAL FORMS

Everything you create is directly related to your experience. If your experiences are slight then you are limited in what you can say, write, draw or make. It may be that your knowledge is restricted to some particular topic, and in this case it is certain that you will be more fluent on this theme than on any other. The more you understand something, the more it can influence what you do.

Throughout the book it has been stressed that to use a tool, a machine or a material to the best advantage you must have a good knowledge and understanding of it. The same thing applies to shape and form; and the more you know about it, the better equipped you are to use it as a design source.

On p. 43 you read how geometric shapes can be broken down in order to create new designs and the same thing applies when you are using natural forms as a starting point. It was suggested that you could develop a shape by (1) changing the outer shape, (2) changing the inner shape, (3) dissecting and replacing, (4) repeating the shape, (5) adding other shapes, (6) adding surface textures, (7) changing the scale.

For clarity, you can consider this as a two-dimensional development, but the same thinking applies equally to three-dimensional forms as can be seen in the photographs on pp. 33 and 45.

You have already done much work of the sort, but most of the shapes were developed from geometric forms. They are easier to work from because they are plainly seen and understood, and this seeing and understanding is the most essential requirement of visual design. It follows that you must make careful preparations before trying to use forms as complex as those in nature. To abstract without understanding means that your solutions will be superficial and lacking in the characteristics which were inherent in the object.

As an example you can take a simple leaf and examine its potential as a starting point for further designs (Fig. 10.1).

PROBLEMS
1 (a) Find an interesting natural object. This could be a bone, pebble, leaf, twig, fruit, shell; in fact, anything natural which you find interesting.

(b) Do not decide what the final design is going to be yet or this will influence your study.

(c) Make numerous sketches of the object. Draw the whole thing and draw small areas, as seen through a magnifying glass. If possible, cut the object in two and make sketches of the sections and construction. Do not try to abstract shape or form at this stage, just study the object so that you can understand the structure and why it is made as it is. Find out and record what you discover about the surface, what it looks like and what it feels like.

(d) Possibly at this stage, you can decide what your end product will be. It may be an aluminium casting, or a structure. It could be a piece of jewellery or a wall panel, possibly a machined unit or a forged screen. When you have decided what you are designing for, the metal you are going to use, and the process you are going to employ, you will then have to choose sketches which can be developed to conform to these limitations.

(e) These sketches should be developed in the systematic way which has been outlined on p. 165.

2 Design from natural form a three-dimensional shape which can be cast using expanded polystyrene as a pattern. This casting should be visually interesting from all angles and should not include a base so that it can be placed down in more than one position.

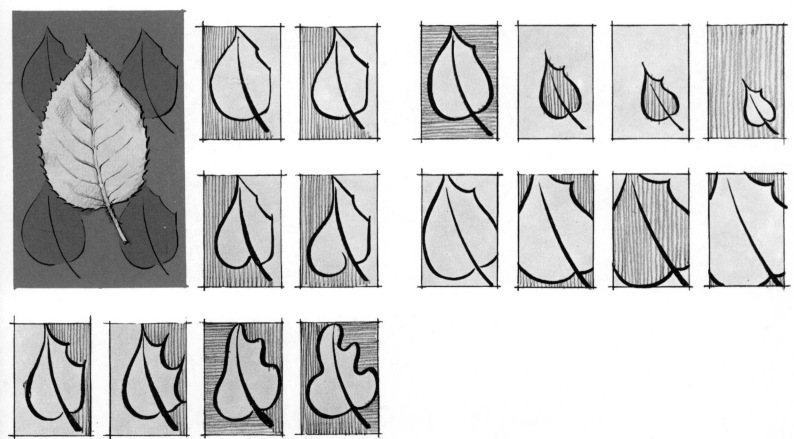

Fig. 10.1

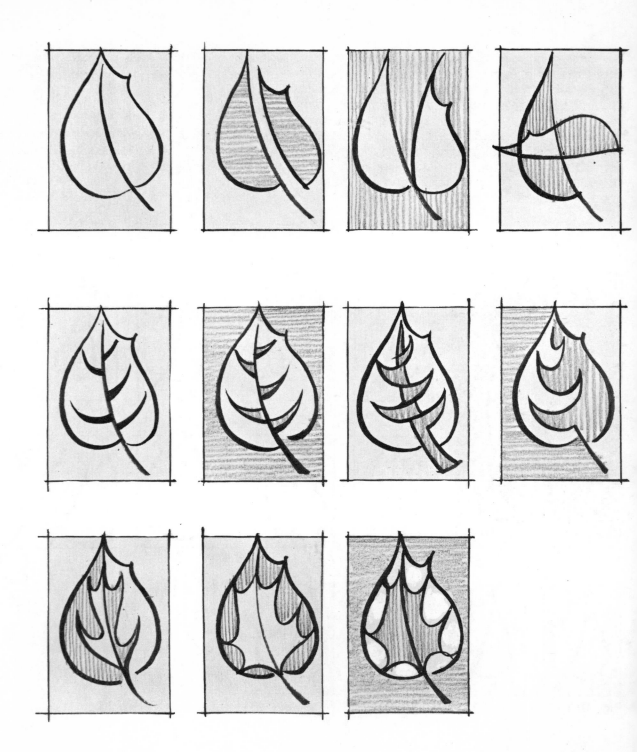

Fig. 10.2

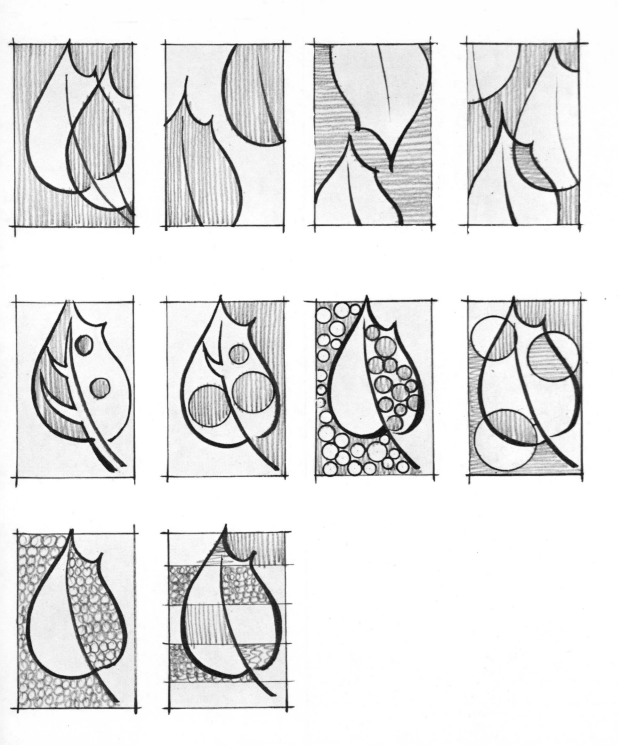

Appendix A

SURFACE TREATMENTS

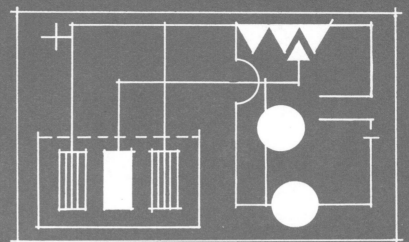

This book would not be complete without some mention of the surface treatments which can be applied to metals and some suggestions of ways in which they can be used to further your scope when designing.

The study of surface treatments is too large a topic to be covered in detail by this book. However, a general outline of the methods most likely to be of immediate interest to the reader is given, together with books and other sources of information, which will allow for more intensive study.

TEXTURES

Mention was made in Chapter 7 of textures by deep, regular machined cuts to relieve the plain surface of metal objects. They also added visual interest by introducing new shapes to the form and the resulting side effects of patterns caused by the increased light and shadow helped to make this a major feature in the overall design of the objects concerned. Hand tools can also be used to texture surfaces in both regular and irregular ways as shown in Fig. A(A).1. Texturing is also possible by substituting a steel or brass scratch brush for the usual soft mop on the polishing machine. This produces a sheen on the workpiece but also lightly scratches it all over, making it more serviceable if the article is to be in constant use in situations that would

normally scratch it periodically. This is known as a butler finish.

A high polish from soft mops is another surface treatment that should be mentioned here. Different grades of finish are possible on different metals by using varying combinations of polishing compounds and mops. Generally speaking, of the more usual calico mops, the stitched ones cut harder than the unstitched and a swansdown mop cuts least of all and therefore produces the finest finish. The usual abrasives used in schools for polishing are tripoli compound for normal work and rouge for fine polishing. Further details of the full range of possibilities can be obtained from W. Canning and Co., Ltd., Gt. Hampton Street, Birmingham 18.

Textures can also be created by the reverse process of applying decoration instead of by cutting away. Such features as rivet heads, lengths of welding rod, lengths of soft copper wire perhaps hammered flat in places (textured) or cut shapes can be soldered on to a preconceived design.

Experiment with several or all of these techniques by producing a sample strip of copper on which each is represented to serve as a three dimensional record for your design folder. This will be valuable to you when faced with future design problems. Keep method notes also in your technology notebook for future reference.

169

Tool	Method	Application
Scoring tool	Used against straight edge. Produces straight lines only.	Normal use of scoring comes prior to bending and soldering an edge (see p. 000). Otherwise can be used on outside surfaces as lined decoration. Such lines can be left or later filled with enamel or resins. Easy to use.
Chasing tool or chaser	Work held on pitch block and chaser tapped with light hammer.	Normally used with repoussé work, but can be used on its own to cut straight or curved lines; quite easy to use.
Engraving tool or graver	Can be of different shapes. Hand controlled	Difficult to use, but produces intricate patterns; similar in effect to chiselling. Very skilled craftsmen can produce emphasized effects of highlights and shadows by angling the tool in use.
Blind punches and chisels	Work supported on hard surface and tool hit with hammer. Blind punches should have highly polished faces. Infinite variety of shapes possible.	Easy to design and make as required, and easy to use. Pattern can be later filled with enamel or coloured resins if required.
Ground hammer faces	Peen of hammer ground and tried until desired effect is achieved.	Very easy to use. Similar effect to ground punches.
Grinding paste — Different grades of abrasive grit available.	Applied manually or on end of dowel rod which is revolved in a wheel brace or drilling machine.	Easy to use; needs no careful planning and therefore lacks definition. Generally associated more with ferrous metals where it also serves to provide minute oil reservoirs which prevent rusting.

Fig. A(A).1

An interesting exercise is to make a 55 mm cube from sheet metal and to texture each of the six faces using a different technique on each face.

ETCHING

Acids that attack different metals can also be used to provide a textured surface finish similar in appearance to that produced by the small burrs and grinding wheels mentioned earlier. This process is called etching.

Complete immersion of the metal into the acid will produce an overall eroded surface, and a partial immersion will only affect the areas immersed. However, erosion can be reduced if an acid-resisting medium can be painted onto the metal first to a pre-planned design leaving exposed surfaces. On immersion in the acid, only these exposed areas are attacked, thereby producing the desired effect.

Proprietary brands of acid-resisting varnishes can be obtained but, with care, common paraffin wax or beeswax will suffice. The varnishes are carefully painted onto the work to the prepared design. The waxes are usually applied to the workpiece *overall* when warm so that they melt and run evenly over the surfaces concerned, and the unwanted wax is later scraped off the design area.

A light etching can be obtained by applying the acid to the area being worked by means of a stick as shown in Fig. A(A).2(a) but if a deeper etch is required, the workpiece should be completely immersed in the etching solution. In such cases, great care must be taken to protect all surfaces, especially the corners and edges, from the

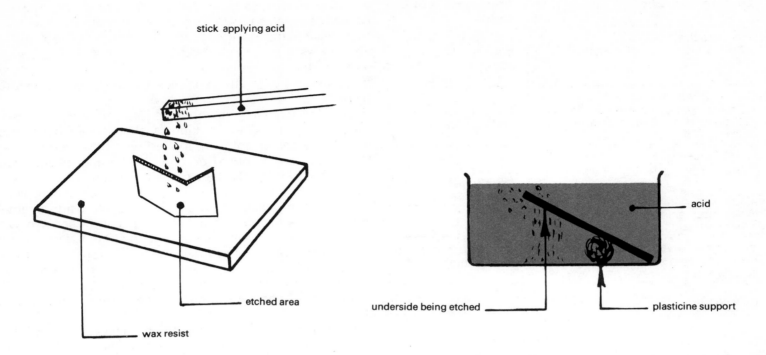

stick applying acid

etched area

wax resist

acid

underside being etched

plasticine support

Fig. A(A).2(a)

Fig. A(A).2(b)

attack of the acid. Definition is improved if the work is immersed as shown in Fig. A(A).2(b) so that the resulting silt falls away from the etched area and does not retard the action of the acid.

The table (Fig. A(A)3) gives the more popular etching solutions and the metals on which they are normally used.

ENAMELLING

Metals can also be coloured by fusing a layer of vitreous enamel—or glass—on the surface, which provides decoration and protection from corrosion and abrasion. Such a process is usually referred to simply as enamelling

Enamelling on an industrial scale is used mainly on items of household equipment such as cookers, washing mach-

ines, sinks and baths, where it is done for protection. Ferrous metals are usually associated with work of this kind, whereas decorative work is usually applied to copper, or (to a lesser extent) silver and to a special stainless steel now being developed for this purpose.

As this appendix is intended merely to introduce you to the process of enamelling, the following text refers solely to work on copper, all of which is possible with the most humble equipment.

Enamelling implies a coating of low melting point glass, compounded from a wide variety of chemicals, the proportions of which are varied to provide enamels of different colours and characteristics such as transparent or opaque, hard or soft.

The enamel is applied to the metal in a powder form

171

Etching Solutions	Metals on which used
Iron perchloride— dissolve lumps in hot water to cover.	Iron, steel, copper, brass, gilding metal, aluminium, stainless steel.
Dutch Mordant— 60 fl. oz. water, 12 fl. oz. hydrochloric acid, 2½ fl. g. potassium chlorate.	Copper, brass, gilding metal.
Nitric Acid— 3 parts water, 1 part nitric acid.	Copper, brass, gilding metal, silver, iron, steel.
Weak nitric acid for a sharp edge. 5 parts water, 1 part nitric acid.	Silver
Remember always to add the acid SLOWLY to the water and never the reverse. Do NOT put a stopper in a bottle until the solution has cooled.	

Fig. A(A)3

known as **frit** which can be coarsely or finely ground. Much time is saved if the enamels are bought pre-ground although these will need several washings if the colours are to appear true. They should be washed and the water changed regularly until the water no longer appears milky.

For the fusion to take place, the surface of the workpiece must first be chemically cleaned as described in appendix A p. 176. The area to be enamelled is then covered with a thin layer of adhesive such as gum tragacanth or Polycell which burn away without trace when the enamel is fired. The enamel is sieved, dusted or painted onto this surface. The workpiece is fired either by a bunsen burner, gas and air torch, or in a gas or electrically fired kiln. A thermostatically controlled kiln is preferable as different enamels fuse at different temperatures between 620°C and 830°C, but it is by no means essential. Firing normally takes approximately three minutes but a short firing in a hot kiln gives a better colour than a long firing at a gentle heat.

When different colours are required, separate firings

are needed for each and the adhesive again helps to control the placing of the different colours according to the prepared design. If the enamel cools too quickly and cracks it can be re-fired and thus restored. Likewise, if the surface of the fused enamel has to be ground down to finish flush with other surfaces, the glaze can be restored by re-firing.

Three enamelling techniques are worthy of special mention. **Painted** enamelling is almost self explanatory after these earlier notes. If applied wet, however, to attain fine definition, it should be dried in the area of the warm kiln before firing. **Cloisonné** enamelling entails making cells with fine wire for the retention of the enamel. These may be either soldered onto the workpiece using enamelling solder—because of the melting point—or fixed with the adhesive and ultimately held by the fused enamel. In **Champlevé** enamelling, the cells for the different coloured enamels are scored, graved, chiselled, punched or etched out as mentioned in Fig. A(A).2 p. 171. The sequence of the enamelling process then continues as before.

On large pieces of enamelling, a counter enamel—usually colourless—should always be used on the underside of shallow articles such as dishes and plates. This not only gives a more finished appearance, but equalizes the strain caused by the enamel on the other side, thus preventing chipping or cracking.

Jigs should be designed to hold or support the work during firing with a minimum contact area, thereby allowing a full circulation of heat around the workpiece.

Strings of enamel can be made for use during second and later firings where straight lines are required in the design. These are made by fusing frit in a hollow within a charcoal block and when molten, squeezing some between the jaws of tweezers and pulling outwards. It cools quickly and can then be broken into short lengths for use.

Experiment fully with this medium as it offers tremendous scope for decorative work. Once the basic technique has been mastered, plan simple units for enamelling using design techniques described earlier in the book. Keep a strict record of all your experiments for future use when designing.

COLOURING

The application of other chemicals to metals—particularly copper and its alloys—produces calculated reactions with the parent metals resulting in a change of surface colour.

The success of exact colouring depends both upon keeping rigidly to the recommended chemical formula and agreed procedure and upon the skill of the craftsmen concerned. Variables such as these, plus the exact composition and general condition of the metal, make the production or reproduction of an exact colour very difficult, but general colouring for overall decorative purposes to contrast with other areas within a designed piece of work, is very easy to achieve in a small workshop.

In schools, the blueing of steel—oxidising its surface by heating until the desired colour is attained followed by immediate immersion in oil—is the most generally known method of colouring metal.

However, copper and its alloys—or silver—provide much more scope for experimental work and the reader is therefore advised to experiment widely with these materials along the lines now indicated. The methods of chemical colouring may be divided into three categories: (a) immersion in a solution, (b) application by brush, swab or spray, and (c) application and removal of a paste. The general principles of these are now given.

As the desired effect in each case depends upon a direct chemical reaction between the chemical solution and the parent metal, it is *essential* that the workpiece is chemically clean before the process is commenced. This can be achieved by either etching or pickling and careful washing. Great care must be taken to avoid finger marks at the conclusion of this stage.

Immersion

After the general cleaning described earlier, the workpiece is immersed in a stoneware, enamelled or glass bath containing the required chemical solution and washed according to the instructions given. The many proprietary brands available give explicit instructions to be followed, but where a student prefers to experiment with his own chemical preparations the following notes will be helpful.

To produce *black* a solution of sodium hydroxide (50 g/l) is boiled and to this is added the workpiece and a solution of potassium persulphate (10 g/l). The workpiece should be agitated in this mixture for 5 to 10 minutes. After colouring, the piece is rinsed, wiped and lacquered. For brass the sodium hydroxide content should be doubled.

To produce *red* and *brown*, a solution of liver of sulphur in water (10 g/l) made slightly alkaline with sodium hydroxide or ammonia is heated to approximately 80°C and the workpiece immersed until the required colour is reached.

Brass should be dipped alternately in this mixture and in water made slightly acidic by the addition of sulphuric acid and a little copper sulphate.

A *green* patina can be produced by immersing the workpiece in a solution containing 0.9 kg of copper nitrate, 1.4 kg ammonia, 1.8 kg ammonium chloride, 1.8 kg sodium acetate and 4.5 l water. This should be allowed to dry on the surface. The film can be wiped off and the process repeated until the required intensity of colour is obtained. This patina resembles that seen on copper roofs after they have been exposed to the atmosphere for some time.

If the quantities of these solutions are reduced, the separate ingredients should be reduced proportionally.

Brushing and Spraying

This method is particularly popular on an industrial scale as it is not restricted by the size of the workpiece. However, in schools, it is also particularly useful for treatment to the individual piece of work as it normally prevents the necessity of preparing a large amount of colouring solution.

The pre-cleaning requirements remain as for the immersion method.

Dilute ammonium chloride or dilute sodium chloride will colour copper, gilding metal and silver if brushed on until the required colour is obtained and then left to dry before rinsing and drying carefully.

A suitable solution for brushing or spraying to obtain a *green* patina is as follows: 0.3 kg ammonium chloride, 0.1 kg sodium chloride, 0.1 kg cream of tartar, 0.1 kg copper acetate, 1.25 l acetic acid and 1.25 l water. When the workpiece has been sprayed, it should be left to dry for twenty-four hours, preferably in a warm place, and the process should then be repeated several times until the desired colour is obtained. Although the green compounds are quickly developed, they do not immediately adhere to the workpiece. If undisturbed, however, the salts gradually key themselves into the metal and become truly adherent after one year. It is, therefore, necessary to protect this patina with lacquer during this initial period.

Use of Paste

This method has been developed mainly for builders and architects who may want to treat metals already used on buildings. Yet it can be used equally well in a small workshop. The bronzing powders used are usually of a proprietary brand and after being mixed into a paste are applied to the workpiece with a brush. The paste is brushed off when dry. Differences in colour and tone can be obtained by varying the consistency of the paste, the duration of its contact with the metal and the number of applications.

The following table (Fig. A(A)4), is a summary of immediate possibilities that should be helpful to you whilst experimenting.

As with all processes mentioned earlier in the book, you should experiment freely with this method of colouring metals and record your experiences carefully in your technology note book for future reference. A full range of possibilities can be obtained from W. Cannings and Co. and the Copper Development Association at 55 South Audley Street, London W.1.

ANODISING

The colouring—or dyeing—of pure aluminium can also be done if the natural oxide film is first thickened. This can be done artificially by making the workpiece the anode in an electrolyte. Such a process takes the name anodising.

Briefly, this consists of depositing a film of aluminium hydroxide on the surfaces of the workpiece in order to protect it from corrosion. Its main value, however, lies in the ability of this anodic film to absorb dyes, which means that many highly decorative effects can be obtained.

The workpiece is first highly polished and then degreased, using carbon tetrachloride. After this, it is washed

Colour	Metal	Method
all shades of brown	copper gunmetal gilding metal brass	immersion, brush or paste
black	copper gunmetal	immersion
	gilding metal brass zinc based alloy (Kayem)	brush immersion brush
blue blue-black	brass nickel silver steel copper gunmetal	immersion immersion
blue-grey	gilding metal brass	immersion
green patinas	copper gunmetal gilding metal	brush
red/brown	copper	immersion

Fig. A(A).4

in hot, soapy water and then hung from the anode bar of an electro-plating tank using pure aluminium connectors. It is advisable to use cathodes on both sides of the workpiece to ensure an even coating of oxide, so two or more lead plates are hung from the cathode bars, this time using lead connectors. Fig. A(A).5 shows the general layout of the plant used.

The electrolyte is made from:
          0.14 kg/l of sulphuric acid—by volume
          0.055 kg/l sodium sulphate (Glauber salts)
          remainder—water

The sodium sulphate is dissolved in three-quarters of the water and the sulphuric acid is added slowly, stirring constantly. As this generates heat, the solution should be cooled to between 12°C and 20°C. This is now added to the plating tank and the DC current used should be in

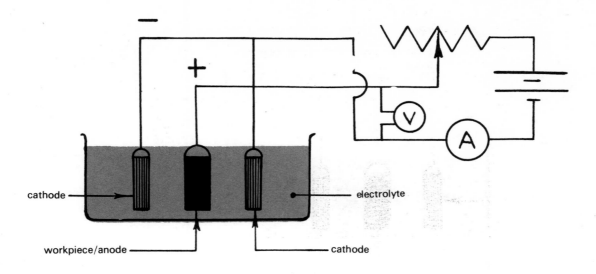

Fig. A(A).5

the neighbourhood of 2 amp per square decimetre. About 10 volts are required and this will have to be adjusted after about 20 minutes as it gradually decreases as the oxide thickens on the anode. The total time taken is approximately 30 to 40 minutes, at the end of which the workpiece is withdrawn and rinsed in cold water. The oxides thus deposited are converted into the complex hydroxides by boiling in clean water, to which the dye can be added if a coloured surface is required.

Experiment with ordinary household dyes for this— they are usually found very satisfactory providing no other substance is added to serve as a fixative. The aluminium hydroxide serves this purpose itself.

Finally, the workpiece should be boiled in clean water to wash off any excess dye which has not been fixed. To protect this surface, lacquers of the cellulose type are often used.

Experiment also with techniques for masking certain areas with sticky tapes before anodising and dyeing to see the potential of this process for the designer.

You can see that the equipment needed is very simple and can be easily improvised. A 12 volt car battery provides an excellent source of current and many domestic goods are sold in good quality plastic containers which serve well

as tanks.

This method of oxidising is the simplest of all those possible. For further details apply to the Aluminium Federation, Portland House, Stag Place, London, S.W.1.

Electrolytic deposition of this kind is more familiarly associated with electro-plating or the application of another metallic coating to the workpiece.

ELECTROPLATING

This is a process in which the workpiece is immersed in a solution called the electrolyte and is connected to the negative in a low voltage direct current, thereby making it the cathode. To complete the circuit, as shown in Fig. A(A).6, anodes are immersed in the electrolyte and connected to the positive lead.

The electrolyte provides the source of metal ions which are deposited on the cathode. The anodes may be insoluble as in the case of chromium plating solutions, or may be of the metal to be deposited as in the case of nickel, copper and zinc plating. In the case of the latter, the metal dissolves to maintain the metallic content of the solution, as well as acting as an electrode to complete the electrical circuit.

To electroplate an article, it is not sufficient merely to

175

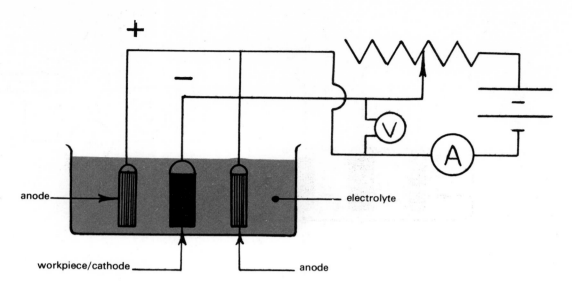

Fig. A(A).6

anode

workpiece/cathode

anode

electrolyte

immerse it in a plating solution and then apply a low voltage direct current. As with the other surface treatments previously described, which relied upon a chemical reaction, it is necessary to remove all traces of grease or oxide and to ensure that the surface is chemically active. If the surface is not properly prepared, the plated deposit will not be satisfactory.

Preparation of metals to be plated

It is not the intention of this appendix to cover the technique of plating completely but to provide just sufficient information to encourage you to experiment with the more simple techniques.

As different metals (bases) require different treatments when plating, the preparatory processes mentioned earlier must now be described in detail so that they can be thoroughly understood and applied before plating commences.

A *Smoothing* is a straightforward process whereby all the dents, scratches etc. are removed by filing, stoning and polishing with emery cloth or buffing machine as appropriate.

B (i) *Cleaning with an acid dip*. The workpiece (base) is immersed in the following solution at room temperature for five minutes:

sulphuric acid, pure	1,300 ml
hydrochloric acid, pure	52 ml
nitric acid, pure	78 ml
water	1,560 ml

(ii) *Cleaning with an alkaline dip*

caustic soda, pure	42 g
sodium carbonate	42 g
sodium cyanide 13%	28 g
water to make	1,136 ml

This is quite a dangerous mix to make and the following instructions should be closely followed: Mix the water, nitric acid and hydrochloric acid. Add a quarter of the sulphuric and cool thoroughly. When cold, add a further quarter of the sulphuric and again cool. Do not add the remainder of the acid until the mixture is quite cool. This solution should be kept in a glass container with a glass stopper.

C *De-greasing*. This is done carefully with rag soaked in carbon tetrachloride or similar agent, after which the workpiece should be washed in hot water and household soap, but *not* toilet soap as this contains too much grease itself.

D (i) *Etching of non-ferrous* metals is done by making

the workpiece the anode and immersing it in the following solution at 70°C:

citric acid	208 ml
water	2,250 ml

Mix these and add a strong ammonia solution, stirring continuously until the mixture just smells of ammonia, then add:

citric acid	78 ml
water to make	4,500 ml in all

A DC current of 2 amp per square decimetre should then be passed through it for three minutes using steel or copper cathodes.

(ii) *Etching ferrous* metals is identical to the above method but the solution used is replaced by:

sulphuric acid, pure	130 ml
hydrochloric acid, pure	130 ml
water to make	4,500 ml

Ideally, the cathodes should be copper and the current extended to five minutes.

Note. Etching provides a very fine matt surface to which the plating adheres.

E *Quicksilvering* is used solely on copper and brass, when silver plating, to stop the silver from lifting. A thin film of mercury on the base ensures perfect ·adhesion between the copper and the silver.

Base	A	B(i)	B(ii)	C	D(i)	D(ii)	E	Rinse in water
Wrought iron and steel for **all** bases	1		6	2		4		3, 5, 7
Copper and brass for silver plate	1		2				4	3
Copper for nickel plate	1	4			2			3, 5

Fig. A(A). 7

This enables swabbing the workpiece with a clean rag liberally soaked in the prepared solution, rinsing in clean water and then immediately proceeding with the silver plating. Any delay at this stage should not exceed ten minutes, during which time the workpiece should be kept under clean water.

Solution:

perchloride of mercury	3.54 g
sodium cyanide, 13%	14.20 g
water to make	4,500 ml

The solution is used cold and should be kept in a glass container when not in use.

Fig. A(A).7 shows a table giving the correct sequence of operations—shown numerically—for preparing the various bases for the more common plates.

ELECTROLYTES

The next consideration is the preparation of the different electrolytes necessary. It is of the utmost importance that these are made from pure chemicals, all of which are obtainable from most school chemistry laboratories, or from local pharmacists. The cyanide and salts of mercury are HIGHLY POISONOUS and it may, therefore, be difficult to purchase them, but they will be obtainable through any school. These must NEVER be allowed to come into contact with any acid as they will give off the highly poisonous prussic acid gas. If any small spot is spilt, it should be immediately wiped up.

The following electrolytes are recommended and general notes are given as appropriate.

Copper No. 1, in g/l.

copper sulphate crystals	62.40 g
sulphuric acid	6.24 ml
sodium sulphocarbolate	0.80 g

Pour the acid into three times its volume of cold water and stir carefully. Add the sodium sulphocarbolate while the mixture retains the heat caused by the first mixing. Boil very gently in an enamelled pan for three minutes, then pour into three-quarters of the total amount of water. Add the copper sulphate and make up the volume with water.

plating temperature	cold (12°C—20°C)
plating current	1—1½ amp per square decimetre
anodes	sheet copper, twice the area of the base

time	eight minutes at $1\frac{1}{2}$ amp will deposit 0.0025 mm
storage after use	should not be in a galvanised container

Copper No. 2, in g/l:

copper sulphate crystals	15.60 g
sodium cyanide	24.96 g
sodium bisulphite	18.72 g
sodium carbonate	12.48 g
caustic soda	1.56 g

Dissolve the copper sulphate in half the water and the sodium cyanide in a quarter. Stirring constantly, add the former to the latter in successive *small* amounts. The final mixture should be brown in colour with no trace of green at all. If this is not so, add a little more cyanide solution. Dissolve the caustic soda, sodium carbonate and the bisulphite into this solution in that order and make it up to 4,546 litres by adding water.

plating temperature	55°C
plating current	$\frac{1}{4}$ amp per square decimetre
anodes	as for copper no. 1
time	forty-five minutes deposits approx. 0.0025 mm
storage after use	should not be in a galvanised container

Nickel, in g/l:

nickel sulphate crystals	74.88 g
Epsom salts	24.96 g
boric acid	9.36 g
ammonium chloride	6.24 g
glucose	6.24 g

Mix the boric acid with one-eighth of the water and boil in an enamelled pan until dissolved. When this has cooled to about 80°C pour into three-quarters of the water. Dissolve into this the nickel, Epsom and ammonium salts, and finally the glucose. Allow this to cool and strain through fine linen.

plating temperature	cold (12°C—20°C)
plating current	$\frac{1}{2}$ amp per square decimetre
anodes	nickel bars, three-quarters of the area of the workpiece
time	thirty minutes will deposit approx 0.0025 mm
storage	any convenient clean container

Silver, in g/l:

silver nitrate	25.00 g
sodium cyanide	37.50 g
sodium carbonate	18.75 g
caustic soda	6.25 g

Dissolve the silver salt in one quarter of the water and the cyanide in one half. Pour the former into the latter and stir constantly. Dissolve the sodium carbonate and the caustic soda and make up to volume with water.

plating temperature	30°C—35°C
plating current	$\frac{2}{3}$ amp per square decimetre
anodes	silver sheet or foil the same area as the workpiece or steel
time	fifteen minutes will deposit approx. 0.0025 mm
storage	any non-metallic container

Note. As silver anodes are not readily available, steel is suggested but, if these are used, it is necessary to replace the silver in the solution from time to time. This is done by dissolving 20 g of silver nitrate in a litre of water and adding it to the solution with constant stirring. This should be followed by the addition of 10 g of sodium cyanide in a little water. These additions can be made about four times before the solution should be discarded.

Figures A(A).8 and A(A).9 show tables giving the sequence of operations necessary for copper, nickel and silver plating on bases of steel.

Experiment now with this process using both direct and masking techniques. As with anodising, the equipment can be easily improvised and if great care is taken with the handling of the dangerous chemicals, it has tremendous scope for the designer as it offers both decorative and metallurgical opportunities.

Further information can be obtained from the Copper Development Association, the Aluminium Federation and W. Canning and Co. as before.

For the plastic coating of metals see *Design and Technology—Plastic.*

PLATING ON STEEL

Plating Required	Copper	Nickel	Silver
Process 1	No. 2 copper to required thickness	Use nickel electrolyte to required thickness	Nickel plate for 10 minutes.
Process 2	Rinse dry and polish.	Rinse dry and polish.	Rinse.
Process 3			Plate to required thickness with silver electrolyte.
Process 4			Rinse dry and polish.

Fig. A(A).8

PLATING ON COPPER OR BRASS

Plating Required	Copper	Nickel	Silver
Process 1	No. 1 copper to required thickness.	Polish	Quicksilver
Process 2	Rinse dry and polish.	No. 1 copper for 5 minutes.	Plate direct to required thickness.
Process 3		Rinse thoroughly.	Rinse dry and polish.
Process 4		Plate to required thickness.	
Process 5		Rinse dry and polish.	

Fig. A(A).9

Appendix B

DESIGN PROBLEMS

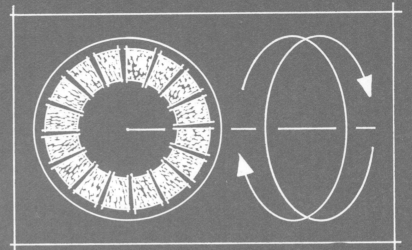

1 The paved patio area of a garden lacks interest. Design and make a unit that will prove visually interesting in this setting and indicate also the direction of the prevailing wind.

2 When scaling up a drawing or decoration from a design sheet, it is difficult to reproduce all the required detail to the same proportion. Design and make a piece of apparatus that will ensure this while using either a pencil or a scriber.

3 When the window is open in the Headmaster's study, the papers on his desk tend to get blown away when the door is opened. Design and make something that he can use to prevent this and which will be visually interesting to his visitors.

4 A white candle measuring 45 mm diameter and 220 mm long is to be used in a home for decorative purposes. Design and make a unit that will keep this stable when in a vertical position and will also add to its visual appeal.

5 When taking vertical measurements from a surface plate, it is essential to keep the rule upright. Design and make a tool that will overcome this difficulty, and allow two hands free for other operations.

6 Design and make a desk calendar for use by the Headmaster in his study which will be both visually interesting to him when viewed with the other articles in his room, and also give an indication to visitors of the work done by senior pupils studying Design and Technology.

7 Removing circlips from an assembled unit is often very difficult until the clip is opened. Design and make a simple tool for this purpose.

8 Design and make a base for a table lamp to be used in your home. (You may think it necessary to design the whole unit with the shade as well.)

9 When working in strip materials such as wood, metal or plastic, it is often necessary to mark a centre line along the length. Design and make a tool, to take either a pencil or a scriber, which is self-centring on material between 25 and 100 mm wide.

10 Names or numbers to identify a house should be bold and easily read from the road and should be pleasant and interesting to look at. Using this specification, design and make such a unit for your house.

11 When setting-up lathe tools for turning operations, it

is essential to set the cutting tip to the height of the spindle axis of the lathe. Design and make a tool that will indicate this height to the tool setter of any lathe in your school workshop. It should be usable from the top slide of the lathe.

12 The base of a casserole dish is circular in shape and 250 mm in diameter. When the casserole is hot, it might damage the surface finish of the dining table. Design and make something to overcome this problem and which will add to the attractive setting of the table.

13 When equipping a home workshop, it is helpful to have the drills and taps relevant to five preferred sizes of threads to be accommodated in a single unit. Design and make such a unit that will allow these tools to be immediately available and arranged in the most convenient manner for use.

14 Design and make a unit to hold up to ten paperback books. It should be free-standing and pleasant to look at even when only partially filled with books.

15 When casting into plaster moulds, it is helpful if steam pressure can be used to force the metal into the cavity. Design and make a simple piece of apparatus that will make this possible.

16 Drawer handles should be pleasant to look at, pleasant to touch and should provide an efficient means of exerting the required force to open the drawer. Working from this specification, design and make a drawer pull for use on a drawer in your kitchen.

17 Soft vice clamps made from metals such as lead or 'Kayem' are very useful in the workshop but, as they are easily distorted in use, they should be die cast for ease of reproduction. Design and make a die for this purpose.

18 Door pulls should be pleasant to look at, pleasant to touch and should provide an efficient means of exerting the required force to open the door. Design and make a door pull for any door in your bedroom.

19 A pinholder as used in flower arrangements consists of a lead base with protruding spikes for securing the flowers. This makes it possible to keep the flowers in their set position and also gives stability to the arrangement. Design and make a pinholder 50 mm in diameter which fulfils this specification.

20 When books are housed on an open shelf, unless the whole shelf is used, the last books fall over causing the whole unit to look unsightly. Design and make something to overcome this.

21 When working from a recipe book in a kitchen, a cook prefers to have the book in a vertical position but finds that this causes either the pages to turn or the book to fall over. Design and make a device for overcoming this problem.

22 Storing toothbrushes in a bathroom is a problem requiring careful consideration as it must be visually appealing and essentially functional. Design and make such a unit.

23 Something is required to house the open bottle of wine at a dinner party which will make it easy to pass amongst the guests and make pouring easy. Design and make such an article.

24 A support for a fishing-rod is needed while fishing, to lift the tip end of the rod above the river whilst the handle, or butt, rests on the ground. When in use the height above ground level should be easily adjustable between 200 mm and 350 mm. Design and make such a support.

25 Design and make a collapsible stool that could be used while fishing. It should be of such a size that it can be carried on the back when cycling.

26 When examining the engine of a car to do a repair or trace a fault, insufficient direct light adds to the difficulty.

Chess pieces from copper tubing

Design and make an inspection lamp to overcome this problem.

27 Storing ties in a wardrobe is seldom satisfactory because they usually cover each other as the collection grows, thereby making selection difficult. Design and make a unit to overcome this.

28 Design and make a unit for storing all your shoes and boots within your wardrobe.

29 175 mm EP records should be stored in such a way as to remain flat and yet be easily recognisable and available for selection. Working from this specification, design and make some device to meet the demands of this problem.

30 Design and make a device for pruning the taller branches of fruit trees and/or a device for harvesting the fruit from the highest branches without bruising or damaging the fruit in any way.

31 Long hair can be a disadvantage unless it is fixed back from the face. Design something attractive which will do this.

32 When one is dressed formally, it is desirable to prevent the two ends of a neck tie separating, and separating from the shirt. Design and make a device for overcoming both of these difficulties.

33 Design a method of fixing shirt cuffs together, which adds decoration to the cuff edge.

34 Use a natural object as the design source of a pendant.

35 Scale down the design used in the last question to make earrings.

36 Consider using a similar motif to the one used in answer to the two previous questions and design a ring to be worn with the other pieces.

37 Take as a motif the geometric shape of the circle or square, or use them together to design and make a hanging mobile to decorate your bedroom.

38 Design and make a receptacle for use by smokers in the house.

39 A holder for a table napkin should be easily identified by the owner even though it forms part of a family set. Design such a set of holders and make the one you would prefer to use yourself.

40 When indoor plants are watered, the water tends to drain from the bottom of the flower pot onto the furniture. Design and make a device for preventing this.

41 Attractive indoor plants are often spoilt as means of decoration because of the ugly, predominant flowerpot. Design and make a method of overcoming this.

42 Design and make a tool to be used for easing on well-fitting shoes to prevent them from becoming damaged at the backs.

43 Design a holder for a single boiled egg for use at the dining table. It should be stackable in shape so that several similar units can be stored in the smallest possible space when not in use.

44 When fixing several sheets of note-paper together with a conventional tag fastener it is necessary to produce a hole in the top corner of each sheet at a point 20 mm from the top and 20 mm from the edge. Design and make a device for locating and producing such a hole.

45 When fixing sheets of note-paper into a loose leaf file, two holes are required in a specific location to comply with the sizes and spacing of the spring clip in the folder. Determine these specific facts and then design a tool for producing the required holes in the paper.

46 As a car is driven into a domestic garage it is essential that the door does not swing onto it. Design and make a fitting for the door of your garage, or one that is known to you, that will prevent this from happening.

47 When several members of a family own bicycles, they became difficult to store tidily outside the house during the day. Design and make a storage rack for your bicycle which can be fitted to the house. It should hold the bicycle firmly, away from the wall thereby preventing other cycles from being rested against it.

48 Art and craft materials are often supplied to schools in strong cardboard boxes which are stapled together. To open these quickly and easily during lesson time is difficult. Design and make a tool for cutting the top open which will leave a hinged lid, rendering the box still useful for other purposes. The tool should be perfectly safe in use.

49 Design and make a jig, to be used in a vice, for holding pieces of irregularly shaped thin metal whilst drawfiling.

50 Running water represents a source of power which can be harnessed for other purposes. Design and make a device for converting water power into electrical power.

51 Design and make a fitment to house a spirit level bubble so that it can be used with accuracy to check both vertical and horizontal planes.

52 Bending metal to an even curvature and at an exact location can be a difficult task. Design and make a bending jig to overcome this difficulty to operate within the following limitations: maximum cross section of metal to be bent = 10 mm × 10 mm and maximum/minimum radius of curvature = 50 mm/10 mm.

53 Design a unit for storing magazines neatly when not in use. Begin by selecting a specific location in which the unit is to be used and work from this and the magazines concerned.

54 Design and make a device which makes possible the convenient and economical use of sticky tape when wrapping parcels.

55 Design a tool for use on the Headmaster's desk for the efficient opening of envelopes, which allows the envelopes to be used again for internal mail within the school.

56 Housewives often experience difficulty when trying to inform their milkman of a change in their regular order and also in carrying indoors several bottles of milk at once. Design and make a device for overcoming both of these difficulties.

57 Fifty metres of fine fishing line are to be attached to a rod when fishing. They should be held to the rod in such a way that the line can be easily cast into the water in the first instance, but not pulled free if a fish is hooked and swims strongly away from the rod. Determine a method of achieving this.

58 Birds are a source of great annoyance to gardeners when they persist in eating newly-sown seed. Design a wind-driven device that could be erected in a garden at such a time which would drive the birds away. As a feature of the garden, it should also be visually interesting.

59 Holiday makers often take ciné films of their journey from a moving car. It is difficult to hold the camera steady in such a situation. Design a unit that could be fitted to the open window of the car, which would hold the camera firmly but allow panning.

60 Elderly people and shopkeepers often experience considerable difficulty in getting objects down from high shelves. Design and make a method of overcoming such a difficulty.

61 Housewives often find it very difficult to unscrew the tops of glass, screw-topped jars and bottles when working in the kitchen. Design and make a safe method of overcoming this problem.

62 Design and make a cruet set for use in your home.

63 Design and make any of the following items for use in your home, a drinking beaker, flower vase, candle holder, jam spoon, butter dish and knife.

64 Design and make a container to hold two packs of playing cards.

65 Design and make a utensil or utensils for taking pieces of salad from a salad bowl during a meal.

66 Design and make a utensil for taking a single piece of lump sugar from a sugar bowl.

67 Physically handicapped people who are confined to wheel chairs, have great difficulty in picking things up from the floor. Design and make a device to overcome this problem.

68 To shorten a bicycle chain is a difficult task because of the problem of removing the retaining pins. Design and make a tool which will overcome this difficulty.

69 Design and make a revolving table which a potter could use when modelling circular forms.

70 Design and make a device for generating centrifugal force onto a small casting the moment the metal is poured, to encourage the molten metal to reach the extreme parts of the mould cavity.

71 Design and make a tool which will make it easy to bend sheet metal along straight lines. Work within the following limitations: the thickest metal to be bent = 2 mm and the greatest width = 220 mm.

72 Energy can be obtained from a falling weight which

unwinds itself from an axle. Use such a source of power to activate a moving sculpture. Control the rate of this movement in such a way that it could be used as a time piece.

73 Electrically operated chime bars provide a pleasant way of announcing the arrival of a visitor to the outside door of a house. Design a make such a unit.

74 Thin sheet plastic material can be formed to shape if softened by gentle heat then subjected to a vacuum, which sucks it to the shape of a prearranged pattern. Design and make a piece of apparatus which will do this.

75 Thin sheet plastic material can be formed to shape shape if softened by heat then blown into the shape of a prearranged mould. Design and make a piece of apparatus which will do this.

76 Design a utensil that can be used for watering indoor plants. As it is to be kept in a lounge, it should be visually interesting.

77 A thaumatrope is a device which uses the persistence of visual impressions. A disc with two different figures drawn on the two sides is rotated rapidly, the axis of rotation being a diameter of the disc. The two figures apparently combine (see Fig. A(B).1). Design and make a mechanism whereby discs may be rapidly rotated about a diametric axis.

78 When a series of figures representing successive positions of a moving object are arranged on the inner surface of a cylinder, or around the periphery of a large disc, and the cylinder or disc is rapidly rotated, the object appears to be in motion. This device is called a zoetrope (see Fig. A(B).2). Design and make a mechanism to operate a zoetrope.

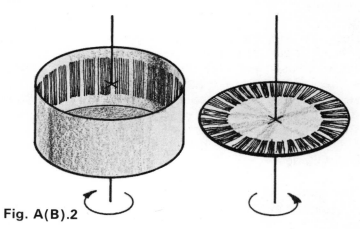

Fig. A(B).2

79 Small pebbles may be mounted as pieces of jewellery. They can be polished by a process called tumbling. The pebbles and polishing media are placed in a rubber-lined cylindrical, octagonal or hexagonal container or plastic bottle which is rotated slowly about its axis (see Fig. A(B).3).

150 mm diameter at 55 rpm	150 mm A/F at 35 rpm
200 mm diameter at 48 rpm	200 mm A/F at 30 rpm
300 mm diameter at 38 rpm	300 mm A/F at 25 rpm

Design and make a tumbler polisher which may be operated continuously for several weeks.

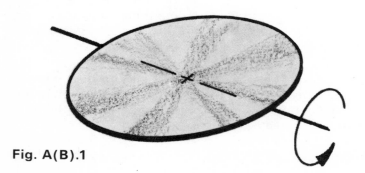

Fig. A(B).1

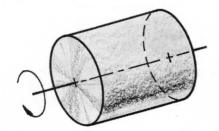

Fig. A(B).3

80 In order to operate the blanking tool discussed in Chapter 8, considerable pressure must be applied to the punch. For this purpose, design and make a press utilizing one or more of the different mechanisms discussed in Chapter 9 (ie. levers, toggles, pulleys—falling weight— cranks, cams, gears—including the rack and pinion, and screw threads).

81 Sheet material is often awkward to hold on the table of a drilling machine. Design and make a clamp to be mounted on the cylindrical column of a drilling machine and capable of being easily moved out of the way when another work-holding device is in use.

82 Design and make a mechanical table-tennis ball server which can be clamped to the table and used in practice and training sessions.

83 An object intended to amuse or interest the user for a limited period of time could be located in either of the following, contrasting, situations:
(a)   a dentist's waiting room,
(b)   a child's nursery.
   As movement invariably arouses interest, make this factor the basic feature of a device or 'toy' which,
(i)   is mechanically operated (by means of a spring, falling weight, pendulum, etc.),
(ii)   functions for approximately five minutes,
(iii)   is either a 'table model' or wall-mounted,
(iv)   creates visual or sonorous interest suitable for either of the locations mentioned.

Index